Teachers of Multiple Languages

PSYCHOLOGY OF LANGUAGE LEARNING AND TEACHING

Series Editors: **Sarah Mercer**, *Universität Graz, Austria* and **Stephen Ryan**, *Waseda University, Japan*

This international, interdisciplinary book series explores the exciting, emerging field of Psychology of Language Learning and Teaching. It is a series that aims to bring together works which address a diverse range of psychological constructs from a multitude of empirical and theoretical perspectives, but always with a clear focus on their applications within the domain of language learning and teaching. The field is one that integrates various areas of research that have been traditionally discussed as distinct entities, such as motivation, identity, beliefs, strategies and self-regulation, and it also explores other less familiar concepts for a language education audience, such as emotions, the self and positive psychology approaches. In theoretical terms, the new field represents a dynamic interface between psychology and foreign language education and books in the series draw on work from diverse branches of psychology, while remaining determinedly focused on their pedagogic value. In methodological terms, sociocultural and complexity perspectives have drawn attention to the relationships between individuals and their social worlds, leading to a field now marked by methodological pluralism. In view of this, books encompassing quantitative, qualitative and mixed methods studies are all welcomed.

All books in this series are externally peer-reviewed.

Full details of all the books in this series and of all our other publications can be found on http://www.multilingual-matters.com, or by writing to Multilingual Matters, St Nicholas House, 31-34 High Street, Bristol, BS1 2AW, UK.

PSYCHOLOGY OF LANGUAGE LEARNING AND TEACHING: 20

Teachers of Multiple Languages

Identities, Beliefs and Emotions

Eric K. Ku

MULTILINGUAL MATTERS
Bristol • Jackson

DOI https://doi.org/10.21832/KU4525
Library of Congress Cataloging in Publication Data
A catalog record for this book is available from the Library of Congress.
Names: Ku, Eric K., author.
Title: Teachers of Multiple Languages: Identities, Beliefs and
   Emotions/Eric K. Ku
Description: Bristol; Jackson: Multilingual Matters, [2023] | Series: Psychology of
   Language Learning and Teaching: 20 | Includes bibliographical references
   and index. | Summary: "This book presents narrative research on individual
   teachers of multiple languages (TMLs). It uncovers what makes TMLs
   unique and reveals the complex identities, beliefs and emotions involved in
   being a TML. The author offers new, globally-relevant insights for language
   teaching research at individual, pedagogical and institutional level"—
   Provided by publisher.
Identifiers: LCCN 2023010358 (print) | LCCN 2023010359 (ebook) |
   ISBN 9781800414525 (hbk : alk. paper) | ISBN 9781800414518 (pbk : alk. paper) |
   ISBN 9781800414549 (epub) | ISBN 9781800414532 (pdf)
Subjects: LCSH: Language and languages—Study and teaching. |
   Language teachers. | Multilingual education.
Classification: LCC P53.85 .K8 2023 (print) | LCC P53.85 (ebook) |
   DDC 407.1—dc23/eng/20230413
LC record available at https://lccn.loc.gov/2023010358
LC ebook record available at https://lccn.loc.gov/2023010359

British Library Cataloguing in Publication Data
A catalogue entry for this book is available from the British Library.

ISBN-13: 978-1-80041-452-5 (hbk)
ISBN-13: 978-1-80041-451-8 (pbk)

Multilingual Matters
UK: St Nicholas House, 31-34 High Street, Bristol, BS1 2AW, UK.
USA: Ingram, Jackson, TN, USA.

Website: www.multilingual-matters.com
Twitter: Multi_Ling_Mat
Facebook: https://www.facebook.com/multilingualmatters
Blog: www.channelviewpublications.wordpress.com

The policy of Multilingual Matters/Channel View Publications is to use papers
that are natural, renewable and recyclable products, made from wood grown in
sustainable forests. In the manufacturing process of our books, and to further
support our policy, preference is given to printers that have FSC and PEFC Chain
of Custody certification. The FSC and/or PEFC logos will appear on those books
where full certification has been granted to the printer concerned.

Typeset by Deanta Global Publishing Services, Chennai, India

Contents

Tables and Figures

Acknowledgements

I am indebted to Dr Yeu-Ting Liu not only for offering his invaluable guidance and inspiration in research, but also for exemplifying great wisdom, empathy and compassion toward the bigger picture of what it means to be a scholar and teacher. Much of what can be achieved in academic scholarship rests upon some form of mentorship, often thankless, from those who have come before us. Thank you for your mentorship.

This book would also not be possible without the generosity of the participants, Ann, Haruko and Megan, for investing their precious time and emotional spirit in sharing their personal stories. Conversations with many other colleagues, friends and students also gave me inspiration for this book, including Cheyenne Maechtle, Cynthia Lee and Cho Yi.

I am grateful to Dawn Jin Lucovich for organizing our online writing accountability group. The support I received from the community we created together with Anne, Satchie, Wendy and others was invaluable in the process of composing this book. And finally, I want to thank the anonymous reviewer(s) and editors whose constructive feedback helped me make improvements with each draft and see my own writing from new perspectives.

Abbreviations

CSL	Chinese as a second language
EFL	English as a foreign language
ESL	English as a second language
FLTA	Foreign Language Teaching Assistant
FYC	First year English composition
IBE	Identity-belief-emotion
L1	First language
L2	Second language
LCTL	Less commonly taught languages
LTE	Language teacher education
LTI	Language teacher identity
NEST	Native English speaker teacher
NNEST	Non-native English speaker teacher
NNS	Non-native speaker
NS	Native speaker
TCSOL	Teaching Chinese to speakers of other languages
TESOL	Teaching English to speakers of other languages
TFL	Teaching of foreign languages
TML	Teacher of multiple languages

1 Who are Teachers of Multiple Languages? Naming and Defining the Unseen

No teacher begins a graduate teacher education program with a blank slate.
(Wolff & De Costa, 2017: 76)

Situating the Book

I begin this book by proposing a broadening of the above quote from Wolff and De Costa (2017) beyond graduate teacher education programs; that is, *no teacher begins their teaching with a blank slate*. Even those in their first year of teaching come with a background. A history. A story. And though it is impossible to know everything about language teachers, our investment in acknowledging and understanding their backgrounds, histories and stories sets the stage for what we can know about language teachers and their work.

The origin of this book is inspired by some of my own experiences as a former faculty member at the University of Taipei in the Department of English Instruction. I had begun developing the idea of 'teachers of multiple languages' (TMLs) and started searching for research participants, specifically teachers who had taught or were currently teaching multiple languages. It was then that I realized that I actually did not know if any of my own colleagues had taught any other languages beyond English. I had never thought to ask. And perhaps because we were all part of the 'Department of English Instruction', I had assumed that they were all simply English teachers and ascribed to them that singular label without much thought. But the idea that some of them might be TMLs incognito intrigued me. When I asked my colleagues 'Have you taught other languages before?', some replied 'No', but others had responses that were more nuanced. One colleague initially said 'No', but explained that prior to being a professor of English, she was an elementary school teacher who had taught Mandarin Chinese. Another colleague also replied 'No', but mentioned that in addition to teaching English classes at our university, she was also teaching Southern Min (often referred to as 'Taiwanese') at

1

an elementary school. Both colleagues asked me whether those experiences 'counted' as 'teaching multiple languages'. They seemed hesitant to fully commit to the idea that they were legitimate teachers of another language alongside English, despite the experience they had that proved otherwise. I realized from these interactions (and other similar interactions from searching for research participants) that unlike the identity of being a teacher of a *single* language (e.g. an English teacher), or even a *speaker* of multiple languages (e.g. being multilingual), identifying as a *teacher* of *multiple* languages was uncharted territory.

This led me to wonder, how many of the language teachers we meet and know in our everyday encounters as colleagues, students, administrators, employers and friends have histories or present realities in teaching multiple languages that we do not know about because it is never asked or talked about? Why is it that we rarely consider the experiences of language teachers beyond the single identity we first come to know them by? This is where I begin this book – highlighting who TMLs are through their stories and experiences, and exploring what that means for language teaching research.

Purpose of the Book

The purpose of this book is to argue for the visibility and significance of TMLs as a demographic group of language teachers that has been largely overlooked in language teaching research. In both research and teaching contexts, they have been assumed to have the same teaching experiences as teachers of a single language but doubled. For instance, a teacher who has taught Japanese and Korean is generally considered to be a teacher who has taught an additional language in comparison to a teacher of Japanese. This book argues that special focus should be paid to TMLs because the experience of teaching multiple languages is unique from teaching a single language and impacts who teachers become and how they teach. I argue that *teaching multiple languages is not simply an act of teaching a greater number of languages or an additional set of coursework, but also an act of navigating more complex worlds and developing additional ways of being through new identities, beliefs and emotions.* Through narratives of individual TMLs, this book aims to understand who TMLs are, what makes TMLs unique and how understanding TMLs paves the way for new perspectives in research on language teachers, language teacher education and multilingualism.

Defining 'Teachers of Multiple Languages'

A TML is *a language teacher who has previously taught or is currently teaching multiple languages.* TMLs are 'a growing subset of the language teacher population in many countries' (Calafato, 2020: 604), and are thus quite diverse; one cannot isolate one specific image of who

TMLs are. One reason is because TMLs' careers often involve teaching different student populations in various educational settings depending on the languages they have taught, as language teachers in today's neoliberal education market are increasingly seeking careers beyond their local educational systems (Li & Lai, 2022). Therefore, the broad landscape of teaching multiple languages involves a wide range of educational institutions, geographical settings, language pedagogies, language policies and cultural ideologies. For example, the following are sample career profiles of several TMLs with different career trajectories:

- TML #1: A language teacher from the US who primarily taught adults English as a second language (ESL) as a part-time adjunct instructor at a community college and took on a second part-time job teaching German at a corporate office.
- TML #2: A language teacher in Norway teaching German and Spanish at an upper-secondary school.
- TML #3: A language teacher from Japan who taught Japanese heritage language classes in the US while studying for a master's (MA) in teaching English to speakers of other languages (TESOL) program, and after obtaining her MA in TESOL, returned to Japan to teach English as a foreign language (EFL).
- TML #4: A language teacher from Turkey who taught EFL in Turkey, traveled to the US to temporarily teach Turkish at a US university for one year through a government-sponsored program, and returned to Turkey to continue teaching EFL.

TML #1 and #2 are examples of teachers who are simultaneously teaching more than one language in their career, while TML #3 and #4 are examples of teachers who have taught multiple languages sequentially, transitioning from teaching one language into another. There may even be TMLs who are a combination of TML #1/#2 and #3/#4 (i.e. having taught multiple languages simultaneously and sequentially), such as a teacher who has taught English and Spanish simultaneously and switched careers to teaching Chinese. Certainly, other combinations of TMLs are possible as these categories largely depend on the circumstances of a TML's career: what languages they teach, what contexts they are teaching in and when in their career they are teaching those languages. This also means that there can be great differences in the background and experience of one TML compared to another. The main point here is that teaching multiple languages looks different in different teaching contexts; there is a great diversity of means and pathways that can lead to the teaching of multiple languages. Despite the wide variation of circumstances, what many TMLs have in common is the *multiplicity* and *non-linearity* of TMLs' careers that comes from teaching multiple languages as part of a 'changing global workforce outside of the traditional teacher workforce that is usually conceived within a single subject area or school setting' (Li & Lai, 2022). In other words, with each language TMLs teach, they are engaging with different linguistic systems, teaching methods, student demographics, classroom contexts, institutional systems, sociohistorical contexts and language ideologies – often not in a neat, linear manner. The experience of learning to navigate this multiplicity and non-linearity influences who TMLs are and how they teach, and is, ultimately, what makes them distinct from teachers who have only taught one language.

The Need for a New Term: TML and Existing Terms

Existing terms describing language teachers

Research in applied linguistics has explored a plethora of terms to label and identify language teachers of various backgrounds. The diversity of ways we describe language teachers is no accident – the terminology that researchers and practitioners develop to conceptualize who teachers are and who they perceive themselves to be is an attempt to account for the realities that language teachers experience in their everyday lives (Darvin & Norton, 2015; Douglas Fir Group, 2016). In particular, multiple terms have been introduced within the past two decades to recognize language teachers in relation to using multiple languages, originally with the intent of providing alternatives for the term 'non-native English speaker' (Jain, 2018). These terms include 'bilingual teachers' (Lemberger, 1997; Rubio et al., 2021; Varghese, 2001), 'multilingual teachers' (Higgins & Ponte, 2017; Pavlenko, 2003), 'the multilingual instructor' (Kramsch & Zhang, 2018), 'plurilingual teachers' (Ellis, 2016; Maddamsetti, 2020), multicompetent teachers (Cook, 1999, 2016; Pavlenko, 2003) and translingual teachers (Jain, 2014; Menard-Warwick et al., 2019; Motha et al., 2012).

While these existing terms all address some aspect of language teachers who *know* and *use* multiple languages in their teaching and non-teaching lives, none of the existing terms specifically addresses the experience of teachers who *have taught* multiple languages as separate subjects. In fact, these existing terms have quite a different focus than the term 'TML'. Terms like 'multilingual teachers' and 'translingual teachers' aim to account for the *knowledge and use of* multiple languages *in any subject* that they may be teaching. García (2009: 193) refers to this as 'multiple multilingual education', or the use of more than two languages to educate, where 'programs weave languages in and out of the curriculum, dropping them, expanding them, and using them for one function or the other'. In other words, these are educational contexts in which multiple languages are being used to teach subject content, such as mathematics, science, history or the visual arts. Scholars have been actively documenting where and how such education models are being implemented, such as bilingual or trilingual education in Hong Kong

(Wang & Kirkpatrick, 2019) and Taiwan (Graham & Yeh, 2022; Pineda & Tsou, 2021), mother tongue language as instruction in Ghana (Ansah, 2014; Kioko *et al.*, 2014), dual language programs in the United States (Arias & Fee, 2018; Christian, 2016; Domínguez-Fret & Oberto, 2022) or English as a medium of instruction classes in global higher education (Brown, 2014; Kim, 2017). These educational models challenge the long-standing assumption that teachers should only use one language to teach a subject and create learning environments that value multiple languages, though the format, implementation, impact and perceptions of multilingual education can vary widely.

Why is there a need for the term 'TML'?

In contrast to multilingual teachers, the term 'TML' describes teachers who are teaching more than one language as a subject. While TMLs are multilingual individuals, they may or may not use multiple languages when teaching a language. That is, the term 'TML' does not describe *how* one teaches, but simply that one has taught more than one language as a subject in their career. While it is possible that TMLs are also multilingual teachers in that they teach multiple languages using multiple languages in each classroom, that may not be the case for many TMLs.

Fundamentally, there is so far no common, established term to characterize teachers who have taught multiple languages. Without a common term, TMLs remain invisible in research, in the workplace and in their own self-conceptions. After all, how does one talk about or self-identify as a language teacher with the job experience of teaching multiple languages without a term like 'TML'? The argument for introducing new professional, identity-based labels has been made before for recognizing instructors' ability to speak multiple languages, which had previously been unaddressed and left invisible. While terms like 'native' or 'non-native' had been commonly used to describe language teachers, there were no terms that allowed teachers to be identified as multilingual. For example, in the following excerpt, Kramsch and Zhang (2018) remind us that for multilingual instructors, introducing new labels for language teachers may challenge language teachers' conceptualizations of themselves and might make them feel uncomfortable, but could also introduce new ways of seeing themselves:

> Indeed, even though as individuals they might speak several languages and be members of several different cultures, as instructors they are trained to present themselves as monolingual and monocultural representatives of a nation-state. Such training, too, is the product of history and the effect of institutional power. Calling them 'multilingual instructors' might be a programmatic metaphor for the researcher and, as Lihua remarks in the Preface, it might open up for them new ways of seeing

themselves, though some of them might feel uncomfortable with such a characterization and argue that they are in fact required to act as monolingual instructors. (Kramsch & Zhang, 2018)

In line with Kramsch and Zhang (2018), one of the primary motivations and goals for this book and introducing the term 'TML' is to provide the possibility of a new way for TMLs to see themselves.

Ellis (2004: 90) has made a similar argument for the explicit recognition of language teachers' multilingualism, calling it the 'one key aspect of teachers' experience [that] is all but invisible in teacher education, employment and professional development'. Finally, Jessner (2008a: 41) has argued that in the context of teaching third languages, in order to properly take into account the role of the teacher in multilingual learning, 'more than one perspective of that teacher has to be taken into consideration', one of which is 'the teacher who teaches several languages'.

This book makes the case that establishing 'TML' as a new term specifically for identifying teachers of multiple languages is long overdue and necessary in order to (1) begin collecting, curating and contributing research on the teaching of multiple languages; (2) spotlight and learn from the stories and lived experiences of TMLs; and (3) professionalize the careers and identities of TMLs (Elsheikh & Yahia, 2020). Chapter 2 begins to make this case by providing a comprehensive overview of the current state of TML research.

2 The Current State of TML Research

In order to understand language teaching and learning, we need to understand teachers; and in order to understand teachers, we need to have a clearer sense of who they are: the professional, cultural, political, and individual identities which they claim or which are assigned to them.

(Varghese et al., 2005: 22)

Research on teachers of multiple languages (TMLs) is still an emerging landscape. The problem is not that TML studies do not exist. In fact, many studies in applied linguistics, language education and language policy/planning explore the experiences of TMLs or policies and programs relating to TMLs. Tables 2.1 and 2.2 provide a summary of selected studies that examine TMLs or the teaching of multiple languages. These studies are discussed in more detail throughout this chapter, so readers can refer to these tables as needed.

To begin with, one problem is a matter of curation: of finding and cataloguing these studies as 'TML studies' because so far there is no collective term that easily and clearly indicates them as such. Many of these studies are categorized under other topics, such as language teacher identity (LTI), multilingual education or multilingual teachers. Another problem is the way the studies are conducted and reported – that when language teaching studies are conducted, participants who have the experience of teaching multiple languages are rarely treated as distinct from participants who have taught a single language. Unfortunately, there is a common assumption that the teaching of multiple languages is not relevant or significant enough to be provided along with other participant background information. This assumption results in three scenarios in language teaching research:

(1) Currently, there are studies that specifically focus on examining TMLs but are mostly not labeled as such. These studies may have the specific aim of learning more about TMLs (i.e. the teachers' experiences, their teaching practices or the teacher education system) or

Table 2.1 Studies about TMLs or the teaching of multiple languages

Study	Teaching context/languages taught by TMLs	No. of TML participants	Research methodology	Summary of the study
Aslan (2015)	US/English, French, German	1 (of 1)	Interviews, in-class observations	A case study of a foreign language teacher in the US, who had taught French., English and German, investigating her NS/NNS identities, professional identity, teacher cognition and teaching practices.
Blair (2012)	UK/English, German, Spanish	1 (of 6)	Interviews, online discussion	A doctorate thesis on the multiple identities of multilingual, multicultural language teachers, one of whom is a language teacher from Germany who had taught German and Spanish in Spain, and English in Thailand and the United Kingdom.
Calafato (2020)	Norway, Russia/English, French, German, Spanish, Norwegian, Russian	103 (of 460)	Online questionnaire	A study comparing the identities and beliefs of being multilingual of upper-secondary school language teachers from Norway and Russia, a portion of whom taught more than one foreign language.
Calafato (2021a)	Norway, Russia/Chinese, English, French, German, Spanish	11 (of 21)	Interviews	A study on the implementation of multilingual teaching practices by upper-secondary school language teachers from Norway and Russia, a portion of whom reported teaching more than one foreign language.
Calafato (2021b)	Norway, Russia/English, French, German, Spanish	128 (of 517)	Online questionnaire	A study on the implementation of multilingual teaching practices by upper-secondary school language teachers from Norway and Russia, a portion of whom reported teaching more than one foreign language.
De Costa (2015)	US/English, Korean	1 (of 1)	Written reflections, interview	A longitudinal narrative inquiry on the professional identity development of an early career female teacher who had taught English in South Korea and Korean in the US.
Haukås (2016)	Norway/English, French, German, Spanish, Norwegian	11 (of 12)	Focus group discussions	A study on the beliefs about multilingualism and multilingual pedagogy by lower-secondary school language teachers in Norway, most of whom had taught more than one language.
Kayi-Aydar (2015a)	US/English, Spanish	1 (of 1)	Interviews, journal entries	A narrative inquiry of the multiple identities of a language teacher who had originally planned to become a Spanish language teacher, but changed to become an ESL teacher.

Study	Context/Languages	Participants	Data collection	Description
Kim and Smith (2019)	US/English, Japanese, Korean	3 (out of 3)	Interviews	A study on the multiple language teacher identities of international graduate students teaching Korean as a foreign language at American universities. All of the participants were TMLs.
Kim and Smith (2020)	US/English, Japanese, Korean	2 (out of 5)	Interviews	A study on the multiple language teacher identities and emotions of international graduate students teaching Korean as a foreign language at American universities. Two participants were TMLs.
Kramsch and Zhang (2018)	US/Chinese, English, French, German, Spanish, Vietnamese	(24 of 78) + 1 author	Survey, interviews	A book about the experiences of multilingual language teachers and their nativeness/non-nativeness from ecolinguistic theory and complexity theory perspectives.
Li and Lai (2022)	Hong Kong/English, Chinese	3 (out of 3)	Interviews	A narrative study on the professional identities of ESL teachers who transition to teaching CSL as second careers.
Luo and Gao (2017)	US/Chinese, English	25 (out of 25)	Questionnaire, observation notes, written reports and reflections	A study on the experiences of English language teachers from China temporarily teaching Chinese at American universities through the Fulbright Foreign Language Teaching Assistant program.
Mutlu and Ortaçtepe (2016)	Turkey/English, Turkish	5 (of 5)	Questionnaire, journals, interviews	A study on the identities, self-efficacy and beliefs of Turkish EFL teachers participating in a government-sponsored international teacher exchange program to teach Turkish at an American university for one year.
Pessoa et al. (2018)	Brazil/English, Portuguese	7 (of 7)	Questionnaires, written narratives, class activity, reflective session	A study on the discourses of language teacher education and experiences participating in a program developing teachers' English competency from language teachers who had taught Portuguese and English.
Rostami et al. (2021)	Iran/Arabic, English, Persian	11 (of 111)	Interviews	A study on plurilingualism, teacher agency and teacher identity in a language teacher from Canada who taught French and Spanish and participated in a two-week professional development sojourn.
Tavares (2022)	Portuguese, English	1 (of 1)	Memory, teacher journals, textbook	An autoethnography examining the identity-related experiences of a teacher who had taught Portuguese and English.
Wernicke (2018)	Canada/French, Spanish	1 (of 1)	Interviews, focus group	A study on the professional identities of secondary school language teachers in Iran who shifted from teaching Persian or Arabic to teaching English.

focus on investigating some other aspect of language teaching (i.e. heritage language learning, language policy, etc.).

(2) There are some studies that *incidentally* include participants who are TMLs, that is, with no intention to investigate the teaching of multiple languages. Such studies usually only mention the fact that the participant has taught multiple languages as a brief descriptor of their background, leaving unquestioned their background as a TML as a taken-for-granted detail of their profile. No discussion relating to the teaching of multiple languages is provided so the findings may not substantially contribute to TML research, even though they include TML participants. For example, Ruohotie-Lyhty (2013) featured two participants who are indicated as qualified to teach multiple languages. However, throughout the findings and discussion, whether they are teaching multiple languages and what languages they are teaching are not clearly or consistently explained. Therefore, interpreting Ruohotie-Lyhty's (2013) findings as TML research may be misleading. Other examples of such studies include Elmquist (1970), Hurst (2018) and Leonet *et al.* (2017).

(3) Finally, there are likely studies that may include TMLs as participants but are left undiscoverable because many studies do not ask participants about or provide any information about their language teaching backgrounds.

The following section reviews the existing TML research that I have curated through my own search to find TML studies.

Exploring the Experiences and Lives of TMLs: Identities, Emotions, Beliefs

Perhaps the most prolific topic in TML research so far is examining the experiences and lives of TMLs. These studies provide an in-depth look at what it is like for a language teacher to teach another language, often in different educational contexts. While some studies are conducted during a set period of time in which a teacher is experiencing teaching another language temporarily (e.g. when a teacher goes abroad for one year to teach a different language through a language teacher exchange program), other studies take a longer, 'life story' (McAdams, 2008; Park, 2006) approach and have participants reflect on their career experience in teaching multiple languages. Regardless, what makes these studies (and TMLs' experiences) most interesting is that through their lived experience of having taught multiple languages, TMLs can make comparisons between the teaching of different languages – comparisons in their teacher knowledge, identities, beliefs, emotions, practices and students. It is through these comparisons that we can witness the degree of complexity that the teaching of multiple languages requires and why there is reason to distinguish TMLs from teachers of a single language. From a teacher cognition perspective, Aslan (2015: 256) has described the complexity of a TML's teaching experiences as 'dynamic and non-linear, meaning that they caused unpredictable and context-dependent changes'. The following literature review aims to (1) provide a brief overview of current understandings of LTIs, beliefs and emotions; and (2) explore what findings TML studies have found in relation to TMLs' dynamic and non-linear teaching experiences.

Language teacher identities, beliefs and emotions

Language teacher identities

LTIs are the ways that language teachers understand, construct, perform and reflect on who they are and how others perceive them within the context of language teaching. Theoretical understandings of LTIs have only expanded over time as scholars have shared new findings and ways of conceptualizing LTIs. Thus, there is no simple way of defining LTIs. However, Kayi-Aydar (2015a) and Yazan (2018a) present the following definitions that provide a helpful foundation for introducing our discussion of LTIs for TMLs.

> I define identity as multiple presentations of self which are (re)constructed across social contexts and demonstrated through actions and emotions. (Kayi-Aydar, 2015a: 138)

> Teacher identity refers to teachers' dynamic self-conception and imagination of themselves as language teachers, which shifts as they participate in varying communities, interact with other individuals, and position themselves (and are positioned by others) in social contexts. (Yazan, 2018a: 21)

These definitions highlight some of the central themes of LTI that have been consistently reported in LTI research, as have other prominent scholars (Barkhuizen, 2017; Cheung, 2015; Kayi-Aydar, 2019; Sang, 2020; Yazan, 2018a; Yazan & Lindahl, 2020). The following is a summary of current understandings of LTI and areas of LTI research:

(1) LTIs are dynamic, multiple, hybrid and continually evolving (e.g. Aneja, 2016; Kayi-Aydar, 2015a; Racelis & Matsuda, 2015; Yazan, 2018a).
(2) LTIs are a site of conflict and struggle (e.g. Chang, 2018; Kayi-Aydar, 2015b; Phan, 2008; Varghese et al., 2005).
(3) LTIs are individual as well as mediated by social, cultural and political contexts; LTIs are internal and external (e.g. Aoyama, 2021;

Edwards & Burns, 2016; Fogle & Moser, 2017; Pennington & Richards, 2016; Tsui, 2007).

(4) LTIs are inseparable from other social identities, such as race, culture, gender, class and sexuality (e.g. Cooper & Bryan, 2020; Gagné *et al.*, 2018; Ku, 2020; Lander, 2018; Lawrence & Nagashima, 2020; Lin *et al.*, 2004; Menard-Warwick, 2008; Motha, 2006; Park, 2015, 2017; Simon-Maeda, 2004).

(5) LTIs are constructed, maintained, negotiated and performed through membership and participation in communities of practice (e.g. Ajayi, 2011; Clarke, 2008; Pavlenko, 2003; Tsui, 2007; Varghese *et al.*, 2005; Vélez-Rendón, 2010).

(6) LTIs are constructed, maintained, negotiated and performed discursively through narratives and self-authoring (e.g. Kayi-Aydar, 2015b; Liao, 2020; Menard-Warwick *et al.*, 2019; Morrison *et al.*, 2020).

(7) LTIs shape teacher agency and investment, while teacher agency and investment also shape LTIs (e.g. Darvin & Norton, 2015; Haneda & Sherman, 2016; Kayi-Aydar, 2015b; Norton, 2013, 2017; Yazan, 2018c).

(8) LTIs shape the emotions experienced from teaching, while emotions also shape LTIs (e.g. Kim & Smith, 2020; Kocabaş-Gedik & Ortaçtepe Hart, 2021; Reis, 2015; Song, 2016; Wolff & De Costa, 2017).

(9) LTIs can be a pedagogical resource (i.e. 'identity as pedagogy') that can shape language teaching practices, language teacher education curriculum and language teaching policies (e.g. Fairley, 2020; Kanno & Stuart, 2011; Ku & Liu, 2021; Morgan, 2004; Zheng, 2017).

(10) LTIs can be transformative as a source of social change and social justice (e.g. De Costa & Norton, 2017; Fairley, 2020; Miller *et al.*, 2017; Morgan, 2016; Varghese *et al.*, 2016).

The above list is not meant to be exhaustive or definitive. It certainly is not meant to be a checklist of 'what identity is'. Rather, one should approach the above list as what we have observed *so far* about the role that LTIs play as part of language teaching research. Working from the foundation of current conceptualizations of LTIs, we can begin to explore questions relating to what TML research may contribute to LTI research. Of definite interest is to examine what aspects of TML research affirms or challenges current understandings of LTIs. Additionally, how does the added complexity of teaching multiple languages (which perhaps may also involve different teaching contexts, mediums of instruction, teaching methodologies, student populations and/or institutional systems) impact the development of LTIs? For example, a key issue often discussed in TML research is the experience of having been both a native speaker (NS) and a non-native speaker (NNS) teacher and/or transitioning from one to another. These are some of the predominant issues that are discussed in this book.

Language teacher beliefs

Language teacher beliefs can be described as the ideas and theories language teachers have about language teaching and learning. Language teacher beliefs have long been of interest in language teaching research, starting in the mid-1980s with a focus on understanding what beliefs students and teachers have about language learning and teaching (Barcelos & Kalaja, 2011). Although beliefs can be considered universal and relatable in that we all have beliefs about language teaching and learning to a certain extent, beliefs can also be 'messy' (Pajares, 1992: 307), 'elusive' (Barcelos, 2003: 7) and 'notoriously difficult to define' (Mercer, 2011: 336). One reason is because, from a research standpoint, beliefs may not be directly observable because participants may not have the language to describe their own beliefs (Kagan, 1992), may not want to voice some of their beliefs or may not be conscious of them (Borg, 2018; Kamiya, 2018). In addition, what also complicates beliefs is their 'paradoxical nature': beliefs are both fluctuating yet stable, individual yet also contextually mediated and generalizable (Negueruela-Azarola, 2011). Furthermore, Mercer (2011: 343) has shown how beliefs are a complex dynamic system, in which 'the system as a whole can be both self-consistent… but yet different components can also adapt and change across contexts and time and be mediated in potentially unpredictable ways by various self-related processes'.

These issues with conceptualizing beliefs have significant methodological implications. The most common data collection methods for researching language teacher beliefs are questionnaires, interviews, stimulated recall, observations and reflective writing (Song, 2015). In general, qualitative methodologies such as interviews, observations and reflective writing have been recognized for being able to capture the complex and dynamic nature of beliefs in greater depth (Richardson & Placier, 2001). However, the persistent problem that underlies any of these methods is the difficulty of knowing what teachers 'really believe', as mentioned in the previous paragraph (Skott, 2015). To address this dilemma, Song (2015) has emphasized the importance of employing multiple data collection methods to improve research credibility and account for the complexity and multiplicity of teachers' beliefs. In addition, Skott (2015) has recommended that any research on teacher beliefs should also engage with the teachers' educational experiences within and beyond the classroom, emphasizing that beliefs are social and not solely based on individual action.

In addition to researching the nature of beliefs, research on language teacher beliefs has also investigated how beliefs impact language teaching practices and decision-making processes (Borg, 2003; Farrell & Bennis, 2013; Pajares, 1992). This line of research has been prolific in that beliefs have been seen as a way of accessing the reasoning behind language teaching practices and possibly influencing language teaching practices (Song, 2015). However, the opposite has also been of interest, that beliefs might (or might not) be able to be changed through some form of intervention, such as changing teaching practices (Guskey, 2002), teacher education curriculum (Borg, 2011; Kurihara & Samimy, 2007; Phipps, 2007; Urmston, 2003) or reflective practices (Borg, 2011; Farrell & Ives, 2015). However, the reality is that language teaching beliefs and practices have a reciprocal relationship, each influencing the other in complex and sometimes incongruent ways (Basturkmen, 2012; Borg, 2018). A reciprocal relationship, however, does not mean that there is a causal relationship between beliefs and practices. In fact, Borg (2018) has concluded that:

> We know that very often teachers' stated beliefs are not reflected in their classroom practices, that exceptions to this trend can be identified, and that variations in the relationship between beliefs and practices can be explained with reference to both internal factors in the teachers themselves (e.g. biography, awareness, motivation, experience) and external factors (e.g. curricula, time, institutional policy), which may constrain what teachers do. (Borg, 2018: 81)

The discussion around language teacher beliefs in this book does not focus on the nature of what beliefs are or determining the relationship between teacher beliefs and practices. Rather, I approach beliefs in conjunction with its sister constructs, identity and emotions, in order to explore '*how* beliefs develop, fluctuate and interact with actions, emotions, identities or affordances and how they are constructed within the micro and macro-political contexts of learning and teaching languages' (Barcelos & Kalaja, 2011: 282, emphasis in original). Specifically, the discussion of beliefs in relation to the teaching of multiple languages is multi-layered and multi-faceted – TMLs may have different beliefs regarding (1) the experience or work of teaching multiple languages; (2) the teaching practices of different languages; (3) the way beliefs change or are impacted by the transitioning from teaching one language to another; and/or (4) the role of teacher education in teaching multiple languages. Accordingly, the qualitative data collection methodologies employed in this study (i.e. interviews, writing teaching philosophies, photo-elicitation) were designed to best operationalize this approach to teacher beliefs.

Language teacher emotions

In comparison to the previous two constructs, identity and beliefs, language teacher emotions is a relatively more recent topic in language teaching research. In the past two decades, there has been an 'emotional turn' (Barcelos, 2015; De Costa *et al.*, 2019; White, 2018) in applied linguistics, recognizing the significance of emotions in understanding language learning and teaching. Early research focused on emotions in language learning, such as the affective filter (Krashen, 1982; Scovel, 1978) and language learner anxiety (Horwitz *et al.*, 1986). In the 2000s, there was a shift toward examining the emotions of language teachers through research on multilingualism and emotions in a broader sense (Dewaele, 2010; Pavlenko, 2005).

One major area of research on language teacher emotions has come from positive psychology, which has changed the focus of psychology 'from preoccupation only with repairing the worst things in life to also building positive qualities' (Seligman & Csikszentmihalyi, 2000: 5). Moreover, positive psychology emphasizes 'a concern with individuals as holistic beings with potential for trajectories of positive growth' (MacIntyre *et al.*, 2019). Thus, emotions play an important role in the study of the positive psychology of language learning and teaching. Some studies have explored the nature of language teachers' *emotional well-being* (e.g. Gregersen *et al.*, 2020; Jin *et al.*, 2021; Mercer, 2020; Oxford, 2020) and strategies to help manage language teacher wellbeing, also known as 'positive psychology interventions' (e.g. Fresacher, 2016; Gregersen *et al.*, 2016; Helgesen, 2017; Hiver, 2016; Talbot & Mercer, 2018). Closely related to this are studies focusing on *emotional intelligence*, which is 'the ability to understand feelings in the self and others and to use these feelings as informational guides for thinking and action' (Salovey *et al.*, 2011: 238). Studies on language teachers' emotional intelligence focus on measuring levels of emotional intelligence in language teachers, understanding what factors mediate levels of emotional intelligence in language teachers and how emotional intelligence impacts language teaching practices (Dewaele *et al.*, 2018; Gkonou & Mercer, 2017; Kang, 2020). Finally, a number of studies have also explored the role of *empathy* in language learning and teaching (McAlinden, 2014; Mercer, 2016) as well as how language education can play a role in cultivating empathy and social justice (Porto & Zembylas, 2020; Zembylas & Chubbuck, 2009).

Recent research has also expanded to the social and post-structuralist perspectives of language teacher emotions, which approach emotions as 'discursively constructed', 'processes, which shape and are also shaped by the sociocultural context', 'interactive, dynamic, and form a complex' (Barcelos, 2015: 309–310). Furthermore, social and post-structuralist perspectives of language teacher emotions also look at emotion in relation to power, inequality, ideology and politics. A prominent example of this line of research is Benesch's (2017, 2018, 2019, 2020) application of two related constructs: *feeling rules* and *emotional labor*. Feeling rules are defined as 'explicit instructions, formulated by management, about which emotions lower-level workers are expected to display in the workplace', and emotional labor is the 'conflict between feeling rules and employee's internal feelings' (Benesch, 2018: 62). For example, Benesch's (2018) examination of the language used in a university's plagiarism policy revealed implied expectations of how faculty members should respond upon discovering plagiarism, namely 'hypervigilance', 'indignation' and 'retribution'. Emotional labor was involved when language teachers felt conflicted and even resisted the feeling rules of their institution.

The discussion around language teacher emotions in this book focuses on understanding the range and dynamics of emotions experienced by TMLs from teaching multiple languages. In particular, what may be unique about TMLs' experiences of teacher emotions is the need to regulate or manage different emotions depending on each of the different languages they are teaching. This may complicate the emotional labor required of TMLs because they may need to adapt to different expectations of what emotions they are allowed to express based on the different languages they teach. Furthermore, the discussion in this book also examines possible factors involved in the co-construction of emotional experiences, including beliefs and identities. In this way, the language teacher emotions discussed in this book are seen as interactive, dynamic and part of a greater network of teacher development.

The relationship between identities, beliefs and emotions

The relationship between LTIs, beliefs and emotions is neither simple nor clear-cut. Not all scholars agree on how the relationships should be conceptualized or drawn. For example, some scholars approach emotions and beliefs under the larger umbrella of identity work (Barkhuizen & Mendieta, 2020; Schutz *et al.*, 2007; Yazan, 2018a), while others describe identities, beliefs and emotions as working parallel to one another, or as interrelated, overlapping and co-constructed constructs (Barcelos, 2015, 2017; Cross & Hong, 2009).

Although there does not seem to be a singular, simple way to pin down the relationship between identities, beliefs and emotions, many recent studies have described the three constructs in similar ways: as complex, multiple, dynamic, contradictory, interactive and co-constructed (Barcelos, 2015, 2017). Furthermore, scholars have recognized that identities, beliefs and emotions are indeed inextricably connected (Barcelos, 2015; Kalaja *et al.*, 2016; Schutz *et al.*, 2007). More specifically, Barcelos (2015: 315) has suggested the idea of 'beliefs-emotions-identities', in which the three constructs are part of a non-linear, complex system and they 'change and adapt in response to any changes within themselves and within each other'. The discussion around TMLs' identities, beliefs and emotions in this book applies the above approach to identities, beliefs and emotions.

Identities in teaching multiple languages

Many studies have found that in teaching multiple languages, TMLs experience the negotiation of multiple identities changing over time. One major factor influencing the negotiation of multiple identities is having the experience of being both a NS and a NNS language teacher. Research in applied linguistics has long established the terms NS and NNS as perpetuating oversimplified and discriminatory categorizations based on the 'elusive' NS category (Moussu & Llurda, 2008). This has led to the deleterious treatment of language teachers and learners manifesting as native-speakerism (Cook, 1999; Holliday, 2015; Phillipson, 1992), linguicism (Skutnabb-Kangas, 2015) and linguistic racism (Dobinson & Mercieca, 2020; Dovchin, 2020). Here and throughout the rest of this book, I use the terms NS and NNS with an awareness and sensitivity to the greater problem to which they contribute. In the section titled 'Reflexivity: Addressing Choices, Contentions and Limitations' in Chapter 3, I explain in more detail the problems with using the labels NS and NNS. Despite the issues with using the NS and NNS labels, I have chosen to use them with the purpose of (1) examining TMLs' experiences with the NS construct in the different languages they have taught and (2) using terms that the participants were most familiar with and used themselves during the process of data collection.

Although it is certainly possible for a TML to have only been a NNS teacher, what has been more commonly reported in TML research is a situation in which a language teacher shifts roles from being a NS teacher to a NNS teacher, or vice versa. This shift results in language teachers experiencing a different way of perceiving themselves and a different way others perceive them. Furthermore, Li and Lai (2022), in particular, explored the role of 'brokering', or making new connections across different communities of practice, in the context of English as a second language (ESL) teachers transitioning to a second career as Chinese as a second language (CSL) teachers. In their study, Li and Lai (2022) found that when ESL teachers transitioned to CSL teachers, they engaged in acts of language and knowledge brokering (e.g. adapting to new approaches to teacher–student relationship, teacher authority and linguistic practices) to help them become members of their new, second-career communities. Thus, from a teacher identity perspective, brokering played a key role in helping TMLs 'find meaningful connections between different professional experiences and facilitated their alignment with their second-career professional identity' (Li & Lai, 2022: 11).

When NS teachers become NNS teachers

One scenario is when a formerly NS teacher becomes a NNS teacher when teaching another language. Kim and Smith (2019) studied international graduate students teaching Korean at American universities.

For example, a Japanese participant in their study shifted from teaching Japanese as a NS teacher to teaching Korean as a NNS. She reported feeling both positive emotions of empathy as well as negative emotions of anxiety. As a NNS speaker of Korean, she was able to relate with the language learning difficulties her students faced; however, she also reported feeling anxious when she was not able to answer a question or got confused by certain Korean expressions (Kim & Smith, 2019). Also, Fan and de Jong (2019) present an interesting case study of a language teacher from China who, at first, had positive experiences teaching EFL in China, but upon studying for a master's (MA) teaching English to speakers of other languages (TESOL) program in the US, began to feel increasingly unqualified and inadequate in comparison to her NS peers. In this scenario, it was not necessarily the experience of teaching English as a NNS that discouraged her, but the stigma and 'native speaker ideal' that she felt was prevalent in US educational contexts that ultimately pushed her to give up English language teaching in the US.

When NNS teachers become NS teachers

Another scenario is when a formerly NNS teacher becomes a NS teacher when teaching another language. For example, Mutlu and Orta-çtepe (2016) examined TMLs in the context of Turkish EFL teachers participating in a sponsored international education exchange program in which they taught Turkish at an American university for one year. Mutlu and Ortaçtepe's (2016: 565) findings showed that as participants renegotiated their identity from a NNS teacher to a NS teacher, they changed 'the way [they] described themselves, their self-confidence and competence, their perceptions of their abilities as teachers/users of both languages, their views of how their students and colleagues perceived them, and their beliefs about teaching and learning'. More specifically, Mutlu and Ortaçtepe (2016: 565) observed that in adjusting to being a native Turkish teacher, the participants felt 'more confident, safe, and powerful in class [as a native Turkish teacher], while they were more competent in terms of their teaching abilities in the position of a non-native English teacher'. Such feelings of confidence as new NS teachers were also expressed in Aslan (2015) and Kim and Smith (2019). In other words, while the participants associated feelings of confidence, safety and power with their experience as a NS teacher, they also recognized the significance of their English language training that led to feeling competent as a NNS English teacher.

Simultaneously becoming NS and NNS teachers

The examples so far have focused on TML participants who obtained language teacher education in one of the languages they taught but not the other. In other words, they had likely already established a professional LTI in a certain language (whether as a NS or NNS teacher), before exploring a different one. Another scenario that has been studied in TML research is the identity development of pre-service teachers enrolled in TML teacher education programs. These pre-service teachers, often undergraduate students, are working on a degree in teaching two languages and thus, they are simultaneously developing LTIs in both languages. In such cases, where the comparison between how one identifies with one language or the other is immediate and simultaneous, TMLs may experience favoring one language over another. For example, Pessoa *et al.* (2018) examined Brazilian teachers who graduated with an undergraduate degree in English and Portuguese education. Of the seven participants in his study, three only took English classes to fulfill the program's requirements and did not end up teaching English, and four participants eventually did teach English. However, in the study, six participants (out of seven) expressed dissatisfaction with the TML program and avoided identifying as English teachers because they 'focused on the fact that they had not learned how to speak fluently' (Pessoa *et al.*, 2018: 361).

Language learner identities

In addition to shifts between being a NS or NNS language teacher, TMLs also experience changes in their own language *learner* identities, particularly as a result of using a different language of instruction in teaching a different language. For example, in Kim and Smith (2019), all three participants felt their NNS English learner identities were intertwined with their TML teaching even though they were not teaching English. They were aware that having a high level of English proficiency was very important when teaching Korean at an American university, causing anxiety at times. Mutlu and Ortaçtepe (2016) also found that EFL Turkish teachers teaching English at American universities reflected on their English proficiency and this impacted their sense of confidence and competence, even when they were not teaching English. Similarly, Fan and de Jong (2019) featured a language teacher from China who had originally felt confident teaching EFL in China, but upon studying for her MA in TESOL in the US, lost confidence in English teaching because of her Chinese English accent and level of English fluency. These findings suggest that the negotiation of multiple identities and emotions in teaching multiple languages involves not only the languages that are taught, but also the languages used during instruction which may be different for each of the languages a TML teaches.

Cultural identities

Other studies have shown that another layer of identity that can become intertwined with TMLs' LTIs is their cultural identity, especially if they are transitioning from being a NNS teacher in their own country to a NS teacher in a foreign country. One of the observations mentioned by TMLs is the significance of culture in their language teaching in transitioning to the role of a NS teacher (Aslan, 2015; Kim & Smith, 2019; Mutlu & Ortaçtepe, 2016). When teaching as a NS teacher for the first time, some TMLs have reported feelings of cultural legitimacy, such as pride in being able to represent their native culture or country (Kim & Smith, 2019). Furthermore, NNS teachers who are teaching their language as a NS teacher in a different country (e.g. De Costa, 2015; Kim & Smith, 2019; Luo & Gao, 2017; Mutlu & Ortaçtepe, 2016) have reported that their experience living and teaching in the US has given them firsthand experiences with American culture that they believe will benefit their future EFL teaching back in their home country (Luo & Gao, 2017; Mutlu & Ortaçtepe, 2016). In other words, not only did they feel that they were bringing their cultural identities and knowledge to their American students through their new role as a NS teacher, but they also felt that they were gaining new cultural knowledge from living in the US that could benefit them when they returned to their home country and resumed their role as a NNS teacher. Although a positive cultural identity can emerge from the NNS to NS teacher transition, the reverse has also been shown to occur, in which a NS teacher transitioning to the role of a NNS teacher may feel a loss of confidence in no longer knowing about the language and culture firsthand (Fan & de Jong, 2019). Kramsch and Zhang (2018) described an example of this through Damien, a white NNS Chinese instructor in the US who talks with his students about his past travels and EFL teaching in China in order to gain greater cultural legitimacy with his students.

The negotiation of cultural identities can also be framed separately from the NS/NNS dichotomy. For example, one TML participant in Blair (2012) explained not feeling 'just German' because of her multicultural background as someone who has lived in four different countries, taking a bit from each culture, and taught three different languages. Another example can be seen in Rostami *et al.* (2021: 130), in which language teachers in Iran transitioned from teaching Persian or Arabic to teaching English and their new identities as EFL teachers were also associated with becoming more 'global', 'cosmopolitan' and 'academic' (Rostami *et al.*, 2021: 132). According to the participants, this involved 'adapting the norms of English-speaking countries' culture' to the way they teach (Rostami *et al.*, 2021: 130–131) and being 'an open-minded person from a self and social point of view' (Rostami *et al.*, 2021: 132). In fact, for one of Rostami *et al.*'s (2021) participants, changing his major to English teaching greatly benefitted his life far beyond his role as a teacher. His knowledge of English (which he attributed to his training and career as an English teacher and contrasted with his previous role as a Persian teacher) helped him become a successful international businessman and pulled him out of poverty. In turn, the cultural capital he gained as an international businessman helped him become 'a more competent teacher' because he had firsthand experience traveling abroad, meeting people of different cultures and using English for business (Rostami *et al.*, 2021: 133).

Finally, TMLs can also experience differences in the way their cultural identities are perceived and judged by others in the different teaching contexts they inhabit. Tavares (2022) discussed his experience of teaching Portuguese and English, where students from his Portuguese class questioned his legitimacy as a language teacher because he did not teach the variety of Portuguese they had expected and he did not match many of the students' cultural expectations. On the other hand, this issue never came up in the English classes he taught.

Beliefs in teaching multiple languages

The difficulty of being a NS teacher

In conjunction with negotiating multiple identities from teaching multiple languages, studies have also shown that TMLs experience changes in their language teaching beliefs, many of which are not necessarily specific to the teaching of multiple languages. Several studies have found that TMLs who were initially NNS teachers and later became NS teachers discovered that being a NS teacher is not as easy as they had originally believed (Aslan, 2015; Blair, 2012; De Costa, 2015; Kim & Smith, 2019; Mutlu & Ortaçtepe, 2016). For example, in De Costa (2015: 145), the participant, Natasha, described that when she had only been a non-native speaker teacher (NNST) of English in South Korea, she thought being a NS teacher would make teaching easier; however, after having taught her native language in the US, she realized that 'how successful my lesson is has nothing much to do with whether I'm teaching my native language or my second language'. In reflecting on her experience as a TML, Natasha found that her language teaching efficacy did not have to be bound by a LTI that followed the NS/NNS dichotomy; rather, she was able to reconceptualize her LTI in a more holistic sense that did not depend on whether or not she was teaching her native language. The TML participants in Mutlu and Ortaçtepe (2016: 564) made similar observations, noting that 'being a native speaker was not enough to be able teach a language, and being trained in language teaching was more important than being a native or a non-native teacher'.

The benefit of previous teaching experience and training

Studies have also found that the experience of teaching multiple languages can reinforce teachers' perceptions of their previous language teacher education and language teaching experiences (Blair, 2012; Li & Lai, 2022; Luo & Gao, 2017; Mutlu & Ortaçtepe, 2016; Tavares, 2022). In particular, many TMLs felt that their previous teacher training and teaching experience benefitted their teaching of other languages. For example, when the TML participants in Mutlu and Ortaçtepe (2016: 561) moved to the US to teach Turkish as NS teachers, they did not have any formal training or experience in teaching Turkish, but they still felt competent because as EFL teachers in Turkey, they had previously been 'trained in teaching to be equipped with the knowledge and skills to implement methods and teach a language effectively'. Tavares (2022: 9) felt similarly when recalling his own experiences of being able to draw on his 'ESL teaching experiential repertoire to reflect on potentially best ways to create and execute a particular learning activity for Portuguese', or what he described as 'pedagogical synergy'. Of course, studies have also reported TMLs realizing that solely relying on previously learned teaching approaches can have its own drawbacks. For example, in Luo and Gao (2017: 102), their questionnaire asked a question that pertained to the teaching of multiple languages: 'to what degree does your English teaching experience help your role as a Chinese Fulbright TA?'. The results from the 25 respondents showed that participants perceived their past English teaching experience to be 'fairly useful' (i.e. a mean rating of 5.84 out of 7), though their perceived usefulness of their past English teaching experience was also negatively correlated with their perceptions of the overall experience and success of their Chinese teaching (Luo & Gao, 2017: 78). Luo and Gao suggested that participants who deemed their past English teaching experience as more useful may have depended on that when teaching Chinese in the US, rather than testing new teaching approaches, thereby impacting their perceived experience and success of their Chinese teaching.

Adopting new teaching methods

Studies have also shown that the teaching of multiple languages can be an opportunity to experiment with different approaches to language teaching, whether TMLs are teaching within the same educational context (Rostami *et al.*, 2021) or adapting to a different context with different educational expectations (Fan & de Jong, 2019; Luo & Gao, 2017; Mutlu & Ortaçtepe, 2016). This, in turn, can impact their beliefs about effective language teaching practices. Both Luo and Gao (2017) and Mutlu and Ortaçtepe (2016) reported findings from participants who had positive experiences experimenting with new methods of language teaching while teaching a new language abroad at US universities. While it is certainly possible that the opportunity to use new teaching methods is more a result of teaching in a new educational context rather than a new language, what is also true in such cases is that the willingness to teach a new language granted access to the opportunity to teach in a new context (i.e. participate in a government-sponsored teacher exchange program to teach their native language at US universities). For such TMLs, the experience of teaching multiple languages and teaching in a new context abroad is inseparable.

The benefits of being multilingual

In perhaps one of the few large-scale, quantitative TML studies, Calafato (2020) conducted an online questionnaire with 460 language teachers from Norway and Russia, 98 of whom had taught two foreign languages and five of whom had taught three foreign languages. The questionnaire focused on language teacher beliefs on (1) the benefits of being multilingual, (2) the extent to which learning multilingual languages was promoted and (3) the NS ideal. One of Calafato's (2020: 611) findings showed that TMLs 'believed statistically significantly more strongly than did those teaching only one foreign language in the benefits of being or becoming a multilingual teacher in five out of the six items'. This seems in line with findings from Haukås' (2016) focus group study with 12 Norwegian TMLs (i.e. a mix of having taught English, German, Spanish, French or Norwegian), in which she found that the Norwegian teachers believed in the benefit of multilingualism from their own language learning experience, but did not necessarily perceive the same benefit for their students because their students did not seem aware of how to use their multilingualism to benefit their language learning. Furthermore, TMLs have described the way their multilingualism helped them use multilingual teaching practices more effectively, especially if they had a strong metalinguistic knowledge of the languages (Calafato, 2021a). However, Calafato (2021a: 597) also noted that for TMLs, 'metalinguistic knowledge in one [foreign language] did not always contribute to the ability to implement [multilingual teaching practices] in the other [foreign language]'.

The overall benefit of teaching multiple languages

Related to the benefit of experimenting with new approaches while teaching a new language, Luo and Gao (2017) also asked about how their participants perceived the overall experience of teaching multiple languages. This kind of question seems to be less commonly asked in TML research, possibly because in many studies, the teaching of multiple languages is studied as a relatively recent occurrence in the participants' lives and participants did not have the long-term perspective needed to make clear judgements about teaching multiple languages. Another possible explanation is that researchers perhaps did not frame what they were studying as 'the teaching of multiple languages' when they conducted their studies, so participants did not necessarily provide responses framed in that way. In their study, Luo and Guo (2017: 75) conducted a case study on one of their participants, Monica, who they describe as being 'a typical case of Chinese Fulbright TAs in the U.S.'. When asked about her experience teaching Chinese in the program, Monica described a two-way relationship in the way her previous English teaching in China benefitted her Chinese teaching in the US and vice versa. Similarly, Tavares (2022: 18) described his own experience of inhabiting the 'in-between space of teaching two languages' as 'synergetic' and beneficial both in terms of being able to 'critically reflect on [his] dual identity experiences' and interchange pedagogical knowledge from both teaching English and Portuguese. Coming from a slightly different perspective, Li and Lai (2022: 11) commented on the benefits of transitioning from teaching one language into a second career teaching a different language, pointing out that language teachers who had previously taught a different language come equipped with 'more personal, educational, and professional quests'.

Emotions in teaching multiple languages

Emotions are an inseparable part of language teaching and in TML studies, in particular, two major aspects of emotions in teaching multiple languages have been discussed. The first is in comparing the conflicting emotions TMLs feel when teaching one language as opposed to another, and the second is in evaluating emotions that either motivate or demotivate TMLs to teach one language versus another. Furthermore, emotions are often described in connection with TMLs' identity development, for instance, when shifting into new teacher roles as NS/NNS teachers. Song (2018: 463) explained that for non-native-speaking English teachers, emotions should not be seen as 'merely an individual reaction or feeling, but as something that is constituted, shaped, and circulated within social, historical, political, and economic contexts'. For TMLs, those social, historical, political and economic contexts can become even more complex because teaching multiple languages often involves entering and adapting to multiple contexts and institutional systems. Thus, complex, often conflicting, emotions become involved in teaching multiple languages.

When NNS teachers become NS teachers

The emotions associated with NS/NNS teaching are often complex and challenge the assumption of binary experiences (i.e. good vs. bad) between NS and NSS teachers. One of the most common emotions expressed by TMLs who transition from being a NNS teacher to a NS teacher is a new-found confidence (Kim & Smith, 2019; Mutlu & Ortaçtepe, 2016) in their teaching. In addition to confidence, TMLs also associated other positive feelings with transitioning from being a NNS teacher to a NS teacher, including feeling 'cool', 'safe, 'powerful' (Mutlu & Ortaçtepe, 2016: 559) and as 'a wanderer who had returned home after a long journey' (Kramsch & Zhang, 2018).

For example, in Kim and Smith (2019), one participant compared her confidence as a NS Korean teacher (as an international graduate student at an American university) with the frustration of being a NNS Japanese teacher (at private institutions in South Korea). She attributed her confidence as a NS teacher to being able to teach Korean culture and act as 'a model Korean' for her students (Kim & Smith, 2019: 37). In another example, participants in Mutlu and Ortaçtepe (2016: 559) explained that they felt more confident as NS Turkish teachers (as opposed to NNS EFL teachers) because 'their students did not question their knowledge of Turkish or refute what they said, but showed them respect'. Interestingly, Mutlu and Ortaçtepe (2016) found that the participants' newfound confidence as NS Turkish teachers did not negatively impact their feelings about their previous experience of being NNS EFL teachers. In fact, they reported that their experience in NS teaching reaffirmed their sense of confidence in their NNS EFL teaching, because they realized that language teaching is not only dependent on their 'nativeness' but also on their teacher training. However, despite the participants' ability to maintain a certain level of confidence in their NNS teaching after experiencing NS teaching, Mutlu and Ortaçtepe (2016) did point out that participants still held on to NS norms prevalent in Turkey. While their experience as NS Turkish teachers affirmed their confidence in their NNS EFL teaching, it also affirmed their desire to be NSs of English from 'feelings of disappointment at seeing that being a native speaker [of English] was an unattainable goal' (Mutlu & Ortaçtepe, 2016: 562). One might say that being able to compare NNS teaching with NS teaching led TMLs to understand each role relative to the other, establishing a dialogic relationship between the two roles. In other words, their emotions as a NNS teacher informed and shaped their emotions as a NS teacher, and vice versa.

It should be noted that the emotions expressed by participants in Kim and Smith (2019) and Mutlu and Ortaçtepe (2016) are also specific to the context of participants who had only made short-term commitments to be a NNS teacher while putting their NS teacher role on pause. Specifically, participants in Kim and Smith (2019) were teaching undergraduate Korean classes as international graduate students at American universities, and participants in Mutlu and Ortaçtepe (2016) were in a government-sponsored program where EFL teachers can teach their native language at an American university for one year. The participants' emotions in both studies could possibly differ if they were making more long-term career decisions to transition from being a NNS teacher to a NS teacher.

When NS teachers become NNS teachers

In general, the transition from being a NS teacher to a NNS teacher seems to be fraught with more mixed emotions than the reverse situation. Some of the negative emotions expressed by TMLs who shifted from being a NS teacher to a NNS teacher are anxiety, frustration, insecurity, incompetence and discomfort (Fan & de Jong, 2019; Kim & Smith, 2019; Mutlu & Ortaçtepe, 2016). These feelings can come from a variety of sources, such as 'being aware of their own weaknesses in terms of pronunciation and vocabulary, not being able to answer students' questions, and not being equipped with the necessary knowledge to be able to teach about the target language' (Mutlu & Ortaçtepe, 2016: 561). As NNS teachers, negative feelings can also come from feeling a lack of legitimacy, or feeling 'like being an imposter'. For instance, one participant in Kramsch and Zhang's (2018) study, a white NNS Chinese teacher in the US, expressed this feeling after he was constantly assumed to be just a student in the classroom. Furthermore, negative feelings can also derive from the comparative experience of being a NS teacher versus being a NNS teacher. For example, in Fan and de Jong (2019), a TML participant felt a loss of confidence and increasing discouragement as she attempted to transition from being a NS Chinese teacher to a NNS English teacher, causing her to give up on English teaching and return to teaching Chinese as a NS teacher. Finally, some TMLs can also feel that they must work harder than NS teachers, such as spending more time preparing lessons (Blair, 2012; Kim & Smith, 2019; Kramsch & Zhang, 2018). This can be a result of certain negative emotions, such as insecurity, or the awareness of having to work harder can lead to further negative emotions, such as frustration.

Perhaps the most common positive emotion expressed by TMLs transitioning from NS to NNS teaching is the new experience of being able to better empathize with their students because they themselves had once been learners of the language they are teaching (Blair, 2012; De Costa, 2015; Kim & Smith, 2019). For some TMLs, empathy largely acts as a technical skill to facilitate teaching. For example, in De Costa (2015: 144), empathy helped the participant's NNS teaching in allowing her to 'anticipate student difficulties', to the point where she actually felt 'disadvantaged by her nativeness' when she was a NS teacher. However, for other TMLs, empathy is more about an emotional connection that TMLs felt as NNS teachers. For example, a participant in Blair (2012: 119) emphasized 'the positive role model advantage she possesses (over "native" teachers) in teaching EAP and Study Skills, where "there is a better bond" with the students "because they know that I really know how they feel"'. Finally, empathy can also be a way for TMLs to connect with their own second language (L2) learner selves. For example, in Kim and Smith (2019: 37), one participant described his experiences as a NNS teacher as 'fun' because she was able to 'learn more about the language as a teacher… which helps [her] grasp a firm understand of those rules'.

Emotions beyond NS/NNS teaching: Self-growth, status and liberation

Perhaps a more interesting finding from TML studies are TMLs who have described their transition from teaching one language to another as a form of self-growth or a greater improvement in their lives from a macro perspective. These emotions are not necessarily framed under or confined to their NS/NNS teacher identities. For example, the participants in Mutlu and Ortaçtepe (2016: 560) described 'being more complete' from their experiences teaching Turkish at an American university for a year. Their sense of completeness was not simply limited to their classroom teaching, but rather their experiences teaching in a new educational context and meeting new people from different backgrounds, leading them to 'being more open to different people, more patient and tolerant, and more confident while socializing and dealing with the challenges'.

TMLs have also associated their teaching of multiple languages with an increase in prestige and status. Rostami *et al.* (2021) very clearly demonstrated this through a study of NS Arabic and/or Persian teachers from Iran who transitioned to NNS English teaching. Interestingly, the participants did not feel negative emotions from becoming NNS English teachers (as other studies have reported). What these participants felt was a substantial increase in social status, recognition and respect due to the prestige of English. The participants emphasized that 'the pay and benefits system are the same for all teachers' (Rostami *et al.*, 2021: 130), but they felt that by teaching EFL, they were 'involved in something that was more valuable and global' (Rostami *et al.*, 2021: 130) and feeling 'a kind of enthusiasm and admiration from among [their] colleagues' (Rostami *et al.*, 2021: 129).

In addition, TMLs can also feel a sense of liberation or freedom when transitioning from teaching one language to another. Kramsch and Zhang (2018) described one participant (NS German teacher, NNS Spanish teacher) who felt that while teaching German as a NS teacher in the US, she had to withhold sharing her life experiences living and traveling in Germany because she was afraid her passion for German culture would be labeled as a bias. The participant felt that 'being a non-native instructor of Spanish in addition to being a native German instructor liberated her from the emotional drain of having to constantly fight for legitimacy as a teacher of German' (Kramsch & Zhang, 2018). Eventually, she made the decision to only teach Spanish. Kramsch and Zhang's (2018) participant felt that being German and teaching German tied her to the negative perceptions of Germany from the American perspective and to escape that 'emotional drain', she turned to teaching a different language where she could occupy a position that she felt was more neutral.

Emotional labor in teaching multiple languages

So far, the emotions that have been discussed in this section can be perceived as TMLs' emotional reactions to teaching new languages, adopting new identities and adjusting to new contexts. Another dimension of emotions involved in teaching multiple languages is the monitoring and crafting of different emotional demeanors that TMLs may perceive as being expected or favorable for the different languages they are teaching. Scholars have called this 'emotional labor' (Benesch, 2017; Kocabaş-Gedik & Ortaçtepe Hart, 2021; Schutz & Lee, 2014), or the work teachers must put into 'self-monitoring to achieve "appropriate" emotions guided by institutional policies and professional guidelines' (Benesch, 2017: 54). One of the main differences between TMLs' emotional labor and the typical emotions reported by TMLs is that emotional labor involves actively and purposefully enacting certain emotions by the TMLs themselves. For example, in Kim and Smith (2019: 40), one TML participant teaching Korean (as a NS teacher) as an international graduate student at an American university described herself as more 'nice', 'kind', 'outgoing' and 'less sensitive to teacher authority' because that was what they thought they should be while using English to teach in America. This connects with her identity as a NS Korean teacher at an American university where she felt she could be 'more like a friend of my students' (Kim & Smith, 2019: 41). Interestingly, another participant in Kim and Smith (2019) also held the same expectation that teachers at American universities might be more like friends with their students but reacted differently by intentionally distancing herself from her students out of fear that getting closer with students would lead to classroom management problems. In both scenarios presented by Kim and Smith (2019), TMLs see the monitoring of their emotional demeanor as part of their teaching practice and a key aspect of their teaching that could possibly have serious consequences in their classrooms, whether positively or negatively.

Emotional labor may also play a role in helping TMLs adjust to their new roles. For example, in Kramsch and Zhang (2018), one participant (NS English teacher, NSS Chinese teacher) explained how in teaching Chinese in the US as a white NNS teacher, students sometimes did not even realize that he was the teacher when he entered the classroom on the first day of class. Therefore, he tried to address his students' surprise at seeing a Chinese teacher that does not 'look' Chinese by trying to 'make a joke about it', 'lighten it up a little bit' and 'try to make a connection with the students that, um, I'm right there with you, learnin the language' (Kramsch & Zhang, 2018). In this situation, before any language teaching happens, the participant's time is already spent on the emotional labor of 'gaining the personal trust of his students, leveling the playing field, [and] denying the racial difference' (Kramsch &

Zhang, 2018). Li and Lai's (2022) study of ESL teachers who transitioned to teaching CSL also presented examples of TMLs adapting to new ways of being in terms of authority, teacher–student relationships and teacher talk. Li and Lai (2022) described these adaptations as language and knowledge brokering, a key aspect of their transition to new roles as CSL teachers.

How and Why Language Teachers Become TMLs

The studies featured above provide a personal look into the individual, inner lives of TMLs. This section takes a broader look at patterns and trends in the teaching of multiple languages. The following literature review collects information from empirical studies as well as other sources, such as institutional websites.

The teaching of multiple languages covers a wide range of teacher backgrounds and teaching contexts based on the educational institutions, geographical settings, language pedagogies, language policies and cultural ideologies of the languages that TMLs have taught. Therefore, the path that language teachers take in their careers to become TMLs can be highly varied. The question I attempt to address in this section can be rephrased in several ways, including:

- How do language teachers become TMLs?
- Why do language teachers decide to teach multiple languages?
- What factors impact language teachers' decisions to teach multiple languages?

Overall, this section aims to address the main factors influencing language teachers to become TMLs. When a language teacher is deciding whether or not to teach multiple languages, some common scenarios can be (1) a language teacher wanting to expand beyond the language they are currently teaching, essentially taking on a second career; (2) a language teacher adapting to new (sometimes imposed) job expectations where they are expected to teach more than one language; or (3) an aspiring language teacher seeking to improve their job prospects by enrolling in a teacher education program for teaching more than one language. These are scenarios in which language teachers are confronted with difficult choices that likely have a major impact on their career. The following sections explore two main categories of factors that influence language teachers' decision to teach multiple languages: personal factors and institutional factors. It is important to note that here, the personal and institutional do not exist as mutually exclusive categories; in most cases, a language teacher is influenced by both personal and institutional factors in deciding to teach multiple languages. Furthermore, personal factors are inevitably influenced by institutional factors, and vice versa.

Individual factors

Here, individual factors are considered as factors that operate on a personal level, involving the social, psychological or cognitive aspects of language teaching. Individual factors are an important consideration in the career trajectory of any language teacher, and this is no different for TMLs. However, the decision to teach multiple languages presents language teachers with a set of considerations that are distinct from teaching a single language and often overlap with considerations for learning multiple languages.

Motivation, interest or passion

Language teachers might teach multiple languages because they have an interest in learning multiple languages and that interest may have transferred to their teaching career (Blair, 2012). While the relationship between the motivation to learn languages and the motivation to teach languages may not be causal, some TMLs mention that their motivation to teach multiple languages originated from their passion for learning multiple languages. On the other hand, one can also imagine the opposite scenario; if a language teacher has had negative experiences learning multiple languages, they may not be interested in pursuing a career teaching multiple languages.

Career development and linguistic entrepreneurship

Language teachers might teach multiple languages as a strategic decision to improve their careers or career prospects. This perspective can be described as a form of 'linguistic entrepreneurship', which De Costa et al. (2016: 696) define as 'strategically exploit[ing] language-related resources for enhancing one's worth in the world'. From the perspective of the linguistic entrepreneur, teaching multiple languages would be about more than simply language teaching; it would also be about self-development as 'the ideal neoliberal subject', embodying characteristics such as 'initiative, innovation, self-reliance, resilience, and the ability to respond quickly to competition' (De Costa et al., 2021: 139). This market-driven, commodity-based approach to one's teaching career can be a significant motivator in attracting language teachers to teach multiple languages.

There are different ways in which the teaching of multiple languages can be seen as a strategic asset to one's teaching career.

(1) *A general benefit in teaching multiple languages.* The ability and experience of teaching multiple languages in a general sense (without specific reference to which languages are taught) can be seen as a way of increasing a teacher's breadth of experience and knowledge. Tavares (2022) described this eloquently when he explained how teaching two languages (i.e. English and Portuguese) benefitted him as a language teacher:

The opportunity to draw on the experiences from one position (ESL) to design teaching material, manage a group of students, and problem-solve in the other (Portuguese) played an essential role in helping me feel better equipped to teach a different language to an audience whose needs and expectations at times contrasted sharply with what I had been accustomed to. (Tavares, 2022: 18)

In addition, some language teacher education programs have advertised their TML-based degrees as increasing 'marketability' and 'employability' as a language teacher in a globally competitive market (HU University of Applied Sciences Utrecht, 2021a, 2021b, 2021c). This perspective can seem like a natural extension of popular discourse on multilingualism that frames learning multiple languages as beneficial in a variety of ways, regardless of which languages an individual learns. Furthermore, teaching multiple languages can be seen as 'casting a wider net' in order to reach a larger language learner market. For example, from a brief search through popular online language tutoring websites, such as 'iTalki' (https://www .italki.com/) and 'Verbling' (https://www.verbling.com/), one can find teachers advertising themselves on a literal job market as teaching more than one language.

(2) *A specific benefit based on teaching certain languages.* Language teachers might teach a different or additional language due to a perceived benefit of that specific language. The perceived benefit could be in cultural capital (De Costa, 2019), such as gaining greater respect, recognition or status based on shifting from teaching one language to another (Rostami *et al.*, 2021). The benefit could also be financial, such as when a language teacher wants to teach another language because another language is in greater demand and there are simply more language teaching jobs or better compensation for that language (Kayi-Aydar, 2015a). Another scenario could be if a NNS teacher faces job discrimination in the NS language teaching job market, and teaching a language in which they are perceived as a NS provides them with better job prospects (Kramsch & Zhang, 2018; Park, 2006). The perceived benefit could also be more abstract and related to one's professional LTI (Ku, 2020). For example, a language teacher may experience imposter syndrome (Ahns & Deles-clefs, 2020; Bernat, 2008; Kramsch & Zhang, 2018) or feel under-qualified despite being certified (Chang, 2018; Fan & de Jong, 2019; Kayi-Aydar, 2015a) to teach a certain language but feel differently when teaching another language.

Park (2006) presented one example of how issues around LTI and linguistic entrepreneurship may influence a teacher's decision to become a TML. One of the participants in Park's study is Shu-Ming, who grew up in Taiwan, immigrated to the United States with her family at the age of 13, went back to Taiwan to teach English at the age of 30, enrolled in a TESOL graduate program in the United States at the age of 33 and volunteered by teaching ESL at an adult education center during her graduate studies. Although she had not taught another language besides English at the time of Park's study, Shu-Ming explained that after graduating from her graduate TESOL program, she originally hoped to teach English in China, but was met with discouraging prospects on contacting hiring companies in China. She noted that companies in China preferred Caucasian NS English teachers and would pay her as a local Chinese teacher (rather than an expatriate English teacher) since she was ethnically Chinese. She concluded her narrative by saying that she considered teaching Chinese at a university in the United States. Even though Shu-Ming never actually became a TML, she felt that teaching Chinese in the United States might bring her better job prospects than teaching English in China, despite having completed an MA TESOL degree.

Fan and de Jong (2019) featured a language teacher with a similar career trajectory, in which a language teacher from China (with Chinese and English teaching experience in China) moved to the US to study for an MA in TESOL degree, but later gave up on teaching English. She felt she was unqualified to be an ESL teacher in the US because of her non-native English speaker accent and perceived lack of proficiency. Both Park (2006) and Fan and de Jong (2019) showed how the decision to switch from teaching one language to another can involve complex factors such as job market prospects, racial identity and feelings of professional legitimacy.

Global migration and mobility

Language teachers might teach multiple languages as 'an instrument for migration' (Aydarova, 2017). For example, a language teacher may see the teaching of multiple languages or enrollment in language teacher education programs abroad as a way to access language teaching job markets abroad. The opposite may also be true, in which teaching multiple languages does not come as the precursor to migration, but migration happens first, forcing a language teacher to adapt to a different language teaching job market in a different place. For example, Li and Lai (2022) presented narratives of an ESL teacher from mainland China who, upon migrating to Hong Kong, switched to teaching CSL. In these examples, decisions to teach multiple languages are considered in the context of globalization and global flows, where becoming a language teacher often means going beyond local contexts and national borders and engaging with an increasingly interconnected world (Kramsch, 2014; Li & Lai, 2022; Paine et al., 2016). While global migration and mobility does indeed involve societal forces greater than the individual, I have categorized this under 'individual factors' because the decision of language teachers to turn to the teaching of multiple languages in response to global migration and mobility is an individual one.

The unintended, accidental and imposed on

Language teachers might teach multiple languages 'accidentally', a term that Yoshihara (2018: 11) used to describe university language teachers who never intended or wanted to become language teachers but ended up as language teachers due to negative experiences in corporate workplaces and a desire for 'something different and meaningful in their lives'. In other words, in contrast to the previously described factors, language teachers may end up teaching multiple languages without the explicit intention of doing so. This is not necessarily surprising considering that teaching multiple languages is not a commonly named profession, so language teachers may 'accidentally' find themselves teaching multiple languages without having planned it as part of their career. There is also a dark side to the 'accidental' nature of becoming a TML, in that some language teachers may be pressured to teach multiple languages against their desire due to local demand for teachers of a certain language. For example, in schools in under-resourced or rural areas, teaching multiple languages (e.g. English and the local language) may be imposed on a language teacher due to the lack of teacher supply. Even if the teacher is underqualified and teaching multiple languages was originally not part of the teacher's job responsibilities when hired, the teacher may reluctantly agree in order to keep their job. For example, Blachford and Jones (2011) described a language teacher in a small village in China who had taught English and Mandarin classes, despite being underqualified and fearful of teaching English, because the rural school was short-staffed.

Institutional factors

The previous section discussed the personal factors that may lead language teachers to make the decision in their careers to become TMLs. This section discusses the institutional factors intertwined with the personal factors that play a strong role in the path to becoming a TML. In particular, the institutional factors highlight the fact that while teaching multiple languages is a language teacher's personal choice, it is also likely that that choice was made under the influence of greater trends and forces at play, such as new language education policies and access to language teacher education. Moreover, the institutional factors suggest that (1) TMLs are not simply isolated cases; and (2) TMLs are not solely a recent phenomenon, but rather, they have long existed and are now a part of a growing group of language teachers moving toward greater professionalization in the language teaching profession. The following sections cover two main institutional factors: language teacher education programs and language education policies. Like the personal factors, these two institutional factors are interconnected, that is, they exist in relation to one another rather than as isolated entities.

TML-focused language teacher education programs

An important institutional factor influencing language teachers to become TMLs are active language teacher education programs focused on training teachers to teach multiple languages (hereafter 'TML programs') in various parts of the world. Table 2.2 offers examples of active TML programs that I have found as of September 2021. This is by no means an exhaustive list of all the currently active TML programs, since there is no commonly used term to describe such programs. However, the TML programs listed provide a sample of the variety of programs that exist.

It is important to note that these TML programs are primarily *teacher education* programs, meaning that in addition to language proficiency, their curriculum also has a strong focus on language pedagogy, second language acquisition and the teaching of specific language skills (e.g. reading, writing). Some active TML programs have the aim of learning to teach multiple languages explicitly written in the title of the degree (e.g. a dual certificate in TESOL and teaching Chinese to speakers of other languages [TCSOL]) (see Examples 1, 2, 5, 6, 7, 8 in Table 2.2). These TML programs are usually structured as 'double degree' or 'dual certificate' programs. Essentially, institutions have taken existing language teacher education degree programs (e.g. MA in TESOL) and provided the option of pairing them with another language teacher education degree program (e.g. MA in TCSOL). While the option of pairing degrees, such as doing a double major or getting a bachelor's degree with a certificate, is common in many modern higher education institutions, what is different about these TML programs is the institution's *explicit* and *intentional* pairing of two language teacher education degrees on their menu of academic programs. Since all of these programs are paired degree programs, it seems that none of these programs has a curriculum or individual courses specifically designed to address the issues of teaching multiple languages. Rather, they seem to be two individual language teacher education programs pieced together.

In contrast, other active TML programs do not explicitly put the aim of learning to teach multiple languages in the title of the degree, even when it is a part of the curriculum. This means that while the degree may seem like a standard teaching degree (e.g. MA in primary education), the actual curriculum provides some coursework that prepares teachers to teach multiple languages (see Examples 3 and 4 in Table 2.2).

Table 2.2   Examples of active TML programs

Name of institution	Location	TML degree(s) offered
Undergraduate programs		
1 HU University of Applied Sciences Utrecht	Netherlands	Double bachelor's degree in • Teaching English + German (HU University of Applied Sciences Utrecht, 2021b) • Teaching French + another language (University of Applied Sciences Utrecht, 2021a) • Teaching Spanish + another language (University of Applied Sciences Utrecht, 2021c)
2 McGill University, Department of Integrated Studies in Education	Canada	Bachelor of education (BEd) in teaching English as a second language – TESL elementary and secondary + teaching Greek language and culture (McGill University, 2021)
3 Universidade do Estado de Mato Grosso	Brazil	Double undergraduate degree in Portuguese and English language teaching (i.e. *Licenciatura em Letras – Português/Inglês*) (Universidade do Estado de Mato Grosso, 2022)
4 Universidade Federal do Triângulo Mineiro	Brazil	Double undergraduate degree in Portuguese and English language teaching (i.e. *Licenciatura em Letras – Português/Inglês*) (Universidade Federal do Triângulo Mineiro, 2022)
Master's programs		
5 Free University of Bozen-Bolzano	Italy	Trilingual master's degree in primary education (Italian, Latin, German) (Free University of Bozen-Bolzano, 2021)
6 Middlebury Institute of International Studies	US	• Master's degree in TESOL with a specialization in teaching foreign languages (TFL) (Middlebury Institute of International Studies, 2021b) • Master's degree in TFL with a specialization in TESOL (Middlebury Institute of International Studies, 2021a)
7 New York University, Steinhardt School of Culture, Education and Human Development	US	Dual-certification master of arts in world language education and TESOL (prepares you to teach English as a second language for Grades K–12, and Chinese, French, Italian, Japanese or Spanish for Grades 7–12) (New York University, 2021)
Other programs		
8 Teachers College of Columbia University, in collaboration with Osaka Gakuin University and Macau University of Science and Technology	US, Japan, Macau (online)	Dual certificate programs in teaching Chinese and English (TCSOL/TESOL) (Teachers College, 2021a, 2021b)

A few significant features about teaching multiple languages as a career can be observed from current TML programs.

(1) The existence of TML programs means that the path to teach multiple languages as a career is not solely an incidental or individual endeavor; becoming a TML through obtaining an accredited, institution-based degree program has become a viable option in mainstream higher education in some countries. This is not to say that informal paths to become TMLs no longer exist or that those are inferior in some way; rather, the existence of TML programs indicates a level of professionalization that is emerging when it comes to teaching multiple languages as a career.

(2) The location of TML programs across a variety of institutions, countries, languages and degree types shows that the development of teaching multiple languages as a career is happening in various contexts around the world, suggesting that TMLs are geographically spread out, though perhaps not yet widespread.

(3) The way institutions are advertising current TML programs suggests some perceptions of the role that teaching multiple languages may have in the global language teaching market. For example, HU University of Applied Sciences Utrecht promotes getting a double degree in teaching two languages (see Table 2.2) as making students 'stand out in the job market', 'more flexible as a teaching professional' (HU University of Applied Sciences Utrecht, 2021b) and 'boosting your prospects of finding a teaching position' (HU University of Applied Sciences Utrecht, 2021a, 2021c). The emphasis in targeting one's prospects and position in the job market can be seen as a part of the discourse of linguistic entrepreneurship, which can and should be questioned and analyzed with a critical lens. One might ask: how valid are such claims? If those are the benefits of obtaining a TML-based degree, what are the possible downsides?

Overall, these examples of TML programs attest to the fact that there are organized initiatives actively recruiting and training pre-service and in-service teachers to become TMLs. Nowadays, it is not just that people are learning and speaking more than one language (i.e. multilingual education and multilingual societies) or that our language teachers are able to use more than one language in their teaching (i.e. multilingual teachers), language teachers are also expanding their professional expertise beyond teaching a single language for their entire teacher career and becoming TMLs.

Now, if we take a step back and take a broader look at the TML program landscape, the establishment of TML programs may be new in some contexts, bringing with them a sense of innovation or excitement. However, in other contexts, TML programs are not new and their effectiveness has been contested. Krawczyk-Neifar (2017) presented a study on an extramural three-year BA program specializing in teaching English and Spanish as foreign languages at the University of Occupational Safety Management in Katowice in Poland. The study involved using a questionnaire with 10 undergraduate students and interviews with two instructors in the same program in order to elicit their opinions about the efficiency of the bilingual teacher training program. Although the study did not specify whether the two instructors were TMLs (one specialized in teaching English and the other Spanish), the 10 undergraduate students can be seen as pre-service TMLs, being specifically trained to teach both English and Spanish (not just teaching in English or in Spanish). The results showed that most of the students were not interested in becoming foreign language teachers or taking language pedagogy classes. They enrolled in the program with the broader belief that knowing more than one foreign language would benefit their job prospects but did not solely focus on pursuing a teaching career. From the interviews, the two teachers expressed skepticism at the bilingual teacher training program's effectiveness, particularly because they felt that the students did not have the appropriate competence in the two foreign languages to be teachers of the languages. Krawczyk-Neifar (2017: 180) concluded the study by stating that the program was a failure because 'you cannot properly educate a teacher of two languages in a 3-year BA extramural course where the students are at B2 in the case of the first language and at A1/A2 in the case of the second language'.

The effectiveness of TML programs has also been contested in the Brazilian educational context where students can get a double degree in English and Portuguese teacher education. Cox and Assis-Peterson (2008) and Celani (2010) have pointed out the drawbacks of double degree programs, that students often do not gain proficiency in either of the foreign languages and teachers are not prepared to teach (as cited in Pessoa *et al.*, 2018). Brandão (2019, 2021), for example, has shown the challenges of Brazilian language teachers from an undergraduate Portuguese–English language teaching program – that the difficulty was not only a matter of developing language proficiency but also the process of being able to imagine themselves as EFL teachers. Furthermore, Pessoa *et al.* (2018) and Mastrella-de-Andrade and Pessoa (2019) have shown from a critical lens that dominant discourses around TML programs in Brazil often involve failure, dissatisfaction and unpreparedness.

Language education policies and programs

Another institutional factor that influences language teachers to become TMLs are language education policies and programs, often operating in conjunction with TML programs. While there may be some language education policies and programs that are meant to explicitly address the teaching of multiple languages, what seems to be most common are policies and programs meant to address some other aspect of language education and the teaching of multiple languages happens to also be affected. The following list introduces examples of language education policies and programs that have influenced language teachers to teach multiple languages, in effect, becoming TMLs. Like the previous examples of TML programs, this list is not meant to be exhaustive; rather, the aim is to provide a variety of examples that illustrate how language education policies and programs have impacted teachers to teach multiple languages at different historical periods and contexts.

- **Global politics and international relations.** At times, large-scale changes in global politics and international relations have impacted changes in language education policies, in turn, impacting on language teachers' careers. For example, Chinese–Soviet relations in the 1950s and 1960s had a major impact on foreign language education in China. After the founding of the People's Republic of China in 1949, China and the Soviet Union developed a friendly relationship, which led to an increase in Russian language education and a decrease in English language education in higher institutions and secondary schools in China. Thus, in the 1950s, Russia became the primary foreign language in China. However, Chinese–Soviet relations became strained in 1960, leading to a resurgence of English language education. With the sudden shift toward English language education and a shortage of qualified English teachers, in the late 1950s and early 1960s, many Russian language teachers in China were trained to become English language teachers (Cortazzi & Jin, 1996; Hu, 2002; Yang, 1987). Furthermore, while some of these newly trained English teachers 'were quite successful and became qualified for their new jobs', others 'remained limited in English ability', undoubtedly affected by the lack of exposure to English during the Cultural Revolution from 1966 to 1976 (Yang, 1987: 29). This is an example of language teachers becoming TMLs as a result of changes in language education policies tied to global politics. In other words, if there had not been changes in Chinese–Soviet relations, there may not have been a need for Russian language teachers to switch to teaching English in China.
- **Global language and cultural exchanges.** A common way that language teachers inadvertently become TMLs is through studying abroad, particularly as an international graduate student, and taking on opportunities to teach their first language (L1) at the institution where they are studying. This is particularly common in American universities. For these TMLs, studying abroad at an American university is what brought them into the position of teaching multiple languages. De Costa (2015) and Kim and Smith (2019) both featured TMLs in this specific situation.

    Language education policies that have created programs to facilitate foreign language education and exchange have also produced TMLs. Another way to frame this is programs systematically developing TMLs but for the purpose of global language and cultural exchange. The most notable of such programs is the Fulbright Foreign Language Teaching Assistant (FLTA) program funded by the US Department of State with the goal of 'develop[ing] Americans' knowledge of foreign cultures and languages' (Fulbright Foreign Student Program, 2021). Operationally, the program sponsors language teachers from over 50 countries to come to the US for one year to be teaching assistants for foreign language classrooms, 'sharing [their] culture and language with American students' (Fulbright Foreign Student Program, 2021). Interestingly, two of the requirements to be eligible for the program are (1) 'an early career teacher of English or training to become a teacher of English, or are an early career educator in a related field' and (2) 'an interest in teaching your native language and culture to students in the U.S.' (Fulbright Foreign Student Program, 2021). In other words, a preferred FLTA candidate would be currently a pre-service or in-service EFL instructor in their country but with the desire or willingness to teach their native language at a US institution. Essentially, each year, a portion of language teachers participating in the FLTA program (i.e. those who are not teaching their native language in their home country) would be experiencing the teaching of multiple languages for the first time.

An example of an FLTA participant is Andrey, an FLTA from Russia whose story is featured on the Bureau of Educational and Cultural Affairs Exchange Programs (2021) website. Andrey felt that the FLTA program was a 'perfect opportunity' and 'beneficial to [his] future career as an English and German Teacher' (Bureau of Educational and Cultural Affairs Exchange Programs, 2021). He spent his time as an FLTA at Michigan State University teaching Russian. Other examples of FLTAs are described by Luo and Gao (2017) in their study on Chinese Fulbright teaching assistants in the US, and Mutlu and Ortaçtepe (2016) in their study on Turkish teachers (though the latter do not specify the name of the program). In these examples, it is notable that Andrey expressed that he already had aspirations to teach multiple languages (i.e. English and German) prior to being an FLTA, and saw the experience of teaching Russian in the US as contributing toward that goal. From his story, it is not quite clear if he had previous experience teaching English and German; regardless, he saw the FLTA program as contributing to his career goal of being a TML. On the other hand, the participants from Luo and Gao (2017) and Mutlu and Ortaçtepe (2016) started the FLTA program as EFL teachers and finished the FLTA program as TMLs. Both are examples of language teachers participating in the teaching of multiple languages but framed under a program for global language and culture exchange.

- **Improving language teacher qualifications.** Another example of the way language education policies can influence language teachers to become TMLs is through programs that aim to improve language teacher qualifications. Because such programs attempt to ameliorate local problems in language education, the programs can vary widely. An example of a program aimed at improving language teacher qualifications is Brazil's National Development Plan for Teachers in Public Educational Systems and Network (PARFOR). PARFOR was created in 2009 with the aim of helping 400,000 in-service teachers gain the appropriate qualifications to meet the Brazilian government goal of educating 30% of those age 18–24 (Gimenez *et al.*, 2016: 221). In order to achieve this, PARFOR was designed to help 'the large number of in-service teachers who do not hold a degree in the subject they are teaching (e.g., Portuguese language teachers who also teach English without holding a degree in English)' (Gimenez *et al.*, 2016: 221). In the case of PARFOR, TMLs (i.e. Portuguese language teachers who also taught English) had already been teaching in Brazilian schools, though many without adequate qualifications. Thus, PARFOR provided a pathway for TMLs to further professionalize their careers by improving their language teacher qualifications.
- **The teaching of less commonly taught languages (LCTLs).** Language education policies can also target the teaching of LCTLs and involve TMLs as a temporary solution for the lack of qualified teachers of LCTLs. A LCTL is defined as 'a language considered important by the government, but unsustainable by the market' and varies for each country depending on their political situation (Gor & Vatz, 2009: 234). According to Piri (2002) in the 'Guide for the Development of Language Education Policies in Europe: From Linguistic Diversity to Plurilingual Education', one issue with LCTL instruction is the lack of qualified language teachers. Thus, Piri (2002: 21) proposed that 'it may be necessary to make do with… teachers of other languages who have a sufficient command of a smaller language or native speakers of a smaller language who have some teaching qualifications'. In other words, because there are not enough language teachers specializing in teaching LCTLs, language teachers of other languages may have to teach both the language they typically teach (and are qualified to teach) and the LCTL. Thus, the need to address issues of teacher supply in LCTL instruction has often led to language teachers inadvertently becoming TMLs.

   This approach to maintaining LCTL instruction has played out in different contexts. In fact, this is the approach that the aforementioned FLTA program has taken. The FLTA program covers over 50 countries and from those countries, most of the languages that the FLTA participants are expected to teach in the US are categorized as a LCTL by the FLTA program (Fulbright Foreign Student

Program, 2021). In other words, the FLTA program primarily functions by recruiting current EFL teachers from other countries to temporarily teach LCTLs at US universities. Another example of language teachers becoming TMLs from teaching a LCTL is in Taiwan, where the Ministry of Education's local language-in-education policy has provided the opportunity for certified, in-service elementary school teachers who are already teaching Chinese or English to also teach one of Taiwan's local languages (Taiwanese Hokkien, Hakka and aboriginal languages) (Chen, 2006; Scott & Tiun, 2007; Tsao, 2008).

• **Teaching in under-resourced areas.** Parallel to the development of TMLs to address the lack of teachers for LCTL instruction, language education policies may also be enacted for language teachers in under-resourced areas to teach more than one language. For example, in China, TMLs are developed when teachers who teach subjects other than English (e.g. Chinese, mathematics, biology) are relocated to primary schools in rural areas to teach English. This is done in response to the shortage of English teachers in rural areas (Xiong & Xiong, 2017). While this example as well as the two examples from the US and Taiwan of TMLs teaching LCTLs feature large-scale, government-led initiatives, it is also possible that such language education policies are enacted locally at the school or community level. For example, Blachford and Jones (2011) described a language teacher in a small rural community in Yunnan, the most ethnically diverse province in the People's Republic of China with 25 out of the 56 ethnic groups of China living there. Specifically, Blachford and Jones examined the way trilingual education policies have impacted the Wenhai school, a rural Naxi school. The Naxi are one of the ethnic minorities living in Yunnan, and they speak Naxiyu. For many ethnic minorities in China, trilingual education has emerged due to the need to learn Mandarin (which is considered to be 'fundamental to participation in all aspects of Chinese society') (Blachford & Jones, 2011: 233), English (which should be taught starting no later than Grade 3 based on a government policy passed in 2001) (Blachford & Jones, 2011: 228) and their local language (which 'the government has mandated… that national minority children should receive education in their own language') (Blachford & Jones, 2011: 229). Thus, many minority children are using their local language as their L1 as well as learning Mandarin as a L2 and English as a third language. Finally, to make things even more complicated, some schools in Yunnan have students from different ethnic minority groups. For example, the Wenhai school in Blachford and Jones' study has children from both the Naxi and Yi ethnic groups, but since the school does not have teachers who speak Yi, the Yi children learn Mandarin through Naxi and English through Mandarin.

All this is to say that in order for the Wenhai school to tackle the challenge of trilingual education in an under-resourced area, one teacher had to teach both English and Mandarin classes. This was implemented despite the teacher not having received any formal teacher training, having low English proficiency and expressing feelings of fear over teaching English (Blachford & Jones, 2011). The need for the teacher to teach multiple languages seemingly against her desire was due to the overall shortage of teachers in rural areas. This particular case is an example of how language teachers may become TMLs because of schools in under-resourced areas attempting to address new language policies that may become 'an enormous barrier' (Blachford & Jones, 2011: 255) as opposed to a solution for rural schools. Furthermore, in such situations, it is possible for teachers to be coerced into teaching more than they desire or are qualified to teach due to a fear of losing their job and pressure to meet the needs of the community.

Conclusion

I conclude this chapter by briefly summarizing some observations I have made from my experience in attempting to find existing literature in applied linguistics, language teaching and language education policy research. The difficulty lies in the absence of an established, shared term to refer to TMLs. Instead, researching TMLs requires searching for and combing through studies that one might suspect to include TMLs (e.g. multilingual education), and examining whether TMLs are mentioned and what those studies say about TMLs. In general, I would summarize the current state of TML research with the following observations:

- Currently, only a few studies specifically focus on examining TMLs. These studies often originate from a variety of sub-disciplines in applied linguistics, language education or language education policy, and they do not use a common terminology to refer to TMLs. Thus, at first glance, they often do not seem to be directly related to each other.
- Some studies incidentally include participants who are TMLs, usually with the primary aim of studying another facet of the participant (e.g. non-native English speaker teacher [NNEST] identity). These studies rely on the authors specifically disclosing the participants' teaching backgrounds (i.e. how many languages they have taught). Most studies do not disclose this information and leave the question of how many languages participants have taught unknown.
- Furthermore, studies that include a TML participant usually only mention the fact that the teacher has taught multiple languages as a brief descriptor of their background, and leave it unquestioned

and unexplored. Such studies rarely question or explain how some participants' experience of teaching multiple languages may influence the findings and differentiate them from other participants. The assumption tends to be that participants who have taught multiple languages do not need to be distinguished from those who have not taught multiple languages.

3 Researching TMLs through Narratives and Photographs

Chapters 1 and 2 introduced the concept of teachers of multiple languages (TMLs) and discussed issues addressed in TML research, including the complex inner lives of TMLs and multiple factors impacting TMLs' career trajectories. The rest of this book focuses on a qualitative study of three TMLs. I detail the choices made in designing a qualitative study that was able to take into account the complexity of researching not only TMLs from different educational, geographic and cultural backgrounds, but also the different psychological factors of TML lives, namely their identities, beliefs and emotions. This includes a discussion around choosing a conceptual framework, finding participants and applying narrative and visual research methods.

Conceptual Framework: Douglas Fir Group's Framework

This study adapted the Douglas Fir Group's (DFG) (2016) 'Transdisciplinary Framework for SLA in a Multilingual World' (see Figure 3.1) as the conceptual framework for interpreting the narrated experiences and identities of TMLs. This framework was chosen because it breaks down how different levels of social interaction influence one another when it comes to language teaching and learning. Using this framework to interpret TMLs' experiences allows for a multi-layered understanding of how these different elements relate to one another when it comes to the teaching of multiple languages. The DFG's framework was proposed by a group of 15 distinguished scholars across 10 different disciplinary perspectives within second language acquisition (SLA) as a way of understanding how multilingualism in 'a new world order in the 21st century', characterized by increasing globalization, technological advances and mobility, is changing SLA (Douglas Fir Group, 2016: 19). Several phenomena emerge as a result of these new global forces. Communication has become deterritorialized and is no longer limited to one's immediate locality; language use and learning have become more dynamic and open-ended. An increasing number of individuals from a wider range of backgrounds are deciding to learn additional languages, becoming

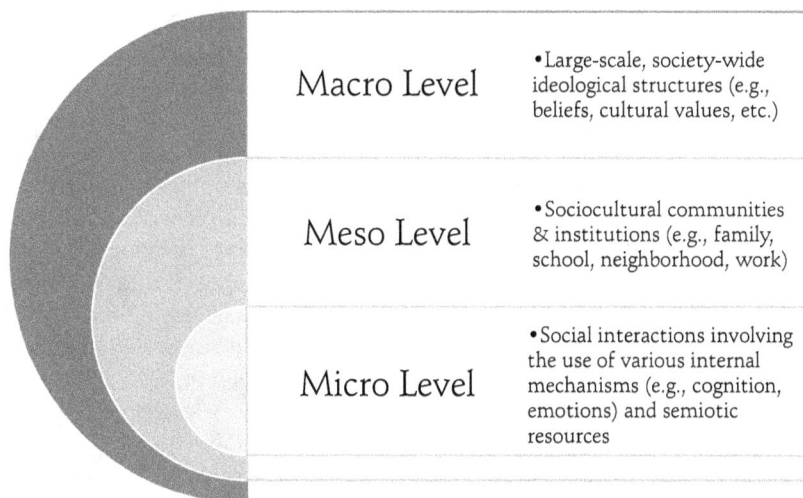

Macro Level	• Large-scale, society-wide ideological structures (e.g., beliefs, cultural values, etc.)
Meso Level	• Sociocultural communities & institutions (e.g., family, school, neighborhood, work)
Micro Level	• Social interactions involving the use of various internal mechanisms (e.g., cognition, emotions) and semiotic resources

Figure 3.1 The Douglas Fir Group's framework (Adapted from Douglas Fir Group, 2016; Copyright 2016 by *The Modern Language Journal*)

multilingual and transcultural. Thus, the DFG's new framework for SLA aims to address the needs of multilingual individuals by examining language learning and teaching from various contextual perspectives (e.g. private vs. public, material vs. digital) in a multilingual world (Douglas Fir Group, 2016).

The DFG framework treats SLA as complex, ever-changing and multi-dimensional, involving the layering of diverse cognitive capabilities and social interactions in a multilingual context (Hall, 2019a). Structurally, the DFG framework provides a new way of conceptualizing SLA by integrating the various levels at which SLA occurs (i.e. micro, meso, macro) with the various disciplinary understandings of SLA (e.g. neural, cognitive, social, ideological) and with the greater context of the globalized, multilingual world that we live in (Douglas Fir Group, 2016). More specifically, the DFG's framework integrates three mutually dependent levels inspired by an ecological framework (Bronfenbrenner, 1979). The three levels can be summarized as:

- Micro level: Internal mechanisms (e.g. cognition, emotions) are used during interaction with others (linguistic, non-verbal, graphic, auditory, semiotic, etc.).
- Meso level: Sociocultural communities and institutions (family, school, neighborhood, work, etc.).
- Macro level: Large-scale, society-wide ideological structures (e.g. beliefs about language use or language learning, cultural values and political values).

According to the Douglas Fir Group (2016), second language (L2) learning begins at the micro level of social activity, in which individual learners manage cognitive and emotional systems during social interactions using any available semiotic resources, such as linguistic, non-verbal, graphic and auditory resources. These micro-level interactions occur within the meso level, shaped by sociocultural communities and institutions, such as family, school, local neighborhood and the workplace. Not all learners are able to experience the same kinds of social interactions at the meso level; the degree to which learners have the power and/or agency to invest their identities and material resources into accessing meso-level communities and institutions is impacted by certain society-wide conditions (e.g. economic class, politics, culture) at the macro level. Thus, the everyday communities and institutions that learners may take part in for language learning are influenced by (and also influence) large-scale, societal ideologies at the macro level of the DFG's framework. Ideologies can be defined as individual and group beliefs and values around the role of forces such as culture, politics and economics in society (Hall, 2019a). The DFG emphasizes that while each of the three levels represents different aspects of language learning, all three levels and mutual interactions among the three levels are essential to fully understanding SLA.

Foundational themes from the DFG framework

From their multi-level framework, the DFG introduced 10 fundamental themes relating to SLA. While these themes originally focused on language learning, De Costa and Norton (2017: 8, emphasis in original) showed that the same themes based on the DFG's framework can be applied to language teaching as well (e.g. from 'language learning is identity work' to 'language *teaching* is identity work'). Below is a brief summary of each of the 10 themes reinterpreted by De Costa and Norton (2017) from the DFG's original 10 fundamental themes through the perspective of language teaching:

(1) 'Language competencies are complex, dynamic, and holistic' (De Costa & Norton, 2017: 8): In contrast to conceptualizing language competencies as fixed, abstract systems, the DFG's framework views language competency as a dynamic system of resources for meaning-making (Hall, 2019a), meaning that language learning and teaching involve the use of the entirety of one's semiotic resources across various languages, varieties and registers, applying them fluidly based on different contexts over a lifetime.

(2) 'Language teaching is semiotic teaching' (De Costa & Norton, 2017: 8): Language teaching involves the application and teaching of a wide range of semiotic resources, including the use of linguistic, visual, graphic and auditory means of expression. In addition, semiotic

resources can be verbal (e.g. turn-taking, intonation, pausing), non-verbal (e.g. gestures, facial expressions, body positioning) or written (e.g. typography). The importance of taking into consideration the different forms of semiotic resources involved in language teaching has also been highlighted in studies looking at the role of multimodality in language teaching (Early *et al.*, 2015). The meaning conveyed by semiotic resources is shaped by meso- and macro-level social institutions, such as family and school, and therefore, are not neutral nor equally accessed (Douglas Fir Group, 2016).

(3) 'Language teaching is situated and attentionally and socially gated' (De Costa & Norton, 2017: 8): Language teaching starts at the micro level, requiring recurring social interaction guided by a range of cognitive activities and emotions (Douglas Fir Group, 2016). During the process of language teaching, these cognitive capabilities help guide patterns of meaning-making, which become more entrenched with more frequent input (Hall, 2019a).

(4) 'Language teaching is multimodal, embodied, and mediated' (De Costa & Norton, 2017: 8): Language teaching involves the application and teaching of multimodal semiotic resources, activating the entire human body as an embodied whole to assist teaching and learning, such as the use of repetition, recast, tone, eye gaze and gesture (Douglas Fir Group, 2016). Language teaching also occurs through the use of cultural tools and resources that make sense of the world (Douglas Fir Group, 2016). Mediational tools used in language teaching range from the use of language itself, to cultural artifacts such as charts, books and technology. Thus, for example, the type of materials used by language teachers can influence the type of interactions and activities a language teacher decides to use.

(5) 'Variability and change are at the heart of language teaching' (De Costa & Norton, 2017: 8): Language teaching is an ever-changing endeavor (Douglas Fir Group, 2016: 29). This means that no two teachers will experience teaching in the same way due to differences in the micro, meso and macro levels of social interaction.

(6) 'Literacy and instruction mediate language teaching' (De Costa & Norton, 2017: 8): Literacy and instruction are important influences on L2 teaching. These include not only the form of instruction and literacy that language teachers have experienced in the languages they know and/or teach, but also the instructional approaches and language pedagogy they have received about language teaching through language teacher education (LTE) programs and other forms of professional development. The mediational relationship between literacy/instruction and language teaching should not be misunderstood as a direct relationship, that is, more instruction equals better language teaching. In fact, literacy and instruction may not influence language teaching in the ways we expect. For example,

language teachers may not find the theoretical nature of what is taught in language teacher programs applicable in everyday teaching contexts (Johnson, 2019).

(7) 'Language teaching is identity work' (De Costa & Norton, 2017: 8): When language teachers teach, they do so with historically situated and contextually influenced social identities (Douglas Fir Group, 2016). These social identities, both as social categories (e.g. ethnicity, nationality, religion) and roles in relation to their interactions with others (e.g. students, native speaker, teachers) influence teachers' motivation and investment in teaching opportunities in various contexts and communities. Language teachers' identities, both real and imagined, fluctuate over time and space, as they are influenced and performed through interaction (Douglas Fir Group, 2016).

(8) 'Agency and transformative power are means and goals for language teaching' (De Costa & Norton, 2017: 8): While language teachers and their practices are shaped by larger societal and institutional forces, they also act as individual agents who have a significant role in influencing those forces themselves. Language teachers may draw upon certain identities over others depending on the context in order to participate in ways that grant them greater agency over teaching opportunities or practices in their career (Douglas Fir Group, 2016).

(9) 'Ideologies permeate all levels of language teaching' (De Costa & Norton, 2017: 8): Ideologies impact the level of access, investment and agency that language teachers may feel the desire, ability or need to exercise in their teaching practices or their overall teaching career. Some of the more common language-based ideologies that impact language teaching are language education policies that influence what languages should or should not be taught, the ideology of monolingualism as the assumed norm (Ortega, 2014) and the fallacy of the native speaker as the ideal model for language teaching and learning (Phillipson, 1992).

(10) 'Emotion and affect matter at all levels of language teaching' (De Costa & Norton, 2017: 8): Language teaching is an emotionally driven process that affects the micro, meso and macro levels of social interaction. At the micro level, emotions impact language perception and cognition. At the meso level, emotions are experienced socially, or are deeply tied to the social interactions and relationships involved in teaching. Emotions also influence and are influenced by society-wide ideologies at the macro level.

Applying the DFG framework

Since the DFG introduced its transdisciplinary framework, applied linguistics scholars from various disciplinary perspectives have sought new ways of applying and extending the DFG's framework in areas such as LTE (Gao, 2019; Johnson, 2019); multilingual socialization (Duff, 2019); multilingualism and social justice (Ortega, 2019); language learner agency from a complex dynamic systems perspective (Larsen-Freeman, 2019); conversation analysis and interactional linguistics (Hall, 2019b); the psycholinguistic development of complexity, accuracy and fluency (LaScotte & Tarone, 2019); multilingualism and translanguaging (Cenoz & Gorter, 2019); raciolinguistics (Flores & Rosa, 2019); and generative approaches to SLA (Slabakova, 2019)

A year after the DFG's framework was first introduced and published in *The Modern Language Journal* (Douglas Fir Group, 2016), De Costa and Norton (2017) edited a special issue of *The Modern Language Journal* focusing on introducing and expanding the application of the DFG's framework for language teacher identity (LTI) research, or what they call 'A Transdisciplinary Approach to Language Teacher Identity'. They argued that applying the DFG's framework to LTI research helps researchers address the ways in which increasing multilingualism and globalization impact the real-life issues relevant to language teachers.

For this study, I believe the DFG's framework is particularly suitable for investigating the teacher lives of TMLs (including identities, beliefs and emotions) for two reasons. First, the framework places an emphasis on the increasing multilingualism around the world, of which TMLs are part. From the perspective of the DFG framework, TMLs are treated as 'people who learn to live—and in fact do live—with more than one language at various points in their lives' and 'the learning and teaching of additional languages across private and public, material and digital social contexts in a multilingual world' (Douglas Fir Group, 2016: 20).

Second, because the DFG's framework is structured into multiple layers that compose a holistic ecology, the framework acknowledges the different sources (e.g. micro: cognitive, emotional, interactional; meso: communities, institutions; macro: beliefs, values) that may influence and be influenced by teaching multiple languages. By taking into consideration multiple sources of influence, the framework allows for a more comprehensive understanding of what makes teaching multiple languages different from teaching a single language. This is important when exploring the experiences of TMLs because TMLs are characterized by an added layer of complexity; namely, to understand TMLs, one must take into account all of the language teaching experiences a TML has in the multiple languages they have taught, not just the current language they are teaching.

Lastly, as a concluding note, it is important to understand that when the DFG proposed their framework and encouraged researchers to apply it to their respective disciplines, the DFG highlighted that they do not expect nor suggest that a researcher attempt to investigate all dimensions of the framework all at once or within the same study (Douglas Fir

Group, 2016). Instead, what the DFG envisioned is that their framework would encourage a transdisciplinary mindset in SLA research, in which researchers integrate different disciplinary perspectives without compromising their own (Douglas Fir Group, 2016). Thus, my approach in applying the DFG framework to this study started with using the structure (i.e. micro, meso, macro) and the broad concepts (i.e. the individual, the sociocultural/institutional, the ideological) of the framework to guide my interpretation and analysis of the participants' narratives.

Narrative Inquiry: Lived Experience as Knowledge

The task of understanding the personal experiences of teaching multiple languages told by TMLs necessitates a methodology oriented toward stories and lived experiences. This study applied narrative inquiry, which can be broadly defined as 'an approach to the study of human lives conceived as a way of honouring lived experience as a source of important knowledge and understanding' (Clandinin, 2016: 17). In other words, researchers conducting narrative inquiry explore their participants' lived experience through the stories told during the researcher–participant interactions. Narrative inquiry can be seen as the process of participants making sense of their past, present and future selves to the researcher as well as to themselves (Barkhuizen *et al.*, 2014).

In this study, I use the terms *story* and *narrative* interchangeably, following Riessman (2008) and Spector-Mersel (2010). While different academic traditions treat the relationship between a story and a narrative differently, using the two terms interchangeably is considered contemporary conventional practice in the social sciences (Spector-Mersel, 2010). In defining what a story is, Barkhuizen (2018) provided specific yet accessible criteria, which I employ in my study:

(1) Stories narrate experiences that have happened in the past or will happen in the future (an imagined future).
(2) Stories include the storytellers' reactions, thoughts and emotions about the narrated experiences.
(3) Stories have a 'temporal dimension' in which 'something happens over a period of time' (Barkhuizen, 2018: 112).
(4) Stories have action. Something happens in a story.
(5) What happens in a story is situated in a social context, characterized by multiple levels (micro, meso, macro) of social interaction and institutional context.
(6) Stories make reference to the who (the characters), the when (the time) and the where (the place).
(7) Stories 'look like stories'; as readers and listeners, 'we have a feel for what a story is and usually these feelings are right' (Barkhuizen, 2018: 121).

Barkhuizen's criteria detail the foundational elements that build a story: temporality, characters, thoughts and emotions, action and social context. Thus, we can see from Barkhuizen's (2018) criteria that these foundational elements also broadly coincide with the foundational elements that the DFG framework consists of, making stories a particularly suitable form of data.

Applying narrative inquiry for researching language teachers

In applied linguistics, narrative inquiry has been recognized as one of the main methodological approaches in past and recent research exploring the lives and experiences of language teachers (Barkhuizen, 2016; Barkhuizen *et al.*, 2014; Benson, 2014; Block, 2015; De Costa & Norton, 2016; Hayes, 2017; Kayi-Aydar, 2019; Norton & De Costa, 2018). As a research methodology, several characteristics of narrative inquiry make it valuable and necessary for language teacher research.

One characteristic pertains to the intimate relationship between narrative inquiry and language teachers as research participants. In contrast to more positivist approaches to research, narrative inquiry places a strong emphasis on the lived experiences of participants and treating them as people whose stories represent ways in which they situate themselves in the world. In the words of Barkhuizen *et al.* (2014: 12), 'narrative inquiry is the only methodology that provides access to language teaching and learning as lived experiences that take place over long periods of time and in multiple settings and contexts'. Stories provide a format to authentically represent how teachers see themselves and their experiences (Clandinin & Connelly, 2000). In the same vein, Clandinin and Caine (2008: 541) referred to narrative inquiry as an 'intimate study' of an individual's experiences. Thus, narrative inquiry provides the kind of full-bodied exploration of language teachers' experiences and the reflective commentary on those experiences needed to produce rich and descriptive findings that incorporate both aspects of teachers' inner lives (e.g. perspectives, beliefs) and social lives (e.g. community membership, social relationships) (Clandinin & Rosiek, 2007; Pomerantz, 2013).

Participants

This study features three participants who have taught multiple languages from different backgrounds (i.e. language, teaching experience, teaching context, nationality and ethnicity). Before conducting this study, the participants had either been past colleagues or past students of mine. It is through my familiarity with their lives as teachers that I knew these participants had taught multiple languages. Like other scholars who have conducted narrative-based studies with language teachers (Barkhuizen, 2009; De Costa, 2015; Kayi-Aydar, 2015a; Park, 2006, 2017), our prior relationship also served as a resource to build rapport during our interviews and grant greater access to their experience of teaching multiple languages (Roiha & Iikkanen, 2022).

Beyond simply knowing them and their teaching circumstances on a personal level, I also recruited these three participants as a form of *unique case sampling*, which is a type of purposeful sampling intended to select 'unique, atypical, perhaps rare attributes or occurrences of the phenomenon of interest' (Merriam & Tisdell, 2016: 97). This was also used by Aslan (2015) to recruit TML participants. Furthermore, I also took into consideration the concept of maximum variation sampling, which maximizes differences to increase the likelihood of findings that reveal different perspectives (Creswell, 2013). In other words, I sought to find participants with the same specific, unique characteristic of having taught multiple languages while also having other different characteristics in order to gain diverse perspectives.

In addition, I also used the stated goal of the DFG framework as a guiding compass for recruiting participants: 'responding to the pressing needs of additional language users, their education, their multilingual and multiliterate development, social integration, and performance across diverse globalized, technologized, and transnational contexts' (Douglas Fir Group, 2016: 24). Thus, the participants recruited for this study were representative of additional language users whose education, multilingual development and social lives have been shaped by the greater forces of globalization and technology (e.g. experiences studying and teaching abroad and integrating innovative technologies into their teaching). Table 3.1 presents the profiles of the participants.

Table 3.1 Demographic profile of participants

Pseudonym		Ann	Megan	Haruko
Gender		Female	Female	Female
Nationality		Taiwan	US	Japan
Age		25	34	33
First language taught	Language	English	English	English
	Location	Taiwan	Germany and US	US and Japan
	No. of years	7	13	9
Second language taught	Language	Chinese	German	Japanese
	Location	Taiwan and US	US	US
	No. of years	3.5	2	1

Data Collection

Collecting data in multiple modes

This study incorporated narrative-based data from different sources (i.e. teaching philosophy, interviews, photographs). Creswell (2013) recommended that when designing procedures for conducting narrative research, one should consider the different mediums through which data collection can be conducted. This is important because narratives in everyday communication are often multimodal or conveyed through multiple modes of expression (i.e. written, verbal, visual); thus, giving participants access to different modes of expression during data collection may produce more comprehensive narratives.

It is important to note that collecting data from different sources and modes does not mean that one should expect a single, consistent conclusion in the findings. In fact, collecting data from different sources and in different modalities (i.e. written, verbal, visual) will likely produce some inconsistencies that are a result of different perspectives and angles on the same phenomenon. However, it is the very act of addressing and interrogating these inconsistencies that increases the credibility of the researcher's findings (Gaskell & Bauer, 2000; Patton, 2015). To summarize, data collection for this study involved collecting narrative-based qualitative data from three different sources in three different modalities (i.e. verbal, written, visual): oral narratives through semi-structured interviews, written teacher philosophy statements and participant-produced photo-narratives through photo-elicitation. Table 3.2 presents a summary of the entire data collection process.

Table 3.2 Summary of data collection process

Task	Month 1	Month 2	Month 3
Informed consent	Issued to and collected from participants	–	–
Photo-elicitation task	Issued to participants	–	Collected from participants
Teaching philosophy	Issued to participants	–	Collected from participants
Semi-structured Interview 1	Conducted with participants	–	–
Semi-structured Interview 2	–	Conducted with participants	
Photo-elicitation interview	–	–	Conducted with participants

Semi-structured interviews

The primary source of narrative data came from semi-structured interviews that specifically focused on asking participants about their teaching experiences in teaching multiple languages over the span of their teaching career. The narrative interview questions were inspired by McAdams' (2008) life story interview guide, which focused on pivotal moments in a person's life, such as high, low and turning points.

However, rather than focusing on the participant's life trajectory, I chose to focus on their teaching career. Nevertheless, this did not mean that the narrative interview did not contain aspects of their life beyond the classroom. Teachers' lived experiences of their own careers are not confined to the classroom. And certainly, events in teachers' lives that may have happened before they became teachers or after they have retired from teaching may influence part of their experience of being a teacher. Therefore, the narrative interviews were not restricted to the period of time when they were actually hired as teachers. Again, the primary focus of the narrative interview is to address pivotal moments in the teachers' lives in relation to their teaching career, as guided by the interview questions adapted from McAdams' (2008) interview guide (see Appendix A).

Interviews were conducted in-person or through Skype and divided into two sessions, one session a month with each session lasting roughly 90 minutes each; 90 minutes is the recommended length of time for interview protocols in qualitative research in order to ensure that there is enough time to go in-depth with participants but not stretch for so long that participants lose focus (Seidman, 2006). The two sessions were spaced one month apart in order to ensure flexibility in accommodating the participants' schedules, all of whom were full-time teachers at the time of the interviews. Seidman (2006) stated that while many variations in the spacing of interviews exist, what is important is that structure is maintained throughout the process. The first session asked participants to answer questions regarding their past and present teaching experiences, and the second session was in regard to their future plans for their teaching career and any follow-up questions to expand on previous points. In the planning stages of my study, I estimated that two sessions were necessary for participants to address all the questions I had planned as well as any additional follow-up questions in enough depth, though I had also planned for a third interview if necessary. Participants were given the choice to conduct interviews in Chinese or English. All interviews were conducted primarily in English and fully transcribed in English. The full interview guide used for all interview session can be found in Appendix A.

Written teaching philosophy statement

Participants were also asked to write a teaching philosophy statement. A teaching philosophy statement is not directly a form of narrative. However, within a teaching philosophy statement, the participant may choose to use narratives in order to show their beliefs or teaching philosophies. Thus, the teaching philosophies can be seen as a type of 'teacher identity text' in the way that it 'provides a forum for the discussion of "self"' (Hallman, 2015: 8). Each participant wrote their own teaching philosophy statement on their own time. The researcher gave participants a month to complete the teaching philosophy to allow participants the time and flexibility for greater reflection, as opposed to immediate face-to-face responses as produced from the interviews. Participants were provided with a guide as to what topics the written teaching philosophy would cover. Participants were free to write as many pages as they liked, as long as they covered all the topics. The main topics for the teaching philosophy were (a) the teacher's beliefs about language learning, (b) the teacher's beliefs about language teaching and (c) how the teacher's beliefs are connected to their teaching. The specific guidelines provided for participants to follow in writing the teaching philosophy can be found in Appendix B.

Photo-elicitation

Photo-elicitation can be considered a specific type of visual elicitation using photographs in research interviews (Barkhuizen *et al.*, 2014; Harper, 2002). Most photo-elicitation studies follow the format of asking participants to take their own photographs, which are used as the subject of discussion during the interview; however, photographs can also be taken by the researcher or collected from an outside source (Barkhuizen, 2018; Barkhuizen *et al.*, 2014). For photo-elicitation, the role that photographs play during research interviews is as a 'a trigger to "telling" whether that is for oneself, in making sense of and remembering experiences past and present, or for others, including researchers' (Harrison, 2002: 108). In language teaching and learning research, photo-elicitation and the use of participant-taken photographs have been applied to explore English language learning in formal and informal contexts (Nikula & Pitkänen-Huhta, 2008), international students' perceptions of their educational environment (Shaw, 2013), the identities and participation of marginalized language learners in L2 communities (Giroir, 2014), international LTIs through narrative inquiry (Cabrera, 2017) and language learners studying abroad (Umino & Benson, 2016, 2019).

In narrative inquiry and life story research, photographs have been considered a rich source of narrative data (Harrison, 2002; Umino & Benson, 2016, 2019). While, like the teaching philosophy statements, photo-elicitation is not directly a narrative form of data collection (in the sense that it is not directly asking participants to share stories), it is a method of using visual expression (i.e. photographs) to elicit stories about the teachers' teaching experiences brought about through a different mode of thinking. Furthermore, Riessman (2008: 4) explained that narrative data is not limited to verbal data collected from interviews, highlighting the fact that 'many kinds of texts can be viewed narratively, including spoken, written and visual materials'.

For this study, I chose to use photo-elicitation because it has the potential to elicit responses from participants that oral-only interviews lack. The following are the four main advantages of using photo-elicitation (as opposed to a traditional oral-based interview), as summarized by Rose (2016):

(1) Photo-elicitation provides different insights. Scholars argue that discussing photographs through an interview can elicit information that researchers may not have otherwise thought about addressing or may not have been aware of (Harper, 2002; Rose, 2016).
(2) Photo-elicitation prompts different types of talk than other interview methods. Scholars argue that photo-elicitation triggers more emotional responses (Harper, 2002; Rose, 2016). Also, since the use of images allows for 'communicating more holistically, and through metaphors, they can enhance empathic understanding, capture the ineffable' (Bagnoli, 2009: 548). Furthermore, Collier (1957) experimented with both verbal-only interviews and verbal interviews with photographs and observed that the use of photographs allowed for the participants' interview responses to be more accurate, while traditional oral interviews were less organized and more open-ended. Lastly, photo-elicitation can be directly connected to the methodology of narrative inquiry in that photographs can be treated as a form of storytelling (Harrison, 2002).
(3) Photo-elicitation helps explore aspects of life that are usually overlooked. Particularly when using participant-taken visual materials, Rose (2016: 316) noted that 'asking [participants] to take photographs of that life, and then to talk about the photos, allows the participants to reflect on their everyday activities in a way that is not usually done; it gives them a distance from what they are usually immersed in and allows them to articulate thoughts and feelings that usually remain implicit'. Mannay (2010: 91) explained that using photo-elicitation allows for both the researcher and the participant to discuss things that may have been taken for granted, describing this process as 'making the familiar strange'. Harrison (2002: 98) suggested that taking a photograph has the special capability of instantly capturing a moment in a format that makes it particularly suitable for the narration of experiences, hence the use of photographs in narrative inquiry.
(4) Photo-elicitation can empower participants. Scholars argue that allowing participants to take their own photos and explain what they mean provides them with the opportunity to share their expertise in the research process (Rose, 2016). Mannay (2010) noticed that using participant-taken visual materials gave participants more control over the data and more time to reflect on the data with less interference from the researcher.

For this study, participant-taken photo-narratives were collected through photo-elicitation procedures. Following Giroir (2014), Langmann and

Pick (2018) and Woodley-Baker (2009), *photo-narratives* was the preferred term used to describe the visual photograph-based data collected
for this study because it most accurately described the importance of the
relationship between the image and the narrative as part of the interpretation of the data. Data collection for the photo-narratives through
photo-elicitation was conducted according to the following steps.

The first step of data collection was describing the photo-elicitation
task to each participant. The prompt was to take and curate a set of 6–12
photographs that represent their everyday lives as language teachers,
defined as people, places, objects, actions, feelings or ideas that appear
or play a role in their daily routines as a language teacher (see Appendix C). The prompt was designed according to common photo-elicitation
practices in providing an appropriate balance of enough direction while
allowing for creative flexibility in what kind of photographs they should
be taking (Rose, 2016). Furthermore, it is also common practice in
photo-elicitation procedures to provide participants with a numerical
range in the number of photographs they should take (Bates *et al.*, 2017;
Langmann & Pick, 2018; Rose, 2016). The number of photographs was
determined by taking into consideration the desired level of depth in the
corresponding photo-elicitation interview. Limiting the number of photographs allows for a researcher to go into more depth when discussing
individual photographs during the photo-elicitation interview, though
it limits the creative expression of the participant. Thus, providing a
numerical range for the number of photographs that participants should
take balances out the restriction by providing the participants with some
creative control over what they produce (Bates *et al.*, 2017; Rose, 2016). I
also gave participants the following specific guidelines to help them better understand the task:

- Photographs did not necessarily have to be restricted to the classroom, as the everyday lives of language teachers may involve situations outside the classroom as well.
- Photographs did not necessarily have to be restricted to images of
  teaching, as the everyday lives of language teachers often involve
  activities beyond simply teaching.
- Photographs could be literal images of their everyday lives as teachers (e.g. a photograph of a classroom) or their photographs might
  be abstract representations of their everyday lives as teachers (e.g. a
  photograph of road traffic as a representation of the workload with
  which a teacher may be dealing).
- Participants were encouraged to take new photographs, though
  the use of existing photographs was allowed. Two of the three
  participants included smartphone or computer screenshots as their
  photographs. Originally, I had not thought about the inclusion
  of screenshots as a possible type of photographic data that the

participants might submit. After looking through the screenshots and referring to academic literature regarding screenshots, I decided to accept the screenshots as a form of 'virtual photography' (Moore, 2014).

- Photographs could be taken with any method or device available to the participant (e.g. smartphones, digital cameras, disposable cameras or polaroid cameras). All three participants ended up using their smartphones to take their photographs.

Overall, I encouraged the participants to treat the prompt openly and creatively, so that they would be able to take ownership and agency of the medium to produce photo-narratives that were meaningful to them. Following ethical research practices in photograph-based research, participants were informed that all personal identifying features (i.e. faces, names, etc.) in the photographs would be blurred to ensure anonymity and protect the privacy of all individuals shown in the photographs (Langmann & Pick, 2018). After I described the photo-elicitation task to the participants, the participants were given the option to join the study by signing a written informed consent.

For the second step of data collection, participants were given two months to take and curate their photographs. At the end of the two-month period, I collected their photographs. Because all of the participants took digital photographs, the photographs were sent to me by email or through an online chat program.

For the third step of data collection, I arranged individual photo-elicitation interviews with each participant. During each interview, I used a prepared interview guide (Appendix A) and asked the participant to describe what each photograph they took is depicting, why they took the photograph and how the photograph pertains to their life as a language teacher. Each photo-elicitation interview lasted 60–90 minutes and all were conducted over an online video chat service. It was through the photo-elicitation interview that I was able to combine the photographs with the participants' oral narratives about the photographs to create the photo-narratives.

Data Analysis

Thematic analysis (Alleyne, 2014; Barkhuizen, 2018; Barkhuizen et al., 2014; Block, 2015; Riessman, 2008) was the primary method of data analysis for this study for all three modes of data (i.e. written, verbal and visual). Thematic analysis has been the most frequently used data analysis approach in narrative inquiry (Barkhuizen, 2018; Barkhuizen et al., 2014; Riessman, 2008). Thematic analysis in narrative inquiry involves a process of analyzing stories for overarching themes (C. Ellis, 2004). In general, thematic analysis consists of three steps: reading through the data multiple times, coding the data for patterns and categorizing the patterns under thematic headings (Barkhuizen *et al.*, 2014). Using thematic analysis in this study allows for not only the analysis of prominent themes in individual TML participant's narratives but also the analysis of recurring themes across all of the TML participants' narratives. In fact, Barkhuizen *et al.* (2014: 77) claimed that 'thematic analysis is probably best suited to multiple case studies, because it opens up the possibility of comparing the narratives in a data set, of establishing shared themes, as well as highlighting individual differences'. In order to achieve this, I adapted Kanno and Stuart's (2011) two-stage approach of using within-case analysis and cross-case analysis for a thematic analysis of all three modes of data:

(1) The first reading consisted of a 'within-case analysis' (Kanno & Stuart, 2011), which means that I read all of the data collected for one participant as a set, before moving on to the data collected for the next participant. These initial readings involved taking notes on recurring issues I observed; assigning codes through open coding based on the micro, meso and macro layers of the DFG's framework; and identifying the greater arch of LTI development for each teacher (Kanno & Stuart, 2011). Also, during the first reading, I began chronologically tracking each participant's teacher story as a timeline. After the first reading, I created a narrative timeline of their teaching career.
(2) The second reading consisted of a 'cross-case analysis' (Kanno & Stuart, 2011), which means that I compared the three participants' individual analysis with each other. This reading also involved taking notes and assigning codes through open coding but focused on grouping the themes from individual participants into collective categories (Kanno & Stuart, 2011). Furthermore, the themes identified from individual participant's narratives in the first readings were cross-compared for patterns and common themes. The second reading was conducted at least a week after the first reading in order to gain a fresh perspective on looking at the data.

Although I used the within-case and cross-case analysis approach for all three modes of data, I had to adopt an additional analytical approach for the analysis of visual data. This was crucial because I needed to address how the participants' photographs should be read and interpreted as visual data. Banks and Zeitlyn (2015) suggested two interrelated elements of reading photographs: the internal narrative and the external narrative. The internal narrative represents the content an image conveys without any knowledge or application of external context. Internal, in this sense, refers to the meaning of the photograph contained within its frame. Thus, the internal narrative is the surface content of the photograph that can be seen by any reader without knowing the intentions or ideas of the photographer. The problem is that the internal narrative is incomplete. As Banks and Zeitlyn (2015) pointed out, what readers can deduce from the internal narrative may not be the same as what the photographer intended to portray. Harrison (2002: 105) also contended that photographs 'only provide an outline of the story' and that 'it is events outside the frame [emphasis added] which gives them meaning'.

Thus, in addition to analyzing an image for the internal narrative, it was also crucial to analyze the image for the external narrative, or the social context the image is situated in (Banks & Zeitlyn, 2015). The external narrative focuses on the surrounding story that cannot be seen by simply looking at the photograph itself. Understanding the external narrative requires input and storytelling from the photographer to fill in the spaces of information that the photograph does not immediately convey. Thus, the external narrative is based on the idea that 'what is absent must be conjured up' (Harrison, 2002: 104) through narratives behind, under, around and about the photographs. By examining both the internal and external narratives when using thematic analysis to analyze the participant-taken photographs, the resulting analysis provides insight into not only what content the images portray as viewed by an external reader (like myself as the researcher) with no knowledge of context but also the participant's interpretation of the image and the social context within which the image was taken.

Validation, Trustworthiness and Verisimilitude

Validation and trustworthiness

Over decades of qualitative research, many perspectives on validation have developed that try to refine what validation means for qualitative research, particularly in relation to traditional concepts of validation based on quantitative research. Some qualitative researchers have proposed new terms and concepts because the terms used in positivist-oriented research cannot be transferred to qualitative research (Ely *et al.*, 1991). For example, Lincoln and Guba (1985) introduced a set of new language concepts that more appropriately addressed qualitative research working under a constructivist paradigm (as opposed to a positivist paradigm). They proposed that naturalistic inquiry should aim to establish trustworthiness instead of rigor, which can be achieved through credibility, transferability, dependability and confirmability as opposed to internal validity, external validity, reliability and objectivity, respectively. How trustworthiness is ensured in this study is explained in the ensuing paragraphs. Lincoln and Guba's alternative language for validation has remained highly influential and is often cited in contemporary qualitative studies. In narrative research, Mischler (1990) also proposed using the term trustworthiness to emphasize knowledge as socially constructed as opposed to knowledge as objective reality.

Verisimilitude

Validation in narrative inquiry studies, in particular, has also been reframed to take into consideration the unique nature of what narrative studies focus on. According to Riessman (2008), narratives are more than a sequence of factual events in that they are shaped around a specific perspective and they seek to persuade the audience of that perspective. Thus, narrative researchers aim not to verify facts but rather to understand the meaning made of those facts by participants (Loh, 2013). This is directly tied to focus in narrative inquiry on using stories as data and what that data is able to provide narrative researchers in terms of interpretation and findings. Polkinghorne (2007) explained that:

> Storied evidence is gathered not to determine if events actually happened but about the meaning experienced by people whether or not the events are accurately described.... Storied texts serve as evidence for personal meaning, not for the factual occurrence of the events reported in the stories. (Polkinghorne, 2007: 479)

Taking into consideration narrative inquiry's focus on understanding the meaning that participants make of their experiences, prominent narrative inquiry researchers (Connelly & Clandinin, 1990) have adopted the term verisimilitude from literary studies as an important criterion for establishing trustworthiness in narrative inquiry. A narrative inquiry study that achieves verisimilitude is 'believable and realistic, accurately reflecting all the complexities that exist in real life and engaging the reader' (Creswell & Poth, 2018: 49). Establishing verisimilitude in a narrative inquiry study is crucial because it allows readers to understand the complexities detailed through the participants' stories and more clearly see the connection between participants' stories, the thematic findings and the theoretical implications made as a result of the study. For this study, I engaged in different ways of ensuring trustworthiness and verisimilitude, namely through generating rich, thick descriptions and exercising reflexivity.

Generating rich, thick descriptions

Rich descriptions in qualitative data are defined as providing ample details when describing and presenting data (Stake, 2010). Providing rich, thick descriptions is important because it ensures transferability, or the ability for data to provide readers with enough information to compare, or transfer, the findings of one case with those of other cases (Schwandt, 2007). In order to provide rich, thick descriptions for each participant's narrative, I provided detailed descriptions as well as direct quotes from the participant data whenever I felt it was important to capture their experience in their own words and stay true to the participant's voice. In paying attention to generating rich, thick descriptions during the process of writing participants' narratives, I found I had to go back and contact participants individually by email to confirm some contextual details I did not collect from the data.

Reflexivity: Addressing choices, contentions and limitations

As qualitative researchers, another way of establishing trustworthiness is being aware of your own biases and subjectivity through reflexivity (Patton, 2015). Reflexivity is key in order for qualitative researchers to produce credible and trustworthy research. Hesse-Biber (2007: 129) defined reflexivity as 'the process through which a researcher recognizes, examines, and understands how his or her own social background and assumptions can intervene in the research process'. The following section discusses specific choices I have made as the author of this book and the implications these choices have on the way this research is presented. The problems I present in this section revolve around (1) my positionality as both insider and outsider; (2) the labeling of separate, countable languages; (3) the limitations of historical and global comparisons; (4) the labeling of 'native' and 'non-native' speakers; and (5) the methodological limitations.

Researcher positionality as both insider and outsider

For narrative inquiry, part of what reflexivity means is that the researcher must be aware of the multi-layered nature of narrative inquiry. One layer of narrative inquiry involves the narratives that participants share with researchers while another layer involves the narratives that researchers create from what the participants share with them (Flowerdew & Miller, 2013). This has direct implications for how researchers should approach data analysis and report narrative inquiry studies. Researchers doing narrative inquiry should guard against the risk of interpreting narratives as objective and generalizable truths. As Riessman (2008) suggested, it is not the role of a researcher in narrative inquiry to find narratives or 'the' story, but rather to participate in the co-construction of multi-vocal narratives in a certain context at a certain time. In this way, it was important for me to acknowledge that narratives are 'socially constructed representations of lived experience' rather than objective truth (Hayes, 2013: 65).

Another crucial aspect of exercising reflexivity is interrogating my own positionality as the researcher of this study. Essentially, this seeks to address the question: How does my position as the researcher impact this study? Similar to Hesse-Biber (2007), Park (2006, 2017) and Rudolph (2012), as the researcher of this study I position my role as *both an insider and outsider*. I was born in Taiwan and immigrated with my family to the United States at a young age. At home in the quiet suburbs of Southern California, my parents were committed to maintaining a strong ethnic Chinese identity through a daily habit of using conversational Mandarin and incorporating common Taiwanese cuisine and cultural traditions in everyday life. When I relocated from the United States to Taiwan as an adult in order to pursue a teaching English to speakers of other languages (TESOL) career in higher education, the cultural capital of 'being Taiwanese' that my parents had sought to retain throughout my upbringing provided me with a partial insider status in Taiwan that other American expatriates in Taiwan may not have had, particularly in interacting with the participant from Taiwan in this book. On the other hand, for the two other participants from the United States and Japan, having Taiwanese heritage may not have granted me any particular insider status. Furthermore, my multiple identities as male, openly gay, Taiwanese American, a Western-educated academic, multilingual and 'native speaker of English' also unavoidably positioned me as an insider to some participants and an outsider to others. Lastly, while my study focused on the experiences of TMLs, I personally have no experience of teaching multiple languages myself and I thus relied on the participants as experts of their own lived experiences.

In order to exercise reflexivity throughout the data collection and analysis process, I was fully transparent with my participants about my background, intentions and research goals. By doing this, I hoped to build trust with my participants (C. Ellis, 2004). I read literature from qualitative studies in not only TESOL but also narrative studies and visual studies in order to gain a greater awareness of the impact my decisions and positionality as a researcher may have on the data and findings of this study. Using what I have learned from other qualitative researchers and qualitative research reference books, I actively engaged with the relationship between how my role as the researcher and the data collection procedures I used influenced the narratives I collected. I think that my personal interactions and relationships with the participants outside of the study made it easier for the participants to share their personal narratives with me. In preparing for the interviews, I considered how I would phrase questions or respond to participants in ways that might prompt or discourage certain responses over others.

The labeling and counting of named languages

Sociolinguists have long recognized problems with modern conceptualizations of languages as countable, singular entities that can be differentiated and named (Cenoz, 2013; Makoni & Pennycook, 2007; Otheguy et al., 2015). This is an issue I want to address because discussion around the teaching of multiple languages involves the labeling and counting of named languages.

The primary problem is that separating languages into independent categories does not reflect the way languages and communication actually happen. For example, when it comes to multilingualism, Cenoz (2013) differentiated between atomistic and holistic views of multilingualism. Atomistic views of multilingualism focus on analyzing languages as separate entities occurring side by side, such as code-switching. In this view, multilinguals are expected to use language as if they were two or more monolinguals. In contrast, holistic views of multilingualism avoid focusing on one language at a time and consider a multilingual person's linguistic repertoire as a whole, emphasizing hybridity and fluid boundaries in the way multilingual speakers use languages. This perspective has led to the proposal of new ways of approaching multilingual communication and education, including concepts such as metrolingualism (Otsuji & Pennycook, 2009), polylingualism (Jørgensen, 2008), plurilingualism (Marshall & Moore, 2018; Taylor & Snoddon, 2013) and perhaps the most well-received of them all, translanguaging (García & Li, 2014). Thus, some may argue that the holistic perspective's emphasis on fluid language boundaries and hybridity more accurately reflects the way multilingual speakers communicate in real life (Cenoz, 2013).

However, for Makoni and Pennycook (2007), even a holistic perspective of multilingualism is problematic, as they argued for the need to 'disinvent' the concept of language altogether. Makoni and Pennycook (2007) began with the premise that modern conceptualizations of language are 'inventions'; that is, the naming and development of languages, such as French or Afrikaans, are part of processes of social construction, often as a result of periods of colonialism. Here, Cenoz (2013) and Makoni and Pennycook (2007) partially overlapped in both challenging the idea of languages as discrete, countable entities; however, the latter explained in greater depth that 'to abstract languages, to count them as discrete objects, and to count the speakers of such languages, is to reproduce a very particular enumerative strategy' (Makoni & Pennycook, 2007: 11) – a strategy that was largely based on European colonization. In addition, Makoni and Pennycook (2007: 27) went further by proposing the 'disinvention and reconstitution' of how we conceptualize language. This means that even concepts such as multilingualism need to be reconsidered. According to Makoni and Pennycook (2007):

> Not only do the notions of language become highly suspect, but so do many related concepts that are premised on a notion of discrete languages, such as language rights, mother tongues, multilingualism or code-switching. It is common in both liberal and more critical approaches to issues in sociolinguistics to insist on plurality, sometimes strengthened by a concept of rights. Thus, there are strong arguments for mother tongue education, for an understanding of multilingualism as the global norm, for understanding the prevalence of code-switching in bilingual and multilingual communities, and for the importance of language rights to provide a moral and legal framework for language

policies. Our position, however, is that although such arguments may be preferable to blinkered views that posit a bizarre and rare state of monolingualism as the norm, they nevertheless remain caught within the same paradigm. They operate with a strategy of pluralization rather than questioning those inventions at the core of the discussion. (Makoni & Pennycook, 2007: 22)

As I write this book, I recognize that this book's discussion on TMLs reinforces the labeling and counting of named languages. This also means that this book and any other TML research participate in atomistic views of multilingualism and perpetuate the colonial invention of languages. I say this not only to show my awareness and respect for research highlighting the blurred boundaries of language, but also to express what in my view is the conundrum of TML research; that in order to spotlight the actual careers of TMLs, the labeling and counting of languages are unavoidable. That is, from a pragmatic perspective, if I want to study teachers who have taught Spanish and Italian, referring to the named languages of 'Spanish' and 'Italian' as separate entities is unavoidable. In addition, as a researcher and writer, retaining the labeling and counting of named languages more authentically reflects the subject matter and aims of this book because the current state of TMLs in language education consists of separate languages. All of these involve, to a certain extent, the acknowledgement of languages as distinct entities. That certainly does not take away from what is also true – that the blurred boundaries between Spanish and Italian are part of the lived experience of teachers who have taught Spanish and Italian. I believe both perspectives can coexist.

The limitations of historical and global comparisons

There can be a tendency to assume that the teaching of multiple languages is a new trend. This kind of ahistorical framing has occurred in many discussions around multilingualism, with some scholars emphasizing the ways that modern multilingualism is different from previous versions (Aronin & Singleton, 2008; Lo Bianco & Aronin, 2020) and other scholars reminding us that multilingualism has been integral in the past around the world, including ancient societies (Adams *et al.*, 2002), the Middle Ages and the Early Modern Age (Classen, 2013; Critten & Dutton, 2021) and precolonial South Asia (Canagarajah & Liyanage, 2012).

In addition, there has been a tendency to assume that multilingualism operates in the same way in any context. Pennycook and Makoni (2020: 102–103) described this as applying a 'northern research gaze' that causes 'the exclusion and invisibility of research from the global South in applied linguistics'. This is particularly relevant when it comes to TML research because one cannot assume that the teaching of multiple languages manifests in the same way in the Global South as it does elsewhere. Pennycook and Makoni (2020) explained that:

> Many students in the early years of schooling in different parts of the world (though particularly in the Global South) attend school without knowing they are 'multilingual'. Being multilingual is something they discover at school through a radical process that alters their self-perception and identity when pedagogy forces them to discover languages as separate entities. [...] The northern understanding of multilingualism as 'multiple monolingualisms' insists on ideas such as a mother tongue or a medium of instruction so that 'African languages, which have existed side by side for significant periods of time, complementing each other in multilingual symbiosis, are suddenly cast as competing for spaces' (Banda, 2009, p. 2). The idea of 'a language' as an educational construct is also reflected in debates as to whether Caribbean Creole (CC) is a variety of English or a separate language. Nero (2006) cites examples of Jamaican speakers of CC who assumed they spoke English until they were assigned to ESL classes, thus challenging their sense of being native speakers of English. (Pennycook & Makoni, 2020: 52)

What this means for TML research is that the way the teaching of multiple languages is implemented in the Global South should not be expected to be the same as the way it has been institutionalized in the Global North, such as through certificates and degrees (see Table 2.2). Pennycook and Makoni (2020) proposed that what is needed is not simply the inclusion of the Global South within existing theoretical frameworks; rather, what is needed is 'to change the predominant terms and assumptions, and to revisit principles upon which the new contexts are included' (Mignolo, 2018: 149, as cited in Pennycook & Makoni, 2020: 103).

One of the points that I want to make clear is that the teaching of multiple languages is not a new phenomenon; rather, what is new is a collective scholarly effort to study it within language teaching research or applied linguistics. After all, as long as there was a need to learn multiple languages for any reason, there may have been teachers who were able to teach multiple languages. There is documentation that suggests the existence of TMLs in some form in various historical eras and contexts around the world, such as a brief mention of teachers of Greek and Latin (Adams, 2004: 692; Biville, 2002: 86) and teachers of English and Russian in China in the 1960s (Cortazzi & Jin, 1996; Hu, 2002; Yang, 1987). However, the problem with searching for historical examples of TMLs and using them to compare with more recent examples of TMLs is that conceptualizations of 'language', 'language education' and 'teaching' have always been changing, as Makoni and Pennycook (2007) have shown in the way conceptualizations of languages have been 'invented'. What may currently be considered to be the teaching of multiple languages may have manifested in a completely different way in the past. Thus, my review of previous TML studies and my own research are limited to modern conceptualizations of 'language', 'language education' and 'teaching', with my earliest example of teaching multiple languages in the 1960s in China. That being said, further research is needed that surveys and clarifies the way conceptualizations of teaching multiple languages have transformed over time and in different contexts. For this book, though I have tried to address the many ways teaching multiple languages manifests across time and contexts, including examples from the Global South, the book mainly focuses on the current iteration of the teaching of multiple languages through examining the lives of three TMLs situated in the Global North.

The labeling of 'native' and 'non-native' speakers

In connection to concerns around the labeling of discrete languages, the use of the labels 'native' and 'non-native' to differentiate speakers has been shown to be problematic as well. The 'native' and 'non-native' speaker labels, often referred to as 'the native nonnative speaker dichotomy' or 'the NS/NNS dichotomy' (Faez, 2011) have been shown to be unhelpful and even inaccurate in several ways. First, scholars have shown that there is no clear definition for the concept of the 'native speaker' (Cook, 1999; Davies, 2003; Moussu & Llurda, 2008). Even then, it is common for native speakers to be assumed as the ideal language teachers, or what Phillipson (1992) called 'the native speaker fallacy'.

Second, the NS/NNS dichotomy perpetuates systems of oppression and discrimination. Much of the research that has been done on this topic has been specifically in relation to English, that is, the status of non-native English speaker teachers (NNESTs) and native English speaker teachers (NESTs) in the field of English teaching (Llurda & Calvet-Terré, 2022; Rivers, 2018). This is likely due to the current status of English as the global lingua franca as well as the most frequently taught language. Furthermore, the fact that NNSs of English exponentially outnumber NSs of English also contributes to the predominance of research questioning the role of native-speakerism in perpetuating oppression and discrimination in English teaching (Llurda & Calvet-Terré, 2022).

Studies show that NNESTs in the TESOL profession face discriminatory hiring practices based on a bias for NESTs, or 'native-speakerism' (Clark & Paran, 2007; Flynn & Gulikers, 2001; Mahboob & Golden, 2013; Mahboob *et al.*, 2004; Medgyes, 1992; Selvi, 2010), and are treated as second-class citizens in the field of TESOL (Rajagopalan, 2005) and 'children of a lesser English' (Mahboob *et al.*, 2004). Internally, native-speakerism can also lead to manifestations of NNEST anxieties, such as the 'I-am-not-a-native-speaker syndrome' (Suarez, 2000) and the imposter syndrome (Bernat, 2008). Even upon securing a job position teaching

English, NNESTs are confronted with further assumptions about what types of English teaching they are probably most suitable for. As highlighted by Selvi (2014), it is not uncommon for NNESTs to be positioned as more suitable for teaching reading and grammar while NESTs are perceived to be more suited to teach speaking, listening and writing skills. Thus, native-speakerism disempowers NNESTs by limiting the potential identities available to them (Yazan, 2018b).

The prevalence of unjust challenges and inequities that NNESTs face in the TESOL profession has resulted in scholars calling for the reconceptualization of the NS/NNS dichotomy. Redefining the conceptual understanding of the NS and NNS involves reframing the relationship between the NS and NNS. Yazan (2018b) cautioned against oversimplifying NESTs and NNESTs as two distinct groups of people, emphasizing the need to recognize the complexities that such identities may entail. Selvi (2014: 584) made a similar point by claiming that one of the prevailing myths is that 'native speakers are from Venus, non-native speakers are from Mars'. While some NNEST research has focused on making the distinction between the skills NESTs and NNESTs have, arguing that NNESTs have assets in language teaching that NESTs lack (Medgyes, 1992), Selvi (2014) suggested that NS/NNS studies are moving toward exploring translinguistic and transcultural identities. This could be a movement toward what some scholars call a 'post-native era' (Blair, 2015; Houghton & Hashimoto, 2018), where language users are no longer framed under singular, overly simplistic notions of nativeness and rather are seen as beyond native (Blair, 2015). Essentially, the NS/NSS dichotomy has become unable to account for the complex, multi-faceted nature of learners' and teachers' diverse backgrounds (Faez, 2011).

Many scholars who feel strongly about reconceptualizing the NS/NNS dichotomy have also introduced alternative terms for NS and NNS learners, such as 'language expert' (Rampton, 1990), 'English-using fellowship' (Kachru, 1992), 'multicompetent speaker' (Cook, 1999), 'competent language user' (Lee, 2005), 'new speaker' (O'Rourke & Pujolar, 2013), 'L1, LX user' (Dewaele, 2018) and 'proficient multilinguals' (Calafato, 2019). Alternative terms have also been introduced for the terms NEST and NNEST, such as 'BEST (bilingual English-speaking teacher)' (Jenkins, 2003), 'transnational English teacher' (Menard-Warwick, 2008), 'multilingual instructor' (Kramsch & Zhang, 2018), 'MET (multilingual English teacher)' (Kirkpatrick, 2010), 'DEST (diverse English-speaking teacher)' (Selvi, 2014) and 'translingual English teacher' (Motha *et al.*, 2012).

One might look at the ever-lengthening list of alternative terms and wonder the purpose of these terms. What are scholars trying to achieve? Jain (2018) argued that these terms (i.e. NNEST and alternative terms) are connected to teacher identities, influencing language teachers' self-perceptions, language ownership, speaker legitimacy and professional credibility. Multiple studies (Golombek & Jordan, 2005; Oxford & Jain, 2010; Pavlenko, 2003; Reis, 2012) have shown that forming new conceptualizations of LTIs can affect NNESTs' teaching practices. For example, Pavlenko (2003) demonstrated with pre-service teachers that by having discussions and readings about multicompetence, bilingualism and the NS/NSS dichotomy through an MA TESOL course, the new identity labels they had just learned (i.e. being a multicompetent speaker or a multilingual speaker) served to offer more positive self-perceptions than using the identity label of being a non-native speaker.

Beyond the TESOL profession, there remains much more research to be done with NS and NNS language teachers of languages other than English. Taking into consideration the specific nature of English in the greater landscape of foreign language teaching as the global lingua franca, one cannot assume that the experiences of NESTs and NNESTs represent the experiences of NS and NNS of languages other than English. In the Foreword to Houghton and Hashimoto's (2018) edited volume on post-native-speakerism, Rivers (2018) called for an expansion in the framing of native-speakerism as a concern for all teachers, including those in other fields and of other languages beyond simply English teaching. Houghton and Hashimoto's (2018) edited volume included several chapters examining native-speakerism in Japanese language teaching (i.e. Bouchard, 2018; Hashimoto, 2018; Kadowaki, 2018; Nomura & Mochizuki, 2018; Nonaka, 2018). Llurda and Calvet-Terré (2022) have made a similar proposal, claiming that English language teaching 'has monopolized most research on this topic' and suggesting that one of future themes of research on native-speakerism should focus on NS and NNS teachers of languages other than English.

In accordance with the recent pivot toward investigating native-speakerism in contexts beyond English language teaching, this book discusses NS and NNS teachers of English as well as Mandarin Chinese, German and Japanese. While I used the terms NEST and NNEST to specifically refer to teachers of English in the above discussion on native-speakerism, the rest of the book uses the terms NS and NNS teachers in order to be inclusive of languages beyond English. Furthermore, as mentioned in Chapter 2, I use the terms 'NS/NNS' in this book with a critical awareness of the problematic issues their use perpetuates. In addition, I have chosen to use 'NS/NNS' for two reasons in particular. First, one of the constructs I aimed to examine was the experience and navigation of 'nativeness' within the career of teaching multiple languages, since many TMLs have experienced both sides of the NS/NNS dichotomy still perpetuated within the profession of language teaching. Therefore, one purpose of using the terms 'NS/NNS' is to pinpoint the NS construct that can then be questioned through a TML lens. The second reason why I have chosen to use the terms 'NS/NSS' is to use terms that the participants used themselves and/or were familiar with in order to facilitate ease of communication and make the discussion more precise.

Limitations in methodological design

Some of the difficulties in designing this study on TMLs was using a methodology that could account for teachers located in three different countries as well as exploring both the teachers' past and present experiences. In particular, in the earlier stages of planning the research design for this study, I had considered classroom observations as one of the possible data collection methods. Classroom observations would have provided more direct insight into TMLs' approaches to teaching different languages, particularly for those who were simultaneously teaching more than one language, as well as TMLs' different classroom contexts. However, classroom observations were ultimately unfeasible because of the logistical and financial challenges of conducting classroom observations in three different countries. Thus, this study relied on retrospective methods that could be conducted by participants in different locations around the world (i.e. Taiwan, Japan and the US).

Ultimately, I have attempted to show that the choices I have made in this book are not without contentions and limitations; they are rooted in particular perspectives and ideologies with which not all agree. I hope that with my explicit discussion of these choices comes a better understanding of how this book is situated and why it is situated in this way.

Introduction to Narrative Chapters

Chapters 4 through 6 present the participants' TML narratives *re-storied* (Creswell, 2008) from the interview transcripts, teaching philosophy and photo-narratives of their lived experiences as TMLs. Each chapter consists of three sections: (1) a descriptive timeline of each TML's language teaching career trajectories (presented as stages); (2) a discussion of the participants' LTIs, beliefs and emotions; and (3) a discussion of other aspects of being a TML. For the timeline of each TML's language teaching career trajectories, two of the participants voluntarily used metaphors to describe the stages of their language teaching career, or 'metaphors of living out the profession' (Brandão, 2021). Finally, photographs from participants' photo-elicitations are also integrated throughout each of the chapters.

4 Ann's Narrative: Accessing Global Dreams as a TML

Ann's Language Teaching Career Trajectory

Figure 4.1 presents an overview of the stages of Ann's language teaching career. The version of her career described in this chapter spanned from 2011 to 2019. The following sections explain in detail each stage of Ann's teaching career.

Stage 1: 'The budding stage' (fall 2011–spring 2013)

Ann's narrative of her teaching career began when she was admitted to an undergraduate English language teacher education (LTE) program at North University (pseudonym) in Taiwan in 2011. This LTE program has a history and reputation for specializing in the preparation of undergraduate students to become elementary school English teachers in Taiwan. When Ann was in high school, 'all [she] wanted was to be admitted to a good university' so when she was admitted to North University, she was 'super excited' and her parents 'were all excited for [her]' (Interview 1, 13 June 2019). Upon getting accepted into the LTE program, she 'knew [she] would be a teacher' (Interview 1, 13 June 2019). Ann was admitted to North University through early admissions, thus giving her 'the advantage of several months before [she] actually started university' (Interview 1, 13 June 2019). With her spare time, Ann decided to try and look for a tutoring job because 'before that, [she] didn't actually have any real teaching experience' (Interview 1, 13 June 2019). She described her first tutoring job in the following excerpt:

Excerpt 1

So I got the advantage of several months before I actually get into the university, so I have a lot of time, and at that time I tried to look for some tutor jobs, but before that, I didn't actually have any real teaching experience. So I found a student to teach, but not only English, because sometimes the students will ask me about other subjects, I also answered, but it wasn't so professional and it was my first tutoring job and my tutoring

Stage 1:"The Budding Stage"
(Fall 2011-Spring 2013, 1.5 yrs.)

Stage 2: "A Small Tree"
(Spring 2013-Fall 2014, 1.5 yrs.)

Stage 3: "Two Stems Tangled Together"
(Fall 2014-Summer 2015, 9 mos.)

Stage 4: "Branching Out to India"
(Summer 2015, 3 mos.)

Stage 5: "Two Trees: English Teaching Tree Grows Slowly, Chinese Teaching Tree Grows Rapidly"
(Summer 2015-Winter 2016, 1.25 yrs.)

Stage 6: "Growing Both Trees, the English Teaching Tree Growing Faster"
(Winter 2016-Summer 2018, 1.5 yrs.)

Stage 7: "Branching Out to America"
(Summer 2018-Summer 2019, 1 yr.)

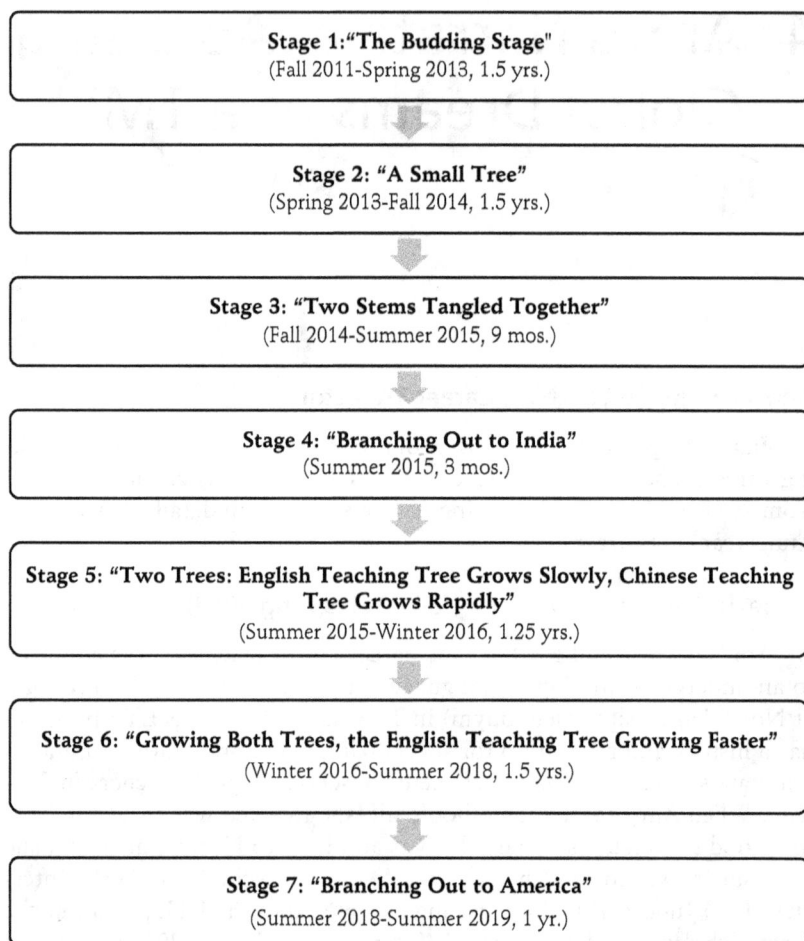

Figure 4.1 Stages of Ann's career trajectory

fee was so cheap and sometimes I just stayed there and accompanied her and if she had some questions she would ask me, that kind of tutoring. (Interview 1, 13 June 2019)

Ann did find a student to teach but the tutoring sessions did not focus exclusively on tutoring English 'because sometimes the student will ask me about other subjects' (Interview 1, 13 June 2019). Even though Ann felt that this 'wasn't so professional', she still tried to answer the student's questions because it was '[her] first tutoring job and [her] tutoring fee was so cheap' (Interview 1, 13 June 2019). Ann recalled that 'sometimes [she] just stayed there and accompanied [the student] and if he had some questions, he would ask me' (Interview 1, 13 June 2019). Ann considered her first tutoring job to be 'that kind of tutoring' (Interview 1, 13

June 2019), implying a certain stigma toward the lack of professionalism that might be associated with individual tutoring sessions. Furthermore, there also seemed to be a lack of agency when Ann tolerated aspects of her first tutoring job that she did not necessarily feel comfortable with, such as teaching subjects other than English and sometimes simply keeping the student company.

Overall, Ann viewed Stage 1 as a time in her career when she was still 'accumulating experience' (Interview 1, 13 June 2019). Once the undergraduate LTE program began, she started her freshman courses, which involved a mix of English-related survey courses (e.g. introduction to Western literature, introduction to linguistics, freshman academic writing) and general education courses (e.g. Chinese, math, education). Ann's goal during her first year was 'to get good grades in all [her] subjects because [she] heard that if [she] got lower grades or failed, then [she] couldn't enroll in the teacher education courses' (Interview 1, 13 June 2019). She continued working as a tutor and despite feeling a lack of professionalism, she mentioned that she 'got fond of it'. Stage 1 ended after the first semester of her second year of the LTE program when she left Taiwan for one semester to study abroad in Shanghai.

Stage 2: 'A small tree' (spring 2013–fall 2014)

Stage 2 began during the second semester of her second year in the LTE program and ended once she had finished her third year in the LTE program. During this period, Ann spent the second semester of her second year in the LTE program studying abroad in Shanghai. For Ann, this study abroad trip marked her first time living abroad for an extended period of time. When she returned to Taipei from Shanghai, she felt conflicted between her interest in becoming an elementary school teacher in Taiwan and her newfound desire to explore teaching opportunities abroad. However, Ann continued to work on her LTE coursework and stay involved in the department's teaching English to speakers of other languages (TESOL-)oriented activities. In particular, Ann indicated that doing English storytelling at elementary schools was a 'big moment' (Interview 1, 13 June 2019) in her teaching career.

Excerpt 2

Our department always holds the English storytelling contest. So I won and then I went to the elementary school across from our university and I also performed in our university auditorium in front of a lot of elementary school students and they laughed. When they laughed I thought all of the practice was worth it. I'm a person who likes kids and I felt satisfied. Though it's not directly related to my teaching job, but I mean it's still related slightly because as a good teacher, when you teach kids, you should be a good storyteller. (Interview 1, 13 June 2019)

This experience was important to Ann not only because she felt that she was successful at English storytelling but also because she was able to gain greater access to the people and places associated with being an elementary school teacher. Furthermore, she gained acclaim and approval not only from the students who enjoyed her storytelling but also from her department. It is important to note that this was an event officially organized and sanctioned by her own department. In winning the contest and doing well during her performances, Ann felt that she was on track to possibly being the 'good teacher' that she had been imagining, as judged not just by herself but others in her community.

Stage 2 ended at the end of her third year in the LTE program. Stage 2 was a time when she began participating in both locally situated activities specifically related to becoming an elementary school English teacher in Taiwan as well as globally situated activities that introduced her to the idea of pursuing a teaching career abroad. At Stage 2, these two paths were not yet clearly differentiated; at this point, Ann had not yet described a divergence in her career pursuits. It was not until Stage 3 that Ann began to feel the need to choose one path over the other.

Stage 3: 'Two stems tangled together' (fall 2014–summer 2015)

Stage 3 began during the first semester of her fourth (and final) year in the undergraduate LTE program. During Stage 3, Ann began to seriously consider what career path she would pursue in terms of becoming an elementary school English teacher in Taiwan or teaching Chinese to speakers of other languages (TCSOL) abroad. Stage 3 was a pivotal time for her and required her to make decisions that would influence what career opportunities would be available to her in the future. Ann was aware that if she wanted to become an elementary school English teacher in Taiwan, this was the time when she had to start preparing for the national teacher certification exam. However, she was also aware that if she wanted to teach Chinese abroad, this was the time when she had to start applying for graduate school in TCSOL. In trying to figure out which career path to prepare for, Ann described the dilemma she faced by characterizing Stage 3 as being 'two stems tangled together'.

Before making any final decisions, she continued to pursue both possibilities. In terms of preparing to become an elementary school English teacher, Ann completed a three-week English as a foreign language (EFL) teaching practicum at an elementary school. Ann considered this another 'big moment' in her teaching career because of its length (a full three weeks working in the same classroom) as well as the experience gained from the practicum. Ann described her experience in the following excerpt:

Excerpt 3

I was assigned to the first grade classroom and then we need to go to the classroom for three weeks and then we need to teach. Because three weeks is much longer than English camp stuff, that's not so impressive compared to the three-week internship because you are really a teacher for them. At first, they are very scared to talk to you because they don't know you but they will find that you're very kind, because they are first graders and they are very innocent and scared of you at first and timid. And then they start to want to know things about you, and every break will swarm around your seat and want to talk to you during the three weeks. When I left, I felt really sad, but I know I can handle it, so I think that was a big moment, and it was during the beginning of senior year. (Interview 1, 13 June 2019)

From the excerpt, we can see that Ann completed the three-week EFL teaching practicum feeling that she was 'really a teacher for them'. Furthermore, she witnessed the transition from students feeling shy around her at first but later getting to know her as part of the classroom. Perhaps what really anchored the three-week practicum as a 'big moment' for Ann was the sadness she felt at the end of the practicum. Her positive experience with the three-week practicum likely made the dilemma of choosing between two different career paths more difficult. If she decided to become an elementary school English teacher, she would have had to start preparing for the national teacher certification exam and complete a half-year teaching practicum after finishing her LTE program.

Also, during her final year in the LTE program, Ann began simultaneously investing in a possible career in TCSOL by enrolling in a TCSOL certification program run by a cram school separate from her university. She spent weekday nights and weekends taking TCSOL courses and eventually obtained a TCSOL certificate. She decided to get a TCSOL certificate because she wanted to 'acquire some knowledge about Chinese teaching' and she was 'thinking about applying for graduate school of teaching Chinese' (Interview 1, 13 June 2019). Furthermore, the TCSOL certificate allowed her to teach Chinese part-time at a cram school. Eventually, she did submit applications to various graduate programs specializing in TCSOL. The 'two stems' of Ann's teaching career eventually converged during her final year in the LTE program when she was admitted to a master's (MA) degree program in TCSOL. It was at this time that she decided to dedicate her time and resources toward getting a master's degree in TCSOL.

Ann made the decision to pursue a master's degree in TCSOL because she wanted a career that would provide her with more opportunities working and traveling abroad. She explained:

Excerpt 4

For me, I just think I love teaching but it depends like, what I teach and the students. Here, I don't have the chance to explore the outside world because I just stay in Taipei. So, I just think that maybe I should change my job to become another teacher. Maybe I can teach Chinese because that can help me go abroad to different countries. (Interview 1, 13 June 2019)

From the excerpt, one can see that Ann perceived teaching TCSOL as a way to gain access to a career abroad, a pathway that she believed would not be available to her if she stuck with teaching English to elementary school students. She explained that as a native speaker (NS) of Chinese, 'if you are a Chinese teacher, most of the teachers will go abroad to teach, and you are the symbol of your country' (Interview 1, 13 June 2019). Despite making the clear decision to invest time and resources into pursuing a master's degree in TCSOL, this did not mean that Ann would never teach English again. In fact, Ann presented a very nuanced explanation of how she viewed herself as a teacher on a broader level:

Excerpt 5

It's very complicated. Because I think teaching English is fun and teaching elementary school children, they are so cute. Like I think being a teacher, you need to inspire others, but I think the important phase to inspire others is in elementary school... So that's why I think if I can graduate from this master's, and my dream is to go a lot of countries to teach, and after I get old, or even I got married, I will come back to Taiwan, so maybe I will go back to teach English. (Interview 1, 13 June 2019)

From this excerpt, we can see a certain level of flexibility when it came to Ann's view of who she is as a teacher. Her career trajectory as a language teacher was very much tied to her life circumstances – to put it simply, if she wanted to travel, she should teach Chinese, and when she wanted to return to Taiwan, she could teach English. It seemed that the primary motivating factor for Ann to pursue degrees and teaching experience in both TESOL and TCSOL was to have the flexibility in her later life to continue language teaching (whether in English or Chinese) in any of the life circumstances she imagined for herself in the future (whether traveling abroad, getting married or returning to Taiwan).

Stage 3 ended once Ann accepted her admissions offer to the graduate program in TCSOL and graduated from her undergraduate LTE program with a bachelor's degree in English instruction.

Stage 4: 'Branching out to India' (summer 2015)

Stage 4 took place during the summer vacation period after Ann had graduated from her undergraduate LTE program and before the first semester of her graduate program in September. During the summer, she participated in a volunteer program teaching Chinese as a second language (CSL) to children in India. While she had taught some Chinese classes at a cram school after getting her TCSOL certificate, teaching CSL in India was the first time Ann had ever taught abroad. According to Ann, 'though it was short compared to the other stages but [teaching in India] had a big influence on [her] so that's why it has its own stage' (Interview 1, 13 June 2019). Ann said that 'just the chance to go abroad was a big moment' so '[she] felt very excited]' and she chose India because she felt that 'when you go to some new country, you'll feel a totally different feeling' (Interview 1, 13 June 2019).

Overall, she had a very positive experience teaching CSL in India. She 'felt touched' because the students 'were very nice to [her]' and 'they studied so hard' (Interview 1, 13 June 2019). One particular moment stood out in Ann's memory:

Excerpt 6

So the most impressive thing was when I taught 'ni hao' (你好) to several classes. For the whole school, I'm their first Chinese teacher and I'm only one person so I cannot teach every class but the class I taught, when they saw me, they would use everything they learned in my class. And then the other students, they really want to know me because I'm a foreigner, so they learned from the other students, so at the end, the whole school learned how to say 'ni hao' (你好) in Chinese, like the whole school, I'm not exaggerating. So, I felt overwhelmed and I was so touched because they know I'm Chinese, my native language is Chinese, so during the break, they would say 'ni hao, ni hao, ni hao' (你好), like everyone, when I go anywhere. It was so touching. (Interview 1, 13 June 2019)

As her first experience teaching abroad, Ann's positive experience teaching 'ni hao' (你好 or 'hello' in Chinese) to children in India showed both similarities and differences to previous positive teaching-related experiences she had, such as her performing English storytelling and teaching during her three-week practicum. Ann's experience in India was similar to her previous experiences in that her recollection and evaluation of success was student centered; that is, when she described her positive experiences related to teaching, many of them were evaluated based on the reactions and behaviors of her students. One major difference in the way she described her teaching experience in India was the relevance of her role as a 'foreigner' and 'NS of Chinese' (Interview 1, 13 June 2019). When teaching in India, these identities were enhanced, and at least from Ann's perspective, played a big role in why the students reacted positively to her teaching of 'ni hao' (你好). In particular, she described the Indian students as being aware that she was a foreigner and a NS of Chinese and that aspect of her presence at their school as being a novelty. Furthermore, she even described her presence at the Indian school as 'a very precious resource for a NS to teach them Chinese' (Interview 1, 13 June

2019). After completing her volunteer program in India, she returned to Taiwan feeling an increased motivation to teach CSL, like 'no matter how hard it's going to be, [she] will learn and become a Chinese teacher' (Interview 1, 13 June 2019).

Stage 4 ended with Ann feeling certain that she had chosen the right path in deciding to pursue TCSOL and preparing to start the first semester of her graduate program in TCSOL. She recalled that her experience in India 'recharged [her], like 100% energy, ready to embrace any obstacles from graduate school' (Interview 1, 13 June 2019). It was with this mindset that Ann started her graduate studies in TCSOL.

Stage 5: 'Two trees: English teaching tree grows slowly, Chinese teaching tree grows rapidly' (summer 2015–winter 2016)

Stage 5 took place mainly during her first year of graduate school in a TCSOL program. The title of Stage 5 continues to use the tree metaphor and conveys an acceleration in her 'Chinese teaching tree' and a stagnation in her 'English teaching tree.' In comparison to Stage 3 in which Ann's two career trajectories were compared to 'two stems tangled together', now it seemed that Ann's two career paths were more clearly differentiated and coexisted parallel to one another, rather than being tangled together. Ann explained that in Stage 5, her 'main focus is on Chinese teaching' (Interview 1, 13 June 2019). During this time, she took on a Chinese tutoring job. Furthermore, from her graduate coursework, she 'learned some philosophy and teaching skills about Chinese teaching, not English teaching' (Interview 1, 13 June 2019). For example, she learned the importance of taking into consideration the linguistic differences between learning English and learning Chinese when designing class activities.

Excerpt 7

When you teach students English, you may want to build up students' phonemic awareness at the beginning, so after that they can differentiate the sounds. And, to help students memorize the vocabulary, some teachers will play a very basic and common game: Hangman. I actually play it whenever I have two or three minutes left in my class. But, can you play it when teaching Chinese? No. And, just like what I mentioned above that for English learners, we will help them build phonemic awareness, but for Chinese learners, after they learn Pinyin system, and they know to mingle sound with Pinyin and can say it correctly, the next part is tone. So we might go through a lot of practice about differentiating the tones, which doesn't even exist in English. So, my main teaching ways for English and Chinese are similar, but it is not exactly the same because they are two distinct language systems, so due to this, my goals in class change, and so do activities. (Teaching philosophy, 20 June 2019)

In this excerpt, Ann showed that in having gone through formal coursework in teaching English and Chinese, she had a pedagogical awareness of how the linguistic differences between the two languages impacted the types of activities she designed for each class. More importantly, Excerpt 7 showed that for Ann, despite the fact that she described her English teaching as 'growing slowly', her acquisition of new pedagogical knowledge, experience and skills in TCSOL was actively engaging with her previous knowledge, experience and skills in TESOL. Because Ann went into the graduate TCSOL program with an undergraduate background in EFL teaching, what she was learning about TCSOL through her coursework and teaching experience was being compared with and contextualized in her previous language teaching experience in TESOL. This was certainly not necessarily the case for the other graduate students in the TCSOL cohort studying alongside Ann. Excerpt 7 is a good example of Ann's early development as a teacher of multiple languages (TML) instructor, as she was analyzing, comparing and coming to certain conclusions about what gaining the knowledge and experience of teaching multiple languages meant for her language teaching on a very practical level.

Stage 5 ended in the middle of the first semester of her second year in the graduate TCSOL program when she got a new job teaching EFL at a cram school.

Stage 6: 'Growing both trees, the English teaching tree growing faster' (winter 2016–summer 2018)

Stage 6 marked a major change during Ann's graduate studies; namely, she was hired at a well-known cram school with a good salary and simultaneously taught EFL while continuing her graduate studies in TCSOL. This is why Ann described Stage 6 as 'growing both trees'. Although this new job had nothing to do with TCSOL, Ann still considered this to be a major milestone in her teaching career. She described her motivation to get this teaching job in the following excerpt:

Excerpt 8

Because I want to make a lot of money, so I started to find some teaching jobs and then opportunities. I was admitted into one English cram school and they paid me very well. I could earn lots of money and it's kind of a big cram school. Some of my classes, I have like 50 students in one classroom. I have my own microphone and my own teaching assistant who always helped me erase the blackboard. Now, my focus was shifting because due to money. (Interview 1, 13 June 2019)

For Ann, this was the most formal teaching position she had taken on so far in her teaching career. Ann pointed out several aspects of this position that made her consider this job as a major upgrade from her previous teaching jobs, such as the size of the cram school, the size of the classes, how much she was getting paid and the equipment and resources provided to her. Despite the fact that it was not a TCSOL position, Ann did not view this teaching job as in conflict with or a digression from her pursuit of a TCSOL career.

In fact, Ann's decision to seek a new EFL teaching job signaled, once again, a willingness to take advantage of opportunities and use both her TESOL and TCSOL experience and skills when needed. In this particular case, by taking on this new EFL teaching job, '[she] didn't need to worry about [her] financial situation, and [she] knew [she] was accumulating English teaching experience too' (Interview 1, 13 June 2019). Because Ann wanted to gain better financial security during her graduate studies, she tapped into her TESOL expertise, which she arguably had a more established foundation in considering her EFL teaching experience. Activating her TESOL expertise for this particular purpose was not in conflict with her greater pursuit of a career in TCSOL that would allow her to travel abroad; in fact, one might argue that her TESOL expertise helped her, financially, to complete her TCSOL studies. In this way, Ann's TML career was characterized by a certain degree of mobility between TESOL and TCSOL, having the ability to easily traverse the two domains as well as occupy them comfortably. This was an ongoing relationship that Ann had built between her two career goals in language teaching and so far, it seemed that she had been able to navigate them to her benefit.

Stage 6 ended at the end of her third year in graduate school when she decided to participate in an internship program allowing her to teach Chinese at an American university for two semesters.

Stage 7: 'Branching out to America' (summer 2018–summer 2019)

Stage 7 began during Ann's third year in graduate school when she was accepted as a participant for a government-sponsored international teacher exchange program called the Fulbright Foreign Language Teaching Assistant (FLTA) program (see Luo & Gao, 2017, for a study of teachers participating in this specific program). This internship program gave her the opportunity to be a teaching assistant for a Chinese language course at an American university for two semesters. Although this program was presented to Ann as an internship opportunity, Ann saw it differently:

Excerpt 9

So that is my internship, so I would say it's a kind of job and it's a lot heavier, and I am well paid so it's like a formal job to me. It is like my first formal job, I would say, because the others are like Chinese tutoring, summer camp, the duration is very short, or some are intensive Chinese teaching, like two or three months, so this one is like my very first formal job of Chinese teaching and then it's in America and it's very long, like two semesters, so 9 months or 10 months. (Interview 1, 13 June 2019)

Again, similar to Stage 6, Ann saw this as an upgrade in her career trajectory, in both the subject she was teaching (i.e. now she gets to teach CSL) and the sense of legitimacy and professionalism she gained from this job, specifically in regard to the length of teaching, how much she was being paid and the educational context of her teaching. However, Ann was unsuccessful in securing the internship right away. In fact, she was not accepted the first time she applied. When she asked the committee members why she had been rejected, they told her that it was mainly because she did not have enough of a 'neutral, formal Chinese accent' suitable for CSL. What the committee members were referring to was that Ann spoke Chinese with a Taiwanese Mandarin or Guoyu (國語) accent rather than a Putonghua (普通話) accent, which is 'the standard variety of Chinese' based on the Beijing dialect. Therefore, when she applied the second time, she adjusted her accent to fit the committee members' preferences and was offered the position.

Stage 7 ended upon Ann completing the two semester-long internship program and returning to Taiwan to finish her graduate studies in TCSOL.

Epilogue: Possible future stages

Ann described several possibilities for future stages in her TML career trajectory. She categorized them into three goals: (1) graduate from her MA TCSOL program, (2) 'learn something new' and (3) 'go abroad again' (Interview 2, 27 July 2019).

First, Ann 'need[ed] to make sure [she] can graduate this year, otherwise [she] can't apply for any jobs abroad' (Interview 2, 27 July 2019). Second, Ann elaborated on the idea of learning something new by explaining that this was something she wanted to do after she had completed her master's degree but before she went abroad for another teaching job, or her 'gap month' as she called it (Interview 2, 27 July 2019).

Excerpt 10

Because I want to stay in Taiwan for a few months to accompany my friends and family. And meanwhile, I want to learn a lot of things I wanted to learn when I was little but I didn't have money. (Interview 2, 27 July 2019)

Specifically, Ann wanted to learn to play the piano, scuba dive, ice skate and paint. Ann explained that she 'really wanted to learn a lot of things, but [she] just didn't have time when [she] was little' (Interview 2, 27 July 2019). Furthermore, '[her] parents didn't let [her] learn a lot of extra-curriculars' (Interview 2, 27 July 2019). These were all extracurricular activities that '[her] parents didn't let [her] learn'. Finally, during her gap month learning new extracurricular activities, Ann planned to apply for jobs abroad. Ann explained her specific plan in the following excerpt:

Excerpt 11

I've been to America and Asia so I have like four continents left. I want to find some good jobs to teach Chinese, first in Europe, because I haven't visited Europe in my life. Second is South America, I haven't visited South America. Third, is Australia, the same reason. Fourth, is Africa. After, if I have four jobs, in the four continents, I'm done and I can just go back to Taiwan, find a job teaching English or Chinese, live a very stable life, and maybe get married or something. After I explore the whole world, then I'm satisfied. (Interview 2, 27 July 2019)

Here, Ann clearly mapped out her plan to travel the world through teaching CSL. It is notable that she was not simply envisioning traveling the world with money she would earn from teaching CSL; rather, she envisioned traveling the world by getting TCSOL jobs abroad. In fact, Ann emphasized her utilitarian view of what motivates her to be a teacher:

Excerpt 12

Some people they want to teach because they want to spread knowledge and help poor kids. Those are very high-level dreams. Not like me, I just want to explore the world. I don't have any holy reasons. (Interview 2, 27 July 2019)

Perhaps what is most interesting about Ann's description of possible future stages in her teaching career is the sense of stoic pragmatism that characterizes her imagined future teaching career, which is in stark contrast to her more inspirational and emotion-based descriptions of her early teaching experiences in the beginning stages of her teaching career. Perhaps that is simply the difference between the nostalgic nature of recollecting past experiences and the practical nature of planning into the future. Another possible explanation is that it was only in the later stages of Ann's teaching career that she realized the opportunities a career in TCSOL provided her, and thus those benefits of potentially giving her access to a globally mobile, cosmopolitan lifestyle of traveling the world were emphasized in her future career plans.

Ann's Identities, Beliefs and Emotions as a TML

Language teacher identities as a TML

Language teacher as a cultural ambassador

While Ann considered teaching any language to be first and foremost 'a job' to her, she also reflected on how she felt her role as an English teacher was different from her role as a Chinese teacher. In fact, she had a much deeper personal connection to the latter. In the following excerpt, she described her views on being a Chinese teacher:

Excerpt 13

If you are a Chinese teacher, most of the teachers will go abroad to teach, and you are the symbol of your country so you cannot do anything bad and if you're friendly and people like you, they will like your country as well. Yeah, it's very important. I think it can be a tool for diplomacy. (Interview 2, 27 July 2019)

The idea of being a 'symbol of your country' and 'a tool for diplomacy' is, on the one hand, part of her perceived role as a Chinese teacher in the US, but also, on the other hand, part of how the FLTA program was framed. In that sense, it is possible that Ann's conceptualization of herself as a cultural ambassador when teaching Chinese may have been partially influenced (directly or indirectly) by the expectations of her program, though there was no indication of this in Ann's interview responses. Ann's photo-narratives present examples of ways that 'Chinese culture' were an important part of her Chinese teaching in the US.

Figures 4.2 and 4.3 in Ann's photo-narratives provide a glimpse of how her identity as a cultural ambassador appears both within and outside of the classroom, formally and informally, in her daily life as a Chinese teacher in the US. For example, in Figure 4.2, six students in Ann's Chinese class are shown holding up finished handwritten pieces of Chinese calligraphy of the word 'chun' (春) on square pieces of red paper. Ann chose this photograph for its focus on what she believed to be the most challenging skill in learning Chinese, which is writing. She explained that to help increase students' motivation for writing Chinese characters and introduce students to Chinese culture, she designed an activity in class where students got to do Chinese calligraphy.

Figure 4.3 features another example of the way Ann's identity as a cultural ambassador appears in her teaching. In Figure 4.3, Ann is taking a selfie with a student while holding up a gift from the student. Ann chose this picture as an example of witnessing her student not only learn Chinese but actually seeing how learning Chinese had influenced the student to take a proactive interest in Chinese culture. She described this particular student's story in the following excerpt:

Excerpt 14

I took a selfie with a student. I'm holding a bookmark of a woman in traditional Chinese clothing. The student was learning Chinese and went to see a Chinese play in America. I think this was a big change for him because he started to have the interest to acquire the culture itself. He

Figure 4.2 Ann's students doing Chinese calligraphy

Figure 4.3 A gift from Ann's student

only understood 10% of the play, but he still learned something, like how the ancient characters behave and talk and how they dressed. He didn't understand what they said but at least he got something. He went to the show and he said he thought of me and got this as a gift. He said, 'Oh when I see the people on stage, I think they are like you and I thought of you.' He's never attended Chinese play before but when he started learning Chinese, he paid for a ticket, even though he didn't understand a lot of Chinese. (Interview 3, 12 August 2019)

Ann's description of her student presents an interesting, reciprocal dynamic between perceptions of Ann as a cultural ambassador from both Ann and her student's perspective. In this situation, Ann felt happy seeing that her student 'started to have the interest to acquire the culture itself' by going to see a Chinese play and her student expressed thinking of Ann when watching the play and even bought a gift for her. In this situation, Ann saw herself through her role as a Chinese teacher. Moreover, the student also reciprocated the idea that Ann played a role in his first experience going to a Chinese play through his buying a gift for her and his desire to retell his experience to her. In other words, Ann's identity as a cultural ambassador through her job as a Chinese teacher was *co-constructed* through her interaction with this student. For Ann, it was not simply 'I see myself as a cultural ambassador', but there was also the external validation of 'We also see you as a cultural ambassador'.

Finally, Figure 4.4 features an example of the way Ann's identity as a cultural ambassador appears outside of her classroom teaching. Ann described the event in the following excerpt:

Excerpt 15

The department has a Chinese club and this is the biggest event of the year. For club events, we want to convey culture. For example, we have the Moon Festival event that was held by the club, and this one is the biggest one. It's for Chinese New Year, and so there are more than a hundred students there. It's a very big room, so I mean, I chose this photo because it's a very big community. We bonded together because we are learning and discussing Chinese. This is our department chair holding the microphone, and she is introducing some Chinese stuff, like what we will eat and zodiac signs. We serve Chinese food, so they can eat, they can learn. And we have different grades who do different performances so they can also enjoy the performances. So it's like a very interactive learning environment and a very interesting one. For the event, I help guide students because they are going to perform and I help them film the video. (Interview 3, 12 August 2019)

We can see that Ann's role as a Chinese teacher at this US university extended beyond the classroom to participating in cultural events

Figure 4.4 The department's Chinese New Year event

organized by the department. From Ann's description, there seems to be an active effort to provide students with an immersive experience of the Chinese New Year, including various 'Chinese stuff' like food, zodiac signs, performances and perhaps even Ann's participation in the event as well.

In contrast to her identity of cultural ambassador as a Chinese teacher, Ann described being an English teacher quite differently:

Excerpt 16

I think being an English teacher, you are the key to open the world to children. Because people live in Taiwan, I think before I learned English, I didn't know what the Western world would be like, even I don't know some culture. They are not like us, so I think teaching English, you can also teach culture. (Interview 2, 27 July 2019)

While Ann viewed being a Chinese teacher as sharing her country and culture with the outside world, she viewed being an English teacher as the opposite – the outside world to Taiwanese children. The former is more like a cultural ambassador of one's own country or culture, while the latter is more like a museum tour guide describing foreign countries or cultures. Furthermore, her language teacher identities (LTIs) connect her national and cultural identity with her self-perceived and socially assigned positions as both an English and a Chinese teacher. As a Chinese teacher, Ann felt her responsibilities went beyond just teaching to include appropriately representing a culture she felt an ownership and a duty to. In contrast, as an English teacher, her sense of responsibility and duty was with providing Taiwanese children access to a foreign culture as part of their foreign language education.

NS/NNS teacher identities

The native speaker/non-native speaker (NS/NNS) dichotomy dictated much of the way Ann thought about her relationship with the languages she taught. Like the other participants in this study, Ann was a particular type of TML who had done language teaching both from the perspective of a NS teacher and a NNS teacher. Her reflections from having been both a NS and NNS teacher show some consistencies with other TMLs from previous studies (Aslan, 2015; Blair, 2012; De Costa, 2015; Kim & Smith, 2019; Mutlu & Ortaçtepe, 2016), in which they found teaching as a NNS teacher easier than teaching as a NS teacher because it was easier for them to empathize with EFL learners' difficulties.

Despite describing her NNS teaching experience as easier than her NS teaching experience, Ann still felt considerable ownership over her NS teaching experience. This may be surprising because Ann described teaching EFL as easier than teaching CSL and that when teaching CSL in the US, Ann was required to change her Chinese accent to match the China-based Putonghua accent. These experiences might lead one to think that Ann may have found teaching CSL frustrating and undesirable. However, the opposite was true. In fact, Ann found teaching CSL in the US to be a very gratifying and fulfilling experience. This sentiment is also echoed in her experience of teaching CSL in India. One probable explanation for why Ann found teaching CSL to be a rewarding experience is because of her ownership of the language as a NS teacher, a testament to the strength and resilience of the NS ideology. This is evident in the way she described her role as a Chinese teacher as 'a symbol of your country' and 'a tool of diplomacy' (Excerpt 13) as explained in the section titled 'Immersion in Teaching Contexts Abroad'. This shows that part of Ann's LTI in teaching CSL was formed by combining a sense of nationalism and cultural duty with the NS ideology; in other words, she felt that as a NS of Chinese, she carried the responsibility to represent not only the Chinese language but also Taiwan as a country and culture in a positive and diplomatic light. The sense of fulfillment from achieving this goal through her CSL teaching is likely what left her feeling impassioned about continuing to teach CSL abroad in the future.

Language teacher beliefs as a TML

Teaching Chinese in the US vs. teaching English in Taiwan

One belief that Ann expressed was that teaching Chinese as a NS teacher in the US was more difficult than teaching English as a NNS teacher in Taiwan. Ann noticed that when she taught English, she might have had to 'prepare for one hour or less than one hour' but when it came to teaching Chinese, she might have had to 'prepare for like three hours' (Interview 2, 27 July 2019). Ann also explained that the extra time spent on lesson preparation was actually part of a much broader issue of having to spend time explicitly learning Chinese grammar:

Excerpt 17

I think because when I teach Chinese, I have a lot of preparation work, but it doesn't come from preparing this specific lesson. It comes from even when I got into my MA, I need to study Chinese grammar, so that's a long, long process. (Interview 2, 27 July 2019)

One factor that influenced the time she spent on lesson preparation was the expectations of the local education context in which she was teaching English and Chinese. When teaching English at cram schools in Taiwan, she was able to explain English grammar using the students' first language (L1; Chinese). However, when teaching Chinese at an American university, she was discouraged from using the students' L1 (English) to teach Chinese; Ann explained that she 'would use Chinese to teach, even though the students don't understand Chinese' (Interview 2, 27 July 2019). That meant that Ann had to incorporate other methods of helping her students understand her lessons, such as 'visual aids, actions, and ways to get them to understand, just not using English' (Interview 2, 27 July 2019). In this way, the difficulties she associated with teaching Chinese in the US were in part related to her being a NS teacher (i.e. needing to explicitly learn Chinese grammar) while also related to the job expectations of the institution where she taught.

Approaches to teaching English and Chinese

Ann described the relationship between her approach to teaching English and teaching Chinese as using the same teaching method but with different activities. She explained that in teaching both English and Chinese, she used communicative and task-based methods; however, she would design different activities because the linguistic characteristics of English and Chinese are different from one another. For example, Ann described using the common spelling game 'Hangman' when teaching English. 'Hangman' requires students to guess a word that their teacher has chosen, letter by letter; each incorrect guess leads to a specific body part being 'hanged' and thus, too many incorrect guesses lead to a complete man being hanged and the end of the game. Ann explained that although she commonly used this game in her English classes, she knew she could not use 'Hangman' in her Chinese classes because Chinese is an ideographic language, not an alphabetic one.

The benefits of having taught both English and Chinese

From a broader point of view, Ann believed that teaching both English and Chinese benefitted her as a teacher. Part of this comes from teaching abroad in a completely new context and in a position that required more teaching hours from her. For instance, Ann learned general teaching skills from teaching Chinese in the US, such as 'how to connect and communicate with students, how to be more familiar and close to them, and how to have good time management' (Interview 2, 27 July 2019).

In addition, Ann discovered that having taught multiple languages made her a more 'persuasive' and 'charismatic' teacher:

Excerpt 18

When I teach English, a lot of students will ask me some dumb questions about 'Why? Why is English like this?' and I will use a lot of Chinese descriptions to explain it. So, I can be more persuasive because I will give them Chinese examples, like even in Chinese, we have this, this and this, and that means the same thing. Also, I want to mention that some students, I mean sometimes, if you experience more things, it will add points to your personality. Like, when they know you taught in a lot of countries, and when they want to know more about you, you have charisma. Sometimes, that's more persuasive because you know, like, the culture in America, because when they want to learn English, they want to know what is happening in America right now, but if you haven't been to the country, maybe they wouldn't ask you a lot of things. So it adds points to your teaching. (Interview 2, 27 July 2019)

For Ann, knowledge and experience in teaching multiple languages contributed not only to her expertise in terms of being able to provide cross-linguistic comparisons for her students but also in becoming a more persuasive and charismatic teacher by being able to share her experiences teaching abroad and presenting herself as a kind of expert of a foreign culture. This can be seen as Ann's perception and awareness that being a TML brings her cultural capital.

Language teacher emotions as a TML

Empathy as a NNS teacher

The ability to empathize with the learner's perspective was also a major factor that differentiated Ann's experience of teaching English from teaching Chinese. In the following excerpt, Ann described the transition from teaching English to teaching Chinese:

Excerpt 19

I think it was a big transition because I knew nothing about Chinese grammar so I needed to learn that grammar. Chinese is my native language so sometimes I don't understand why students can't understand this, why students will make those mistakes. But when I was teaching

English, I totally understand that 'oh, this grammar, when students learn this, they often make this kind of mistake' because I'm also a learner. But when it comes to Chinese, it's totally different because I was born to speak this language so I don't even know why I don't understand it. And some questions, I haven't ever thought about it before. So sometimes, we need to figure it out and sometimes, that's just the way we say it. Nobody knows the answer, there are no regular rules, so I think it's harder to teach Chinese. (Interview 2, 27 July 2019)

For Ann, learning to teach Chinese was more difficult than learning to teach English because Ann had already experienced the process of learning English as an academic subject so when she taught, she was able to tap into her personal experience as an English learner to help inform her English teaching. However, for Chinese, she had only ever experienced the language from the perspective of a NS, and so she was not able to draw from her own experience as a learner and had to depend on pedagogical knowledge learned from coursework and teaching experiences. From this perspective, having the experience of being a language learner of the language she was teaching helped her more than being a NS. This echoes her previously mentioned opinion that teaching Chinese in America as a NS teacher was more difficult than teaching English in Taiwan as a NNS teacher (see the section titled 'Language Teacher Beliefs as a TML').

Ann was also able to empathize with student struggles when it came to a class assignment where students needed to perform a skit based on a Chinese folktale (see Figure 4.5). The students had a difficult time and Ann expressed her ability to empathize with their struggles:

Excerpt 20

They are resistant because they also need to memorize the script and perform it. Memorizing is hard. The activity was designed by a professor. I'm the one who helped them practice, so I can understand how they felt because they would whine 'Oh gosh, how can I memorize those words!' (Interview 3, 12 August 2019)

Positive emotions from students learning Chinese

One noticeable pattern in the way Ann talked about her experience teaching Chinese and English was a deeper emotional investment in her Chinese teaching. This was apparent in her descriptions of students from her Chinese class learning Chinese. It seemed that she was more likely to be happy, excited or impressed by her students in her Chinese class, as opposed to the students in her English class. For example, Ann described (in the section titled 'Stage 4: "Branching Out to India"') how 'overwhelmed' and 'touched' she felt when her students in India greeted her by saying 'hello' in Chinese.

Figure 4.5 Ann's students practicing for a skit

Another example of Ann experiencing positive emotions from students learning Chinese was previously mentioned in the section titled 'Language Teacher Identities as a TML', in which one of her students went to watch a Chinese play and bought her a gift. Finally, Ann provided a screenshot of an email she received from a student in her Chinese class (see Figure 4.6). Ann described the email as something that keeps her motivated to be a language teacher.

All of these are examples of how Ann seemed to be more emotionally invested in her Chinese teaching than her English teaching. This may be tied to the way being a Chinese teacher links her teacher identity and her cultural identity as a Taiwanese person. Therefore, when her students successfully learned Chinese and Chinese culture, she experienced greater satisfaction and fulfillment.

Other Aspects of Being a TML from the DFG Framework

In addition to examining Ann's identities, beliefs and emotions as a TML, there are other aspects of being a TML that can provide a more holistic picture of Ann's experience of teaching multiple languages.

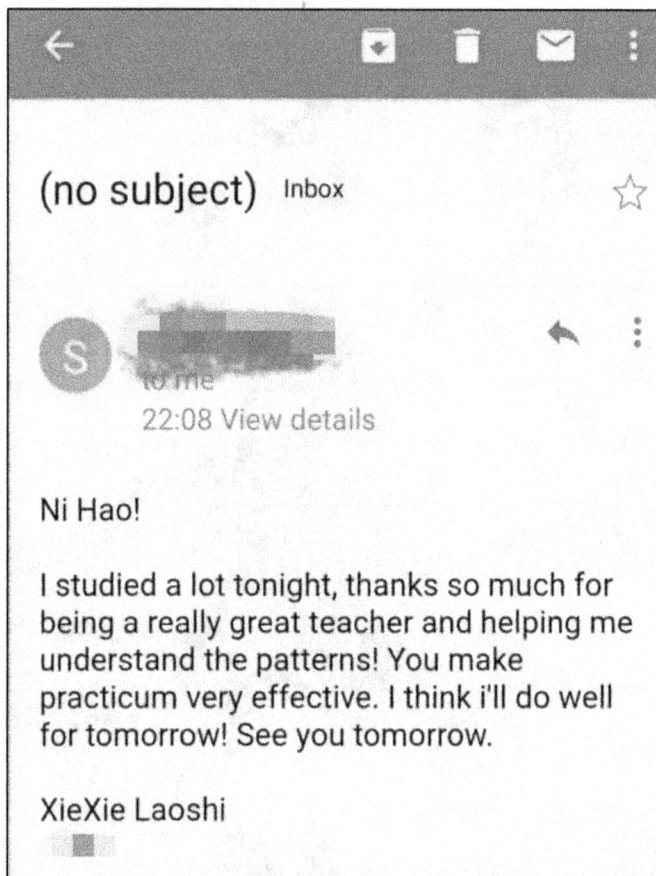

Figure 4.6 An email from Ann's student

The micro level of the DFG framework

At the micro level of the Douglas Fir Group (DFG) framework, one can observe connections between identities, beliefs and emotions and other foundational internal mechanisms involved in Ann's process of becoming and being a TML.

Development of teacher knowledge

Ann's development of teacher knowledge can be considered as the primary internal mechanism underlying the process of becoming a TML. The development of teacher knowledge was a longitudinal process that occurred over the different stages of her TML trajectory, from when she began her undergraduate English LTE program to her various English and Chinese teaching jobs to her graduate coursework in TCSOL.

Specifically, the development of teacher knowledge involved learning the differences between the multiple language systems she was teaching, understanding how those differences impacted her teaching and gaining a greater awareness for the origins of the different sources of her teacher knowledge.

Primarily, Ann's teacher knowledge involved learning and comparing the different language systems and their respective teaching methodologies necessary for her to be able to teach multiple languages. In other words, Ann's teacher knowledge as a TML required understanding how the differences between the linguistic systems of English and Chinese would impact her language teaching. For example, in Excerpt 7, Ann described learning to use the game 'Hangman' in her EFL teaching in order to help her beginning learners build phonemic awareness and expand their vocabulary. She found the game to be useful, especially when there was extra time to spare at the end of class. When Ann began teaching Chinese, she found that this game was not applicable because for Chinese learners, her priority with beginning learners was to learn the Pinyin system and learn to differentiate tones, which do not exist in English, as she remarked. This is an example of Ann expanding her teacher knowledge by understanding the linguistic differences between English and Chinese and how she had to adapt her teaching methods in accordance with those differences.

In addition to learning linguistic differences and their teaching implications, the development of Ann's teacher knowledge also involved acquiring an awareness of the different sources of her teacher knowledge and how that impacted her teaching. For example, in Excerpt 17, Ann notes that learning to teach Chinese was a big transition from teaching English because, as a NS, she lacked explicit grammatical knowledge of Chinese. In fact, she found it easier to teach English because she was able to use her experience as an English learner to answer her students' questions about English. This is an example of Ann gaining a more complex understanding of how her own experiences as a Chinese NS and an EFL learner led to different types of teacher knowledge and an awareness that particularly because she was a NS of Chinese, she needed to explicitly learn Chinese grammar from a pedagogical perspective in order to be a successful Chinese teacher.

Expansion of semiotic resources

In connection with the development of teacher knowledge, the necessity of having to manage two different language systems as a TML also expanded the role and range of the semiotic resources Ann had to apply in her teaching, much of which she had to adapt depending on the local expectations of the specific teaching context she was in. First, Ann had to change the role of 'English' and 'Chinese' as linguistically-based semiotic resources used in her teaching. Namely, when teaching EFL in Taiwan, 'English' as a visual and auditory semiotic resource was treated as the target language of instruction while 'Chinese' was applied as the medium of instruction. The roles assigned to these two language systems as semiotic resources changed when Ann transitioned to teaching Chinese. One example of this is from Excerpt 20, in which Ann described that she had more preparation work to do when teaching Chinese at the American university than when she taught English or Chinese in Taiwan because the American university required her to use Chinese to teach Chinese, even at beginning levels. In order to do this successfully, she had to prepare bilingual (Chinese and English) visual aids to help her students understand her lessons. Thus, when teaching Chinese at the American university, she had to apply 'Chinese' as both the target language of instruction as well as the medium of instruction through teacher talk and visual aids, while 'English' was applied in a supportive role through visual aids. What this example shows is how the transition from teaching English to teaching Chinese required Ann to juggle and manage the roles that 'English' and 'Chinese' played in her teaching both as the target language and the medium of instruction applied in verbal and visual forms.

Another example of this can be seen in Figure 4.7 in which Ann provided a photograph of a completely new type of CSL textbook and a new methodology for teaching Chinese used by the American university that she had not learned from her CSL graduate coursework in Taiwan. Specifically, in this case, the textbook began by introducing new Chinese vocabulary using the Romanized Pinyin system of writing and gradually transitioned to exposing beginning CSL students to Chinese characters. Again, in order to transition to using not only this bilingual textbook but also this new method of CSL teaching, Ann had to reassign the ways in which 'English' and 'Chinese' would be employed in her language teaching.

Lastly, semiotic resources also played a role in the wide range of ways that Ann experienced 'language teaching' and 'language learning' over the course of her TML career. These semiotic resources acted as cultural artifacts of language teaching that mediated what language teaching and learning looked and felt like as she was learning to become a language teacher. While some of these cultural artifacts appeared as physical objects, others were experienced as embodied experiences engaging with a more holistic sense of Ann's TML self. For example, some of the artifactual experiences that stood out to her were English storytelling with children (Excerpt 2), hearing her students in India collectively saying 'ni hao' (你好) to her (Excerpt 6), getting a teaching position that provided her with her own microphone, a teaching assistant and good pay (Excerpt 8), teaching students to do Chinese calligraphy (Figure 4.2), getting a souvenir from a student who went to his first Chinese play (Figure 4.3, Excerpt 14) and leading a Chinese New Year event (Figure 4.4, Excerpt 15). These are all examples of how the cultural artifacts tied to

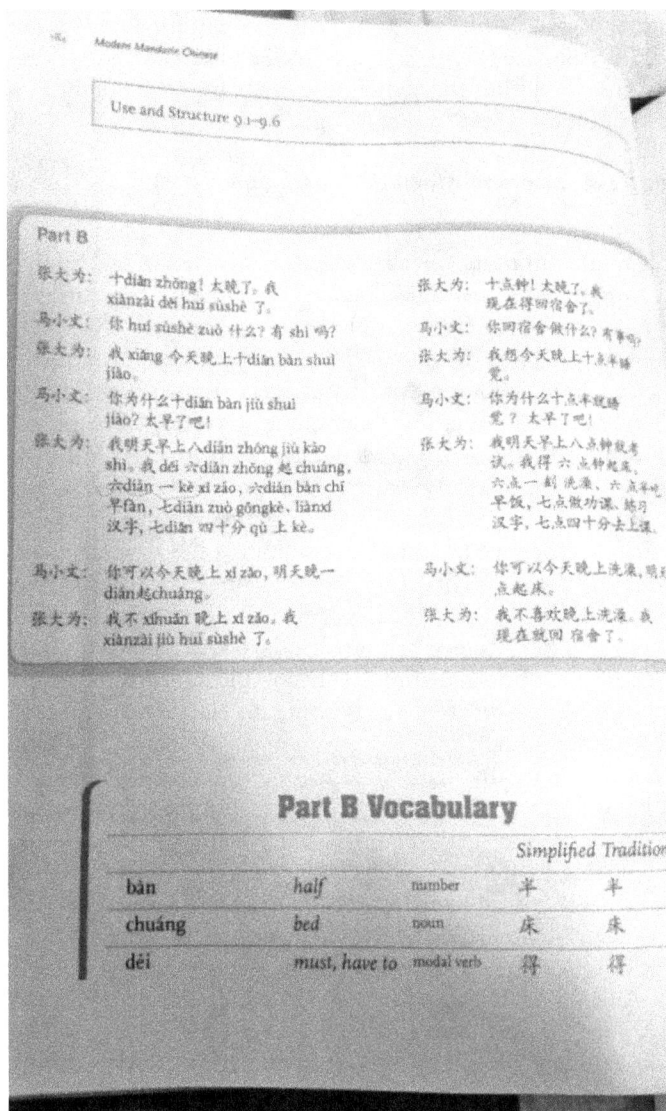

Figure 4.7 The textbook used in Ann's Chinese class

language teaching and learning manifest as the semiotic resources that mediated Ann's experience of teaching multiple languages across different contexts.

The meso level of the DFG framework

The meso level of the DFG framework focuses on the ways in which Ann's participation and membership in certain sociocultural institutions and communities shaped the internal mechanisms discussed at the micro level. In this respect, what was particularly salient for Ann was her ability to navigate various LTE programs as well as immerse herself in various communities in relation to the multiple languages she taught in order to achieve her language teaching career goals.

Navigating LTE programs of multiple languages

For Ann, participating in LTE programs provided her with the basic resources and training to develop teacher knowledge and apply various semiotic resources to multiple languages. Ann received formal LTE in Taiwan in both TESOL from her bachelor's degree and TCSOL from her master's degree, which meant that she received academic coursework in language teaching methodology, pedagogical theory and linguistics for both English and Chinese. For example, in Excerpt 17, Ann mentioned that acquiring this teacher knowledge through formal coursework was particularly important for teaching Chinese because she was a NS of Chinese and had never learned Chinese grammar from a second language pedagogical perspective prior to her graduate TCSOL coursework.

Navigating the different LTE systems meant that Ann had to consider which programs would provide the academic knowledge and credentials that would help her achieve her career goals. During her undergraduate EFL teacher education program, Ann completed various requirements that would have qualified her to become an elementary school English teacher, including a teaching practicum at an elementary school. However, when it eventually came time to take the national teacher certification exams, Ann made the conscious decision to enroll in a master's program in TCSOL instead. For Ann, this was not a decision to give up English teaching as she continued to teach English at cram schools even after entering the graduate TCSOL program. Rather, she decided to enroll in the graduate TCSOL program in order to gain the educational qualifications necessary to apply for Chinese teaching jobs abroad. Thus, the way Ann navigated which language education programs to invest time and money in may be considered a form of *job-crafting* (Haneda & Sherman, 2016), or conscious, informed decisions with her future career aspirations and opportunities in mind.

Immersion in teaching contexts abroad

In addition to navigating different LTE programs, Ann also took advantage of opportunities to travel abroad and do language teaching in other cultural contexts. She did this twice: once when going to India to teach Chinese over the summer before starting her graduate program and a second time when going to the US to teach Chinese at a university for a year. While the LTE programs that Ann attended provided her with explicit training, resources and academic credentials, these opportunities to teach CSL abroad provided her with intensive field experience of teaching Chinese while fully immersed in a foreign language context. But beyond providing her with intensive teaching experiences, these opportunities also enhanced her LTI.

When Ann taught CSL in India and the US, she remarked in both scenarios that she felt like a cultural ambassador or as she put it, 'a symbol of your country' and 'a tool of diplomacy' (Excerpt 13) as a CSL instructor. For her, teaching Chinese was an act of sharing a part of her own culture and native language to foreign learners. In contrast, when teaching EFL in Taiwan, she felt that she was sharing 'the Western world' with Taiwanese children who may not be familiar with that culture (Excerpt 14). In this sense, her identity as an EFL instructor was more akin to being a tour guide rather than a cultural ambassador. For Ann, her experiences of teaching CSL abroad refined her awareness of these differences in her LTIs by being able to experience them not only in Taiwan but also in new, culturally immersive teaching contexts abroad.

While these were indeed enriching experiences for Ann's development as a TML, taking on the identity of a cultural ambassador of the Chinese language also meant that Ann had to conform to decisions in her CSL teaching shaped by greater sociopolitical ideologies outside of her immediate control. For example, in order for her to have the chance to teach CSL in the US, Ann applied through a program sponsored by the Taiwanese government. As described in Stage 7 of Ann's language teaching career trajectory, she was not accepted the first time she applied to the program. She later found out that she had been rejected because she did not speak with the 'proper' Chinese accent, which meant speaking with a Putonghua (普通話) accent based on the Beijing dialect. Essentially, this meant that Ann had to learn to speak Chinese with a completely different accent affiliated with mainland China in order to successfully get the opportunity to teach abroad. Although it conflicted with her identity and everyday use of Chinese as a Taiwanese person, she managed to learn to speak Putonghua and passed the second time she applied. When she started teaching in the US, she also had to conform to teaching CSL using Putonghua, which she did not have to do when teaching CSL in Taiwan or India.

What this shows is that the sociopolitical ideologies that shape the communities and identities associated with the language of instruction also impact the expectations of what kind of teacher Ann should be and how she should teach. One might say that Ann had little teacher agency in this situation, that she was a puppet controlled by a China-centric view of Chinese learning. However, another way to view her situation was that she made the practical decisions that granted her access to the opportunities she wanted for her career, namely the opportunity to teach CSL in the US.

The macro level of the DFG framework

The macro level of the DFG framework focuses on the ways in which large-scale, societal ideologies influence the micro and meso levels of Ann's development as a TML. One of the main ideologies influencing Ann's development as a TML is the NS/NNS dichotomy, which has been discussed in the sections titled 'Language Teacher Identities as a TML' and 'Language Teacher Emotions as a TML'. In addition to the NS/NNS dichotomy, another ideology that was particularly salient for Ann was the concept of a global language market.

Tapping into the global language market

The other large-scale ideology that guided Ann's experience of being a TML is the concept of a global language market (Park & Wee, 2012). According to Park and Wee (2012), the global language market is a neo-liberal concept that frames language skills as a commodity with a negotiated market value in the global job market. For example, the idea of a global language market is often what drives the belief that governments should implement English language education policies so its population will be equipped with proficient English skills in order to become more competitive and marketable for jobs around the world. For Ann, her situation did not completely fit the narrative of using English as a way of accessing jobs abroad.

While Ann certainly recognized English as 'global' when it came to culture and communication, she also saw English as 'local' when it came to her language teaching career as a Taiwanese teacher. Ann did not think it would be possible for her to teach English abroad and thus turned to teaching Chinese as her strategy for getting a teaching job abroad. In other words, Ann felt that her Chinese teaching skills as a native Chinese speaker had greater market value in the global language market than her English teaching skills as a non-native English speaker. However, Ann never abandoned English teaching; in fact, she perceived English teaching as a stable job option that she could continue to do after she finished traveling abroad and returned to Taiwan.

Ann's primary goal in becoming a Chinese teacher was to be able to travel around the world through teaching Chinese in various countries. At the time of her interview, Ann had already been to the US and India through Chinese teaching opportunities and that was before she had officially completed her master's degree. She expected that after completing her master's degree, she would be able to travel to other parts of the world through Chinese teaching. Thus, even though Chinese was 'local' for Ann in the sense that Chinese is the primary language of Taiwan and also her mother tongue, Chinese teaching was also a 'global' pursuit for Ann in the sense that she felt that being a NS teacher of Chinese had greater market value than being a NNS of English in the global language market. Her perception of Chinese teaching as global was also based on her awareness of the increasing influence of the People's Republic of China impacting the increasing demand for Chinese learning both within Taiwan from visiting foreigners and beyond Taiwan. Ann sought to take advantage of the trend toward learning Chinese and her linguistic capital as a NS teacher of Chinese as her way of achieving her dream to travel around the world. Thus, Ann saw teaching Chinese and English as granting her the mobility and flexibility to move back and forth between life in Taiwan and life abroad.

It is important to note that while the increasing demand for Chinese learning provided Ann with an opportunity to expand her language teaching career abroad, there were also difficulties and challenges to pursuing a career in teaching Chinese abroad. At first, this might seem unexpected considering that Ann is a NS of Chinese; however, for Ann, it was actually more difficult for her to qualify as a Chinese teacher abroad than an English teacher in Taiwan. First, the educational qualifications to teach Chinese abroad were higher (i.e. a master's degree) than those for teaching English in Taiwan (i.e. bachelor's degree). Also, because Ann's goal was to teach Chinese abroad (as opposed to teaching Chinese in Taiwan), being a NS of Taiwanese Chinese did not work entirely in her favor. In fact, in order for her to qualify to participate in the Taiwanese government's program for Taiwanese teachers to teach Chinese in the US, Ann had to change the way she spoke Chinese and learn a new linguistic repertoire based on the Chinese used in the People's Republic of China (i.e. reading and writing simplified Chinese characters, using Chinese vocabulary and sayings from the People's Republic of China, speaking with a 'Beijing accent') in order to qualify to teach Chinese abroad. This is because when teaching Chinese in the US, she would be expected to teach the variety of Chinese used in the People's Republic of China, not Taiwan. Yet, Ann did not seem to consider changing her own Chinese usage to be a major difficulty. In fact, Ann voiced greater frustration over what she described as a 'plateau' in her English proficiency or a feeling of not being able to improve no matter how hard she tried, even though this did not have an impact on her English teaching opportunities in Taiwan. Ultimately, while Ann did not figure out a way to move past her plateau in English, she was able to overcome the barriers to Chinese teaching abroad and continued to pursue her aspirations for global and local mobility.

5 Megan's Narrative: Resisting Institutional Inequalities as a TML

Megan's Language Teaching Career Trajectory

Figure 5.1 presents an overview of the stages of Megan's language teaching career. The version of her career described in this chapter spanned from 2006 to 2019. The following sections explain in detail each stage of Megan's teaching career.

Stage 1: 'Teaching before I knew what I was doing' (2006–2009)

Megan began her teacher of multiple languages (TML) career trajectory during the junior year of her undergraduate education pursuing a business degree at an international university in Germany. The reason why Megan was going to college in Germany in the first place had much to do with where she grew up. Megan had grown up in a small rural community in Northern California that she described as 'one of the most economically depressed areas of California' with 'a lot of drug use there, especially meth' (Interview 1, 16 June 2019). Megan had always had a passion for reading and found herself 'reading about all these places where things were happening somewhere in the world' (Interview 1, 16 June 2019). This led her to be 'really into this idea of moving to another country or just getting out of [her] little community' (Interview 1, 16 June 2019). When Megan was in high school, she befriended an exchange student from Germany in her French class and when she was 17, Megan ended up visiting Germany during the summer. She 'fell in love' with Germany, applied to an international university in the German town she wanted to live in and relocated to Germany to attend that university (Interview 1, 16 June 2019).

Although she was not enrolled in a teacher education program, she began teaching English as a foreign language (EFL) in Germany during college in order to make some extra money. She described her early mindset as an EFL teacher in this way:

Excerpt 1

So I have this skill, which is speaking English, that I was able to use to make some extra money. Tutor, teach. I didn't really think much about

```
┌─────────────────────────────────────────────────┐
│  Stage 1:"Teaching Before I Knew What I Was Doing"│
│              (2006-2009, 3 yrs.)                  │
└─────────────────────────────────────────────────┘
                        ⬇
┌─────────────────────────────────────────────────┐
│   Stage 2: "Novice Teaching During my Masters"    │
│              (2009-2012, 3 yrs.)                   │
└─────────────────────────────────────────────────┘
                        ⬇
┌─────────────────────────────────────────────────┐
│        Stage 3: "New Professional"                │
│              (2012-2015)                          │
└─────────────────────────────────────────────────┘
                        ⬇
┌─────────────────────────────────────────────────┐
│  Stage 4: "I Sort of Know What I'm Doing Now"     │
│              (2015-2019)                          │
└─────────────────────────────────────────────────┘
```

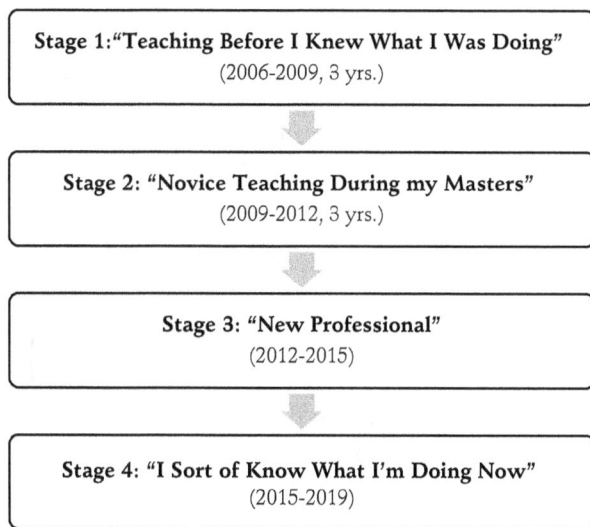

Figure 5.1 Stages of Megan's career trajectory

it. I was given like a real, quick training session at Berlitz, and I just followed the guidelines in the book and I enjoyed it, but I wouldn't say I ever thought very deeply about what I was doing, or why I was doing, or what the purpose of anything was. And then I came up with tricks and methods. I shouldn't make it sound like you know, I've gained no skills. I totally did, but they weren't rooted in any sort of researcher knowledge of pedagogy. (Interview 1, 16 June 2019)

In recollecting the beginnings of her teaching career, Megan described her teaching as lacking professionalism – as something she did not think too deeply about, disconnected from research and pedagogy, and primarily motivated by earning some extra money. Describing her early teaching experiences in this way not only shows what her early teaching experiences were like, but also reveals ideologies she had adopted over time about what she expected from professionally trained teaching.

Megan proceeded to teach EFL in Germany for about three years until 2009 'because the 2008 recession occurred and I couldn't find a job in the United States' (Interview 1, 16 June 2019). Stage 1 ends with Megan having moved back to the US in 2009.

Stage 2: 'Novice teaching during my masters' (2009–2012)

Megan returned to the US and enrolled in a master's (MA) degree program in teaching English to speakers of other languages (TESOL) at an American university. Initially, she decided to pursue an MA TESOL degree for practical reasons relating to her future job prospects:

Excerpt 2

I wouldn't say I was someone who is very prepared for graduate school, or understood even what pedagogy is or what it means. I thought of the masters as more of a means to an end, which is to be qualified for better jobs. So, you know, where I was in Germany, I was able to work at some of these language schools with no qualifications, and I saw a lot of jobs are required qualifications, and I thought, well, you know, I could go get this masters, and then I could move anywhere in the world, and I'd be able to be able to teach officially as a real teacher. So that was my intention. It was more a means to an end. (Interview 1, 16 June 2019)

Megan saw the graduate degree as a way for her not only to be qualified for better jobs, but also to achieve a certain level of professionalism, or 'to teach officially as a real teacher' as she put it. However, her actual experience of the graduate program provided her with more than just the right degree to secure the jobs she wanted. During her graduate program, Megan took coursework on TESOL research and pedagogy as well as teaching English at an intensive English program on campus, which provided her with hands-on teacher training and mentorship from a community of teachers. In the following excerpt, Megan recalled memorable interactions with a mentor during her graduate studies:

Excerpt 3

I have a lot of memories of having an epiphany, of having learned something useful or having had an experience that stood out. So, I just remember during my internship and first semester as a teacher, I had the great fortune of being matched up with Sharon (pseudonym) and having pre- and post-teaching conversations with her, where I felt like I wasn't just talking about future and about life. I was talking about perspectives. Those conversations just helped me so much. There might have been something really, really small that we talked about that had a huge impact. Like, I remember the time Sharon told me, you know, if you put a bunch of, like a big chart on the board, or you have 20 questions on worksheet, you don't have to talk about every single thing on the list. Just because they are numbered in the list doesn't mean they all carried equal weight. You don't have to treat them equally. And I remembered at the time thinking, 'Oh, my God, of course, why did I think otherwise?' Just because they're taking an equal space on a piece of paper doesn't mean they're equally important. And so I suppose that's what I learned to kind of pay more attention to, just to think more critically about the material. So I had some really great small moments like that one, little epiphanies, usually, through conversations with mentors and then resulted in a better outcome. (Interview 2, 22 July 2019)

Although Megan went into the graduate program as a 'means to an end', the actual experience of the graduate program involved a process of development through teaching in the classroom as well as reflecting on her teaching with a mentor, Sharon. Stage 2 ends with Megan graduating from graduate school with a MA TESOL degree.

Stage 3: 'New professional' (2012–2015)

After graduating from the MA TESOL program, over a period of three years, Megan took on a series of English teaching jobs at five different universities in the US. She began with teaching English as a second language (ESL) but soon found the particular type of teaching required of ESL classes to be 'weighing on her personally' and 'exhausting' (Interview 2, 22 July 2019). She explained the complex emotions she felt about teaching ESL in the following excerpt:

Excerpt 4

One is for my sanity, I just felt like in ESL, I found myself constantly repeating myself because students don't necessarily understand, or they're not listening actively… But I just found it bleeding over into my life, where I just felt like I repeated myself all the time, and I didn't mean to and I felt like nobody listened to me. I felt like a broken record. It was just really… I don't know, weighing on me personally. Just having to be so patient and that repetition of saying things over and over again. (Interview 2, 22 July 2019)

Megan's frustration with having to repeat herself over and over again was also connected to her frustration with her students' lack of internal motivation to learn English and her own feelings of hopelessness as an ESL teacher. She expressed these frustrations in the following excerpt:

Excerpt 5

And then at some point, it just feels like we're all pretending here. I mean, what is your motivation for being here in the first place? I mean, I've talked to so many of those students that said, 'Well, my parents like made me come here.' You know, I can imagine learning Chinese and moving to China and sitting in a Chinese university like that must be so terrifying. I mean, so many of the students I've talked to are deeply depressed and they'll just never know that. And I have it like, endless empathy for them. It's just a hard job. It's hard. It's exhausting. (Interview 2, 22 July 2019)

Because of her frustrations with teaching ESL, Megan eventually transitioned from teaching ESL to teaching first-year English composition

(FYC) courses. At first, she taught a mix of a few ESL classes and a few FYC courses, eventually only teaching the latter.

However, even in teaching FYC classes, she still expressed that she often felt like '[she] totally did not know what [she] was doing at all' (Interview 2, 22 July 2019). Several factors influenced her feelings of self-doubt and confusion. One factor was simply the lack of experience that Megan had at the time as a recent graduate entering the adjunct teaching job market, or as the title of this stage suggests, as a 'new professional'. Despite having completed graduate TESOL coursework and receiving training and mentorship on classroom teaching, Megan still experienced a period of learning and adjustment when it came to navigating the job market and new administrative duties. In the following excerpt, Megan described some of the difficulties she faced:

Excerpt 6

I didn't feel comfortable. Like, I walked into this job at University A (pseudonym) with the title of the class, that was all I was given. 'You're teaching written composition one in the rhetoric and language department. Here's a list of textbooks you could use if you want. Here's a syllabus that somebody else made. Have a nice semester.' And I just felt like how can I be expected to build an entire curriculum, assignments, readings, etc., off of nothing? I was so used to being handed curriculums, and putting my own spin on a preexisting curriculum and in a lot of places like University B (pseudonym), I was given a curriculum and I felt like I required a lot of hand-holding. There was a lot of me going to supervisors and asking, 'How would you do this? How would you approach this? How should I do this? Is it okay if I do this?'. So there was a lot of me deferring to superiors at this point where I didn't feel at all prepared to do much more than just teach their curriculums. And I would say that was a few years of that. (Interview 1, 16 June 2019)

In her first few years out of graduate school, Megan had a difficult time figuring out how to teach courses as an adjunct faculty member when she was given few instructions and guidance about what she should actually teach. Rather than seeing this as a lack of structure or organization within the administration, she directed her feelings of incompetency and confusion toward herself, doubting her knowledge and expertise.

Even though Megan seemed to have a difficult time navigating the chaotic waters of adjunct teaching, she was still very engaged in her career as an academic and language teacher; in fact, at one point, she was close to becoming the department chair at one of the universities where she taught:

Excerpt 7

I came close to becoming the chair at University C (pseudonym), and if I had become the chair, I would have totally implemented, like a curriculum across the levels in the classes, because otherwise, you know, if there's no uniformity, I mean, how do you determine when, what's supposed to be learned and how it's going to be taught, etc. (Interview 1, 16 June 2019)

Megan ended up not taking the position as chair because there were plans for the department to split and she felt she could not handle 'all the intricacies' of that kind of administrative change (Interview 1, 16 June 2019). However, it is clear from this excerpt that Megan was trying to work through feeling lost and confused over new adjunct teaching positions and ready to take on leadership positions that may have provided her with the opportunity to improve the way course are structured and assigned to new instructors.

In fact, one of the primary reasons why Megan wanted to take on the position of department chair was because she felt 'pigeonholed' as a certain type of instructor and lacked the leadership and administrative experience to try other job markets. In the following excerpt, she explained her motivations for wanting to take on the role of department chair:

Excerpt 8

I feel like as a FYC instructor, I've pigeonholed myself where I'm only qualified to do exactly what I'm doing now, and I've looked at jobs in other industries, not teaching. I'm doing instructional design, working in training and tech, whatever, just looking, and there's always like all these requirements are on leadership and management, etc. I mean, I just don't have any experience in anything. I mean, I don't particularly want to sell out and work in a tech company, but sometimes I just get so exhausted with what I'm doing. (Interview 1, 16 June 2019)

Considering Megan's feelings of frustration and confusion at taking on adjunct classes without any 'handholding', she had certainly come a long way in just a few years. After having been a FYC instructor for three years, Megan felt constrained in the job opportunities available to her, especially because even several years after earning her graduate degree, she was still stuck with getting adjunct positions. This led her to feel 'pigeonholed' and to start looking for jobs in other industries, such as the tech industry. However, during her job search, she discovered a further lack of qualifications in leadership and management experience as well as an internalized guilt of equating a job at a tech company as 'selling out' (Interview 1, 16 June 2019). Stage 3 ends with Megan having gained more teaching experience as an adjunct instructor of ESL and FYC, but also keeping an eye out for other opportunities in academic leadership and/or other industries.

Stage 4: 'I sort of know what I'm doing now' (2015–2019)

By 2015, Megan had gained enough experience to feel more confident about her teaching. Her higher level of self-confidence came from having more experience with independently designing and teaching classes without much instruction or guidance. Megan described her newly gained experience in this way:

Excerpt 9

I guess I, at this point, as of a couple of years ago, feel comfortable being told, 'Here is the name of the class. Here's kind of what we want you to do,' and then I can walk away and feel confident that I can come up with a curriculum on my own. I can adapt a curriculum. I don't need any help. I mean, I love collaborating. Don't get me wrong, and I'm always happy to collaborate and learn, but I at least feel at this point like I'm able to put a course together and not go into a full panic and need tons and tons of support from supervisors or already made curriculums. (Interview 1, 16 June 2019)

Megan described a type of teacher development based on versatility and resilience, specifically being able to not only adapt and create a curriculum from pre-existing materials or completely from scratch, but also do so on her own without help. She noted that while she was not averse to cooperating with colleagues, learning to work independently was certainly a survival skill she had to learn as an adjunct instructor. Furthermore, Megan was able to take these skills and apply them to teaching German.

During 2018, Megan taught a German class for the first time while simultaneously teaching FYC as an adjunct instructor. She taught German for a German-based company located in Northern California. The class mainly served as an optional extracurricular course provided by the company for employees who wanted to learn German in order to communicate when traveling to Germany for work. Megan described the course in the following excerpt:

Excerpt 10

So I started teaching a German class for the first time a year ago. They kind of told me what they had in mind, and I felt pretty okay with making that happen. Without pressing the panic button and thinking, 'Oh, my God, how do I do this? Who do I talk to?'. You know, I was able to sort of independently plan... So, I teach, well, the class started a year ago. They speak zero words of German. It was a group of people from a company based in Berlin. (Interview 1, 16 June 2019)

When preparing to teach this German class, Megan was very aware of the fact that the kind of class and the language learning goals of the students might be different from the English classes she had been teaching as an adjunct instructor. When teaching English composition courses, she was teaching English for academic purposes and part of a higher education academic institution. The courses were mostly required and part of a degree program. Megan's German classes, however, were voluntary, non-academic courses focusing more on daily conversation language use and were not part of a larger degree program. Megan took these differences into consideration when deciding what teaching method to use when teaching her German class. In the following excerpt, she described her thought process in planning her German course:

Excerpt 11

So it's a voluntary class, and they came in without a word. And so I kind of, you know, I asked several questions about what the goals were, what the objectives were, they're looking for. And they, you know, they didn't want it to be highly academic, and so I decided to use the natural method or the direct method of teaching. So on day one, it was a just a little introductory conversation in German, where we learn how to say 'What's your name? My name is this. Where are you from? I'm from this place. Nice to meet you.' And so, you know, the first day of class, they were asking and answering questions. I mean, a very limited number of questions, but were speaking German and I, you know, I really made the case for, why this isn't a grammar translation class. We're not going to be looking at verb charts and talking about the language. You're going to be using the language. (Interview 1, 16 June 2019)

From the excerpt, Megan chose to use the natural method or the direct method to teach German because she felt it was most appropriate to help them achieve their learning goals. In turn, she avoided teaching based on grammar translation, such as 'looking at verb charts and talking about the language' (Interview 1, 16 June 2019). Her awareness of the students' learning goals also impacted the type of coursework, assignments and activities she designed for this class. In the following excerpt, Megan described her rationale for the way she conducted an exam for her German course:

Excerpt 12

We did an exam, which are written and oral exam, and I brought in a friend of mine from Germany who they had to speak to for ten minutes and just carry on a conversation. We made a joke that it was like a blind date for each of them with her. (Interview 1, 16 June 2019)

By the end of Stage 4, Megan was continuing to simultaneously teach FYC courses and the German class for the German-based company. In addition, she enrolled in a TESOL doctoral program.

At the time of the interview during mid-2019, Megan had become increasingly frustrated with being an adjunct instructor and a certain degree of disillusionment and hopelessness had already influenced her mindset about the current state of her career and the direction she wanted to take it. Megan's frustration with being an adjunct instructor came from the lack of financial and job stability and the overall treatment of adjunct faculty by the departments she worked in. One way in which Megan described her experience as an adjunct instructor is through the metaphor of being 'eggs in an egg carton':

Excerpt 13

Adjuncts are like eggs in an egg carton like, we're all there, but we're all like separated in our own little compartment. Just, it's very isolating. There's no compensation for collaboration. I mean, we're encouraged to collaborate, but nothing about the institution actually supports this. There's no communal workspace, there's no opportunities given to us to like to get together meet. There's no money involved. (Interview 3, 29 August 2019)

Megan recalled a specific example of collaborating with her colleagues to adapt educational technology and incorporate multimodal projects in her classes. While she found benefits to participating in these projects that helped improve her teaching, she also expressed that '[her] biggest issue with it is just the learning curve involved, and also the amount of time it takes, and not being compensated for that time' (Interview 2, 22 July 2019).

In addition to feeling that she was not appropriately compensated for her time and effort as an adjunct instructor, Megan also felt 'undervalued' and 'invisible' as an adjunct instructor. She recalled an incident in which one of her colleagues left an adjunct position she had been teaching at for roughly seven years for a full-time position, and when her colleague left, '[she] didn't even get a goodbye card or a, like a thank you, nothing. They were just sort of like bye, see ya, and her feelings were really hurt' (Interview 2, 22 July 2019). This incident had a major impact on Megan and highlighted her feelings of being 'invisible' as an adjunct instructor:

Excerpt 14

It just sort of made me think about how, I don't know, how undervalued adjuncts are, and how I'll get emails about, you know, the full-time professor of such and such whose mother passed away, and you know condolences, and you know money, memorial funds, and I remember thinking, like, God you know, if I died, I don't think there would be any email that would go out. Like, I just feel like when you're an adjunct, it's made so clear that you don't matter, that we come and go, and we just disappear and appear. There's no kind of, I don't know, commemoration. (Interview 2, 22 July 2019)

The combined feelings of being undervalued financially and socially left Megan feeling 'invisible'. It came as no surprise that at the time of the interview, Megan shared that she was considering an alternative career path to her current position as an adjunct instructor.

Epilogue: Possible future stages

Megan described a three-step plan for possible future stages in her career that she had been considering: (1) 'going corporate' or (2) moving back or staying out of teaching and (3) eventually going back to becoming an adjunct (Interview 3, 29 August 2019). As mentioned in the previous section, the main reasons she had been considering an alternative plan for her career were the lack of proper compensation for her work and the lack of social recognition as part of an academic community. What Megan imagined for her future career was very much shaped by these factors:

Excerpt 15

I'm kind of at the moment looking at not teaching anymore, because of pretty much all the reasons I've told you already, about lack of compensation, feeling like the egg in the egg carton, you know. So what I've been looking at doing is, so next chapter of my life is, I guess, going corporate is looking at being an instructional designer in a corporate setting. So, you know the instructional designer is? An instructional designer is a learning expert, who meets with a subject-matter expert, say, like, an engineer in a company, and helps them plan workshops and trainings for their employees. Very corporatey. So, I would like to do that for a few/couple years, and I could see myself moving around a bit, if I don't feel like the place that I land in the right fit for me, if it's too corporatey. (Interview 3, 29 August 2019)

Megan's interest in changing jobs from an adjunct instructor in higher education to an instructional designer at a company stemmed from her positive experience teaching German for a large corporation. She saw 'going corporate' as a way of finding the financial stability and social recognition that being an adjunct instructor lacked.

It is notable that Megan felt that this was an option she had 'resorted to' because of the frustrations she felt as an adjunct instructor. In many ways, Megan wished she could continue her career in academia because being a teacher had become so intertwined with her identity. Megan shared a story about her friend who worked for a conservation organization as a biologist. While her friend was passionate about her job, she had recently been diagnosed with breast cancer and found herself in a difficult financial situation. Because she didn't earn much as a biologist, she considered going to nursing school to become a nurse, which would have provided her with a better salary. Her friend's dilemma really resonated with Megan. Megan explained:

Excerpt 16

But what she's struggling with, which so resonated with me, is the identity aspect of it, where she's like, I could kind of pride myself on being an academic, of being a biologist and doing something that people go: 'Oh, wow, that's cool. Like, that's such a neat thing that you do'. And to go from that to having a job where people are like: 'Okay, cool, whatever'. There's some like ego wrapped up in it, and I feel the same way, like, I want to be the person who gets to say, smugly, that I'm a teacher, and not the person who says, oh I work at Google, cuz fuck that person, right? I'm like, yeah, there's so much of our egos and identity wrapped up in these professions, and it's hard to say, I'm gonna give up this huge part of my identity that's defined me for so many years, and I'm just doing something different. It's hard, you know? (Interview 3, 29 August 2019)

For Megan, while 'going corporate' seemed to provide better financial compensation and social recognition, she recognized that it also meant a loss of her identity as an academic (as opposed to a corporate employee) that gave her a sense of worth, purpose and status. She recognized that the process of leaving that identity behind would be difficult but it seemed to be a sacrifice she was willing to make.

Megan's plan of getting a corporate job was still tentative and many of her plans were still tenuous, 'maybe, moving back into teaching, or staying out of teaching, depending on how this goes' (Interview 3, 29 August 2019). Furthermore, Megan was not sure whether or not she would continue teaching German. Although she described her overall experience of teaching German at the company as something she 'really enjoyed', 'always walk[ing] out of there happier than when [she] walked in', she was also concerned that her future corporate job might make it difficult to commute and maintain her part-time German teaching job (Interview 3, 29 August 2019). In such a scenario, she would need to make the practical decision of ending her German teaching position with the company. However, she still maintained that 'eventually, when I'm older, [she] would like to go back to doing what [she had been] doing now, once [she had] created more of a stable life for [herself] financially' (Interview 3, 29 August 2019).

Megan's Identities, Beliefs and Emotions as a TML

Megan generally viewed teaching English (both EFL and FYC) as a very different experience from teaching German. Most of the difference was attributed to the fact that she was a native speaker (NS) of English and a second language (L2) learner of German.

Language teacher identities as a TML

Megan's language teacher identities (LTIs) were not necessarily specific to the languages she taught (i.e. English and German); instead, her LTIs were based on the perceived treatment and status she felt from the respective teaching positions she held in teaching English and German.

Being a part-time adjunct instructor

When teaching English, Megan had been employed as a part-time adjunct instructor teaching EFL and FYC at community colleges and universities. As part of the adjunct faculty, she felt that they were poorly compensated for the work expected of them, isolated from one another (Excerpt 13) and 'invisible' and 'undervalued' by the academic institutions they worked for (Interview 2, 22 July 2019). From Excerpt 14 in Megan's TML career trajectory, she recalled a particular incident of receiving a department email notifying her that a full-time professor's mother had passed away. Upon reading the email, she remembered thinking that as an adjunct instructor, if she passed away, no email would be sent to recognize her death. Simply put, she felt that she did not matter to the university.

Megan's identity as an English teacher was strongly impacted by the specific position she held within the institutional hierarchy of academia. Despite her experience as an adjunct instructor seeming to have been mostly negative, Megan had continued to be actively engaged in being an adjunct academic. For example, she had been involved in academic conferences focused on providing adjunct faculty opportunities for professional development and academic recognition.

Furthermore, Megan recalled being part of a FYC professional development project (Figure 5.2). The team consisted of four people, two adjunct and two full-time instructors, and they had to create a new unit that fulfilled a new student learning outcome as mandated by the university department. The new student learning outcome was to incorporate an aspect of oral communication into their FYC classes. The goal was for students to see the difference between spoken and written communication. As a team, they collaborated by meeting once every few weeks and contributing to a running Google document. At the end of the semester,

Figure 5.2 Collaborating with colleagues

they presented their findings. Overall, Megan thought this was 'a great professional development activity and also helped [them] innovate [their] classes to meet the new learning objective' (Interview 2, 22 July 2019). However, she did have a few concerns. One concern was that she was not getting paid extra for doing this project. Another concern was that while she worked well with two members of the team, one member of the team did not contribute anything to the project and this team member was one of the full-time instructors. Megan was frustrated with that team member and felt that it was unfair. In a sense, these kinds of experiences not only helped her further develop her identity and expertise as an academic but also solidified an additional layer of her identity as an adjunct faculty who faced mistreatment and injustice.

Megan's adjunct identity did not stop there. In fact, her own personal experiences and frustrations over the mistreatment of adjunct faculty led her to eventually be a champion for other adjunct faculty. Thus, she saw herself as someone who could enact change and resist the way adjuncts were treated. For example, Megan chose the photograph in Figure 5.3 to portray the mistreatment of adjunct instructors she noticed in academic institutions. The photograph depicts two of Megan's colleagues, Katy and Cynthia (pseudonyms), who were fellow community college ESL teachers. Cynthia had already left her adjunct position for a full-time position at another community college. She had been an adjunct instructor for six or seven years at the community college and when she left, she did not get a goodbye card or a thank you from the department which hurt her feelings. Therefore, when Katy was about to leave her adjunct

Figure 5.3 Celebration with Megan's colleagues

position for a PhD program, Megan decided to do something special for both colleagues to recognize and celebrate their contribution to the community college. Megan bought them gift cards and coffee mugs from the community college, as shown in the photograph. Megan described what motivated her to do this for her colleagues:

Excerpt 17 (extension of Excerpt 14)

I remember thinking, oh the same thing is gonna happen again, nobody's gonna do anything for Katy. And it just sort of made me think about how, I don't know, how undervalued adjuncts are, and how I'll get emails about, you know, the full-time professor of such and such's mother passed away, and you know condolences, and you know money, memorial funds. And I remember thinking, like, God you know, if I died, I don't think there would be any email that would go out, like, I just feel like when you're an adjunct, it's made so clear that you don't matter.

That we come and go, and we just disappear and appear, there's no kind of, I don't know, commemoration. So, anyway, so, like, I roped in a few people, so we need to do like a something for Katy, and then why don't we do something for Cynthia? We'll get Cynthia to come to Katy's like little goodbye, our final semester meeting, and that way we can honor Cynthia as well… And, I don't know. I just like resisting this system of invisible adjuncts, and saying no, we matter, we exist. (Interview 2, 22 July 2019)

Here, we see that Megan frames the small celebration with her co-workers as a greater effort to fight back against the mistreatment of adjunct faculty or 'resisting this system of invisible adjuncts' (Excerpt 17).

Being a part-time teacher at a corporation

The feeling of being unappreciated as an adjunct instructor became even more pronounced when Megan began teaching German in a corporate setting for a German company. Megan's experience as a German instructor at a corporation was vastly different from that of an adjunct English instructor. While she also taught as a part-time instructor, she felt that her skills and teaching were valued at the German company because the purpose of the classes was to provide extracurricular language learning for company employees. Megan interpreted this as 'employee retention' in that 'they don't want people to leave so they provide these fun activities for [the employees]' (Interview 2, 22 July 2019). Furthermore, even beyond simply working as 'employee retention', Megan also felt valued and appreciated in some of the small gestures that occurred in the workplace that did not necessarily have anything to do with her German teaching. For example, she remembered an incident when she showed up at work and found that the company had prepared a 'Happy Birthday' sign, a birthday balloon, flowers and cake (Figure 5.4). Megan was surprised that they remembered her birthday and had put effort into celebrating it because as an adjunct university instructor of English, her birthday had never been recognized by any department. In the following excerpt, Megan described how this incident made her feel:

Excerpt 18

I almost cried because I thought my birthday's never ever been acknowledged anywhere I've worked. Working as an adjunct especially, you know, I'm not gonna tell my students, oh it's my birthday, and I always end up teaching on my birthday, you know unless it's a weekend, because it's right at the beginning of the semester. So, I don't mention it, and, I don't know, I've just never had it acknowledged at work, and because this is like a small community where I teach, it's a small company, and we've built community, and I like them, they like me, that that they got about doing

Figure 5.4 A birthday celebration for Megan

something like this, like really meant something to me. It made me think about how, what it is people want out of work, their work life, and their work environment, and I guess on some level to me, I was like, oh, being acknowledged matters. Like, this didn't really cost them, okay maybe they bought me some flowers and some cake and balloon and probably cost them 20 dollars or 30 dollars, but it wasn't that. It was that I was acknowledged, that my existence was validated. That I was shown that I matter, and that happens so rarely in my other workplaces, especially, yeah, where I teach English like, no, my existence is never validated. (Interview 2, 22 July 2019)

Megan shared this incident because it represented the stark contrast between the way the German company treated her as a part-time German teacher and the way many university academic departments treated her as an adjunct English instructor. For Megan, celebrating her birthday was symbolic for feeling acknowledged and validated; the fact that her birthday had never been celebrated as an adjunct English instructor made her feel that she did not matter in that workplace setting.

Overall, in both her LTIs as a teacher of English and German, neither identity was strongly based on the actual languages she was teaching. Instead, what most strongly impacted her teacher identity was the way she was treated overall as a teacher working and contributing to the workplace. What she wanted to be recognized for was not necessarily her teaching of English or German but her presence and contribution as a fellow colleague or employee.

Language teacher beliefs as a TML

Beliefs on language learning

Megan's beliefs on language learning were centered around language as a tool for communication. For example, Megan believed that learning a language meant 'reaching a point where you can communicate in the target language, that is, express yourself and understand others' (Teaching philosophy, 9 June 2019). Thus, she believed 'the most motivating and quickest way to learn a practical amount of a language is through an emphasis on the direct, or natural method' (Teaching philosophy, 9 June 2019). This belief originated from her own language learning experiences with learning French through a tutor using the natural method and learning German through a romantic relationship. However, Megan did not think that the natural method was the only way to successfully learn a language. She recognized that 'a combination of methods is needed for someone to fully learn enough of a language to claim an advanced level of fluency' (Teaching philosophy, 9 June 2019). She traced this belief back to her experiences learning Arabic in Tunisia and the frustration she felt when an Arabic teacher only used Arabic with the students, even when the students were confused about a grammar point that could have been easily explained using English. Megan believed that 'frustration is a necessary part of learning, but too much of it can be demotivating' (Teaching philosophy, 9 June 2019).

Beliefs on language teaching

Megan attributed her beliefs on language teaching to the 'best teaching practices that [she] learned in graduate school for language learning' (Teaching philosophy, 9 June 2019). Specifically, this included keeping classes student centered, decreasing the amount of teacher talk in favor of more student communication, structuring classes to move from the presentation of a skill to a more controlled practice to a fluency activity,

Figure 5.5 Using an alternative type of assessment

Figure 5.6 Megan's students forming a bond

integrating all skills, providing rationale for course content and adding some of her own humor and personal information. Figure 5.5 features one example of Megan using a non-traditional form of assessment in the German class she taught at the German company. The four people in the photograph were students who had just completed a Jeopardy game activity that Megan had designed in place of an exam. The content of the game was based on what they had learned in the past four months and the company paid for gift card prizes for the winner. For Megan, using a low-stakes competition like the Jeopardy game in place of a traditional exam was more motivating and fun for the students. Megan wanted to create 'a fun, interactive way of testing their knowledge and motivating them, and getting them to interact with each other' (Interview 2, 22 July 2019).

Megan also believed in language teaching and learning as more than just about the language itself; she also considered enjoyment, community, relationships and even social justice as significant goals in her teaching. One might describe these as viewing the classroom as a (potentially) positive, transformative experience, for both the individual and the greater community. For example, in Figure 5.6, Megan is seen showing an activity she designed for her FYC class. For this activity, students formed book groups and were tasked with creating a podcast together determined by a key question based on the book they read. Megan thought the students in

Figure 5.7 A strong sense of community

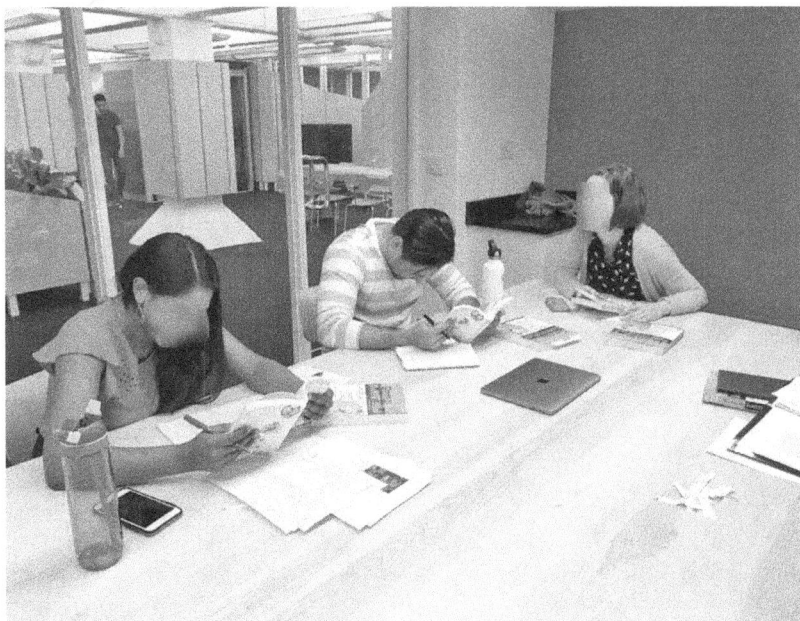

Figure 5.8 A positive learning atmosphere

this photograph in particular did a good job and described their success in the following way:

Excerpt 19

I just really appreciated their interactions and how they sort of formed a bond or a relationship and actually got their work done with all of their personalities coming into play. So, I like to do these sorts of group activities, and it always just sort of, shocks me, surprises me, endlessly interesting to me how good dynamics play out based on personalities. (Interview 2, 22 July 2019)

Figure 5.7 provides a similar example from Megan's community college ESL class, in which the students were not only fellow classmates but they also became friends, even though everyone was from a different background. In other words, this class had built a strong sense of community. There were individuals from Tibet, Thailand, Peru, Mexico, Brazil, Germany and India. Megan had never had such a diverse class with so many countries represented.

Figure 5.8 shows what Megan considered to be 'a positive learning atmosphere', again going beyond simply learning a language to also enjoying the process of learning. The photograph features students from the German class she taught at a German company. Through this

Figure 5.9 The positive social impact of a writing class

photograph, Megan wanted to show how much fun they had together while learning German. Her German students' genuine enjoyment of her German class reminded her of how 'a positive learning environment just makes the learning objectives more attainable, makes the time go by quickly, makes people want to come back, makes its it fun' (Interview 2, 22 July 2019).

Finally, Figure 5.9 shows perhaps the strongest example of Megan's commitment to teaching as community-oriented and transformative. The photograph features a group of students from her FYC class. They were assigned to read a book and make a podcast based on the book (the same assignment as Figure 5.6). This group decided to read about the housing crisis in the US, and for their podcast, they wanted to interview a homeless person who had been evicted. One of the students had been involved in a food recovery student group in which they handed out leftover food from the university cafeteria to the homeless. He invited the rest of the group to participate in a food recovery night, going to a neighborhood to hand out food. Although the rest of the group was nervous at first, they decided to go and were glad that they did so because it gave them a different perspective on homelessness. They were surprised to meet several homeless people who were very eloquent in answering their questions and also homeless people who, in their eyes, were just like them. Megan felt that the student involved with the food recovery group played a major role in making her assignment a meaningful experience for the other students. She described how she viewed the potential impact of her writing assignments in this way:

Excerpt 20

The opportunity was created for him to share. I mean, we're supposed to create writing opportunities that respond to social and ethical issues. And, so, I try to do as much of that as I can, where we talk about real issues that exist. I mean, I try not to get too controversial, like, I don't do gun control, I don't do abortion, but everything else is okay. I mean, I like to create nuanced opportunities. You talk about issues and create opportunities to chat about and write about those things. (Interview 2, 22 July 2019)

In this example, Megan treated her writing class as more than simply about the mechanics of writing; she chose to emphasize the potential a writing class could have in creating a greater positive impact on society.

Language teacher emotions as a TML

Teaching as a NS and NNS teacher

In teaching both English and German, Megan experienced language teaching from the perspective of both a NS teacher and a non-native speaker (NNS) teacher. Megan expressed feeling very different language teacher emotions in these two roles. Megan felt '[her] confidence in teaching English was just so much higher than German' (Interview 1, 16 June 2019). This confidence had impacted her teaching because '[she] can feel if something's right or wrong' without having to do prior research on the topic or look it up after class. In contrast, when it came to teaching German, she described feeling 'more nervous' and 'terrified [she'd] be labeled a fraud' (Teaching philosophy, 9 June 2019). These negative emotions were particularly prominent in instances when she was afraid she would forget a word or when her grammar was incorrect. She specifically recalled an incident when a student asked her how to say the word 'bicycle' in German and she forgot. She 'was nervous' and 'panicked' in that moment, but then looked up the word on her smartphone during class and answered the student's question. Although her students responded light-heartedly and laughed with her about forgetting the word 'bicycle' (Interview 1, 16 June 2019), her overall fear of making mistakes and not being able to answer students' questions still affected her German teaching career in that she felt 'only comfortable teaching basic German' (Teaching philosophy, 9 June 2019). However, not all of her emotions from teaching German were negative. In fact, because she was able to overcome some of the difficulties of teaching German as a NNS, Megan mentioned that she felt 'a sense of accomplishment' from being able to achieve something she did not know she could do (Interview 1, 16 June 2019).

Empathy with language learners

Megan's experience of teaching multiple languages is also characterized by the differences in how much she could empathize with her students, which was connected to her identity as a NS or NNS teacher. When teaching English as a NS, Megan had a more difficult time relating to students' experiences of learning English. She described that 'because English is [her] native language, sometimes it's hard to predict or even have any empathy for the difficulties' (Interview 1, 16 June 2019). In addition, she noticed that as a NS teaching English, '[she was] slightly less perceptive of the students' experience in the classroom' (Teaching philosophy, 9 June 2019). In contrast, Megan was more easily able to relate with her students when teaching German as a NNS. Megan noted that 'because [she] started learning German as an adult, [she's] more aware of what the experience is like to learn as an adult' (Teaching philosophy, 9 June 2019). Furthermore, in addition to having more empathy for her students as L2 learners of German, Megan also expressed having 'a lot more empathy for non-native English speaker teachers' as well. She felt a certain solidarity with NNS teachers of English after having taught German as a NNS.

The differences in Megan's emotions and empathy for her students when teaching English and German impacted her respective approaches to language teaching. In particular, Megan pointed out that her emotions and empathy impacted her teacher talk. When teaching English as a NS, because she felt that she had a more difficult time empathizing with students' English learning experience, Megan explained that she was 'less aware of how quickly [she] speak[s]' or 'whether [she's] used a far too advanced expression or unknown vocabulary and/or grammatical expression to explain a simple concept to a frustrated lower level student' (Teaching philosophy, 9 June 2019). In contrast, when teaching German, Megan was 'much more careful about how [she] expressed [herself]' by 'speaking less and more simply' (Teaching philosophy, 9 June 2019). For example, she described that 'in English, [she] might know eight synonyms for a word' but 'in German, [she] might know one or zero' (Teaching philosophy, 9 June 2019). One strategy she relied on to help her with teacher talk when teaching German was that '[she'd] express [herself] the same way every time in German, mostly because [she didn't] know other ways or [she had] found a way that has been successful for [her] in the past' (Teaching philosophy, 9 June 2019).

Furthermore, Megan observed that when teaching German, she was 'less attached to meaning and more attached to accuracy', while when teaching English, she 'rarely [thought] about accuracy as it was [her] native language' (Teaching philosophy, 9 June 2019). Lastly, when teaching German, Megan felt like 'a lot less of an expert'. So, after having taught German for a while, she 'felt more comfortable not being in complete control of the content' and 'admitting [her] mistakes' (Interview 1, 16 June 2019). Learning to be 'more okay with making mistakes' was a lesson that Megan learned from teaching German but she was also able to apply it more broadly to teaching English as well.

Finally, Megan also discussed having a kind of empathy that was not necessarily specific to language learning or being a NS/NNS. This empathy was the ability to see the humanity in her students and address their issues with kindness, compassion and understanding. She referred to these moments as her putting on her psychologist hat. Megan pointed to one student in particular, who she felt she had a positive impact on as his teacher. The student, named Jay (pseudonym), was taking Megan's FYC class, which is typical for a NS of English. In the first semester of this course, Megan had failed multiple students for plagiarizing their essays through paying other people to write them. Megan saw that Jay had worked very hard that semester on his essays, trying to make improvements in incorporating academic writing skills from one draft to the next, even though he still had difficulties with using English. However, at the end of the semester, he did not submit his final paper. Megan emailed him and asked to talk to him during her office hours. This is how Megan described their interaction:

Excerpt 21

He came to my office hours and then just started bawling, crying. And I shut the door, got him some tissues, and said, 'Don't be embarrassed, you can cry. Don't worry. I won't tell anyone about this or, ask any questions just when you feel ready to talk'. And then he started telling me just how overwhelmed he is. He's a computer science major, he's in over his head. His family is not that wealthy. I mean they're obviously somewhat wealthy. But he just felt like he was failing them, and he felt like, he embarrassed himself in my course because he hadn't turned in the essay, and he failed me and just a lot of emotions, especially in regards to how he's seen by other people. (Interview 2, 22 July 2019)

At this time, Megan 'put on [her] psychologist hat and asked him questions', trying to help him sort through his emotions.

Excerpt 22

So, I was just asking questions and kind of coming around to like, 'Did you want to know what I think of you? Do you want to know about your writing?' you know, and of course, I told him, 'I don't think any of us think badly of you, and I actually have a lot of empathy for you, and I think you're a great writer'. And then he just started crying his eyes out when I told him he was a great writer. And I was like, 'I'm just telling the truth'.

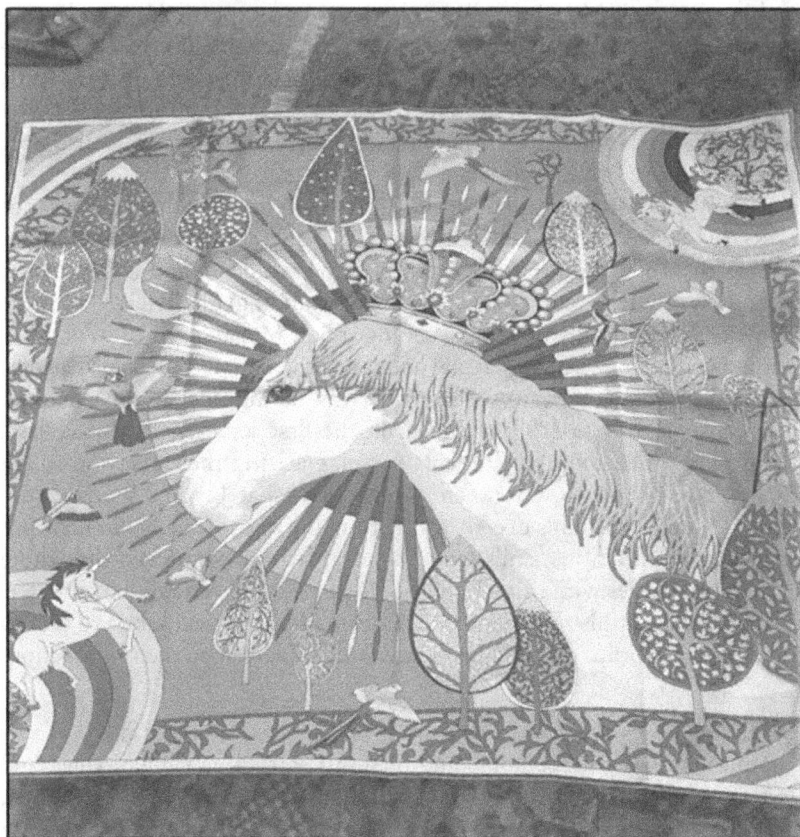

Figure 5.10 A gift from Megan's student

> And I said, 'You know, I'm going to work with you on this, and we'll find it. We'll make an alternative deadline for your paper. I want you to tell me what you think the deadline should be'. (Interview 2, 22 July 2019)

Jay finished his final paper and Megan gave him an A in the class, even though Jay thought that he didn't deserve it. But Megan emphasized that she felt he deserved the A because he truly understood the purpose of the course.

A year later, Jay visited Megan and gave her a gift, the unicorn silk scarf shown in Figure 5.10. Even though Megan said that she would never wear the scarf, it reminded her of what motivates her to be a teacher. She described it in the following way:

Excerpt 23

I think that's why I like being a teacher because I come across students like Jay. And I have the opportunity to maybe offer them a little bit, some sort of wisdom about writing or maybe even life, and that they can move forward with and have a positive impact on their lives. And in this case, he gave me a present which I, you know, will always keep in the shelf. Again, I will never wear it. But being able to make a difference for students is motivating. (Interview 2, 22 July 2019)

Mistreatment as adjunct faculty

Lastly, Megan also experienced strong emotions in relation to feeling frustration and disillusionment over the mistreatment of adjunct faculty. Because she had taught at multiple higher education institutions for nearly 10 years as an adjunct English instructor, Megan strongly identified with the challenges that come with being an adjunct instructor. She described her experience of being an adjunct instructor as being 'eggs in an egg carton' where adjunct instructors were present at the university but were isolated from each other with no sense of community or collaboration (Excerpt 13). One might describe her as experiencing 'teacher burnout', although Megan did not use this term herself. She became increasingly disillusioned with her ability to continue pursuing a career in TESOL in the US because of factors such as job stability in terms of opportunities for acquiring a full-time job position, the heavy workload coupled with low compensation, and feeling invisible and unacknowledged as an adjunct instructor.

Other Aspects of Being a TML from the DFG Framework

The micro level of the DFG framework

At the micro level of the DFG framework, one can observe connections between identities, beliefs and emotions and other foundational internal mechanisms involved in Megan's process of becoming and being a TML.

Development of teacher knowledge

One of the important internal mechanisms that impacted Megan's experience of teaching English and German was managing the linguistic differences and similarities between the two languages. Like Ann, teacher knowledge in this respect involved her own language proficiency in the languages she taught. However, her situation was different from Ann's in that Megan started out her language teaching career teaching her native language, English, and then transitioned to teaching a foreign language, German. Thus, unlike Ann, language proficiency was not an immediate concern to her until later in her career when she started teaching German. Even then, Megan's understanding of the linguistic differences between English and German did not seem to have as much of an impact as Ann's understanding of the linguistic differences between English and Chinese had on their respective teaching practices. In other words, Megan felt that she was able to use similar general teaching methods when teaching both English and German, though the specific curriculum and lesson activities she used differed based on the class context. Thus, while Ann felt that she had to acquire new teacher knowledge to transition from teaching EFL to Chinese as a second language (CSL), hence getting a master's degree in teaching Chinese to speakers of other languages (TCSOL), Megan transitioned from teaching ESL to German without feeling the need to take additional LTE coursework in teaching German. This might be because of the greater linguistic similarities between English and German as well as the different job qualification requirements that Megan and Ann faced, which are explained in more detail in the following 'Meso Level' section.

While Ann described developing strategies for adjusting her EFL teaching to CSL teaching, Megan described developing strategies for monitoring her use of German in the classroom when teaching German at a level comfortable for her proficiency level. For example, she controlled the vocabulary she used during teacher talk when teaching German by using the same words to express herself in German every time, whereas in teaching English, she could more freely use different ways of expressing the same thought. However, even in applying such strategies, she did experience moments in the classroom when she was not able to answer a student's question. She recalled a time when she forgot the German word for 'bicycle' and had to look it up on her smartphone. Despite wanting to exercise greater control of her German teacher talk, in reflecting on her experience of teaching German for roughly two years, Megan felt that over time she did learn to let go of feeling the need to be a complete expert in German. Thus, for Megan, the development of teacher knowledge involved not only learning how to manage the differences in her English and German language proficiency and how that would affect her teaching, but also learning to accept those differences and not let them hinder her teaching.

Expansion of semiotic resources

While many of the semiotic resources mentioned in Ann's narratives were related to the linguistic differences between English and Chinese, the semiotic resources relevant to Megan's narratives were not as language specific. Rather, one of the main semiotic resources Megan mentioned in both her ESL, FYC and German teaching was the integration of technology into her teaching. For example, this is evident in Megan's use of a podcasting assignment in her FYC class (Figures 5.6 and 5.9) and the use of a digital Jeopardy game as an alternative assessment method for her German class (Figure 5.5). Symbolically, Megan used the photograph in Figure 5.11 to represent her relationship with technology in language teaching. The photograph features Megan's car, which is a 'hybrid', or a car that is powered by both gasoline and electricity. For Megan, this photograph was an abstract representation of having to adapt to new

Figure 5.11 Megan's relationship with using technology in language teaching

educational technology such as teaching hybrid classes, flipped learning and asynchronous classes. She also had to learn how to incorporate multimodal projects in her classes, such as assignments that involved podcasting or websites.

Interestingly, the need to keep up with the latest educational technology and work with colleagues to integrate them into her curriculum was a source of both frustration and fulfillment. Particularly when teaching FYC, Megan felt frustrated because she found herself spending too much unpaid time doing extra tasks such as setting her required online learning platform site and having meetings with colleagues on incorporating a digital multimodal project into their curriculum (Figure 5.2). However, Megan also thought that, in general, having to keep up with these new technology-based forms of teaching led to positive changes in her classes, such as creating dynamic and motivating assignments (Figures 5.6 and 5.9) as well as creating alternative assessment methods more suitable for teaching less academically oriented language classes, as with teaching German (Figure 5.5).

At the time of the interview, Megan stated that she felt disillusioned with language teaching in higher education institutions and expressed an interest in finding an education-based job in the corporate sector. Specifically, she was seeking opportunities in 'instructional design', which involved designing both digital and non-digital instructional materials for companies. Thus, 'technology' can be seen as a broad semiotic resource mediating the development of Megan's teacher knowledge as both a teaching methodology and a teacher skillset. In other words, 'technology' played an important role in influencing how Megan's language teaching manifested (e.g. on digital platforms and websites), what language teaching consisted of (e.g. podcasting, alternative assessment methods) and what language teaching career opportunities Megan foresaw as possibilities in her future.

The meso level of the DFG framework

The meso level of the DFG framework focuses on the ways in which Megan's participation and membership in certain sociocultural institutions and communities shaped the internal mechanisms discussed at the micro level. While Ann went through undergraduate and graduate LTE programs and taught in multiple foreign language contexts, Megan only went through a master's program in TESOL and taught mainly in the US. Neither of these social contexts seemed to be salient factors in her narratives. Instead, the kinds of sociocultural institutions and communities that Megan highlighted dealt with different instructional positions within higher education and then transitioning beyond higher education. For Megan, this shift in moving from teaching within higher education to the corporate sector paralleled the shift from teaching English to teaching German.

Teaching within higher education

Megan spent over 10 years teaching English as an adjunct instructor in higher education. During this time, she gradually shifted from teaching ESL to FYC because she found that some of her habits and mannerisms in communicating with ESL learners, such as simplifying her language or repeating teacher talk, affected her personal life and caused her frustration (Excerpt 4). When teaching FYC, most of her students were NSs of English so she could communicate with them 'naturally' and focus her efforts on teaching other skills such as rhetoric and critical thinking. However, after having taught FYC for a while, she felt that she was pigeonholed into only teaching FYC which would make it more difficult for Megan to branch out into other types of education-related careers (Excerpt 8). Furthermore, Megan simultaneously felt frustrated at the mistreatment of adjunct instructors and hopeless about the limited prospects of acquiring a full-time position teaching English in higher education. Thus, it was Megan's disillusionment with the subject matter of teaching ESL and FYC coupled with the position of being an adjunct instructor that motivated her to seek other career opportunities beyond teaching English within higher education.

Teaching in the corporate sector

As mentioned previously, Megan had spent many years working as an adjunct faculty teaching English in various higher education institutions. Over time, Megan grew increasingly frustrated by the lack of opportunities for full-time positions and considered education-related jobs beyond higher education. At the same time, Megan began teaching German as a part-time teacher at a German company and her experience there was thoroughly positive, specifically in terms of the feelings of acknowledgement and validation from her employer (Figure 5.4, Excerpt 19). Her positive experience pushed her to question what path she might have taken in going forward with her teaching career; this was evident when Megan discussed the possibility of 'going corporate' by getting a job in instructional design, a career option her colleague had taken, also in frustration with higher education institutions (Excerpt 15).

At the time of the interview, Megan had only introduced the slight possibility of working in the corporate sector; in fact, she felt very conflicted about leaving higher education. She felt a certain sense of pride and honor in the identity associated with working at an academic institution and felt averse to the stereotype of working within a corporation (Excerpt 16). Interestingly, Megan did not interpret her positive experience teaching German as pushing her toward a career in teaching German; rather, her comparatively positive and negative experiences in teaching English and German, respectively, were based more on workplace conditions rather than differences in the teaching of different languages. Thus, Megan felt most conflicted about her position as an adjunct instructor versus her position as an employee of a company, rather than teaching English versus teaching German. One might conclude that she more strongly identified with her workplace position as an adjunct instructor rather than the language she taught.

The macro level of the DFG framework

The macro level of the DFG framework focuses on the ways in which large-scale, societal ideologies influence the micro and meso levels of Megan's development as a TML. The two ideologies that are particularly salient for Megan are the NS/NNS dichotomy and social/economic inequality.

The NS/NNS dichotomy

So far, Megan's experiences as a NS and NNS teacher have been mentioned many times and influenced Megan's career as a TML in multiple ways. To summarize, as a NS teacher of English, Megan felt more confident as an expert in her own native language. However, this also meant that she had a harder time understanding the difficulties of her EFL and ESL students because Megan had not been an English learner herself. This gradually caused her greater frustration because she found that the type of communication skills and teacher talk necessary for her to help her ESL students learn began to affect the way she communicated in her personal life (Excerpt 4).

As a NNS teacher of German, Megan felt more anxious and often feared being seen as a fraud because of her proficient but non-instinctual grasp of the German language. This led to her using certain coping mechanisms, such as restricting the vocabulary she used in her teacher talk and only teaching beginning German classes. However, she found that her experience as a NNS teacher of German helped her learn to accept making mistakes in her teaching. Also, she had closer relationships with the students in her German class because Megan could better empathize with their learning difficulties, as she had once been a German L2 learner herself.

Like Ann, Megan's reflections of her NS/NNS LTIs in her narratives show that the experience of teaching multiple languages served to complicate Megan's conceptualization of what being a NS/NNS teacher meant. Megan's understanding of her NS/NNS LTIs did not fit into simple black-and-white dichotomies of good versus bad, easy versus hard, natural versus unnatural or novice versus expert. Rather, Megan expressed having both positive and negative experiences in both positions of being a NS and a NNS teacher. However, also like Ann, Megan's narratives seemed to operate within the NS/NNS dichotomy; in other words, her narratives show that she understood her teaching experiences, identities and students in terms of the NS/NNS structure. What changed for Megan over time from teaching multiple languages was that the binary NS/NNS structure began to take on more complexity.

Awareness of social and economic inequalities

In her narratives, Megan consistently conveyed an awareness of how her experiences in teaching English and German were part of a greater system of inequality and struggle, particularly in educational institutions, which informed how she perceived her role as a language teacher toward her students and colleagues as well as how she could use her teaching to have a positive impact on her students.

Perhaps the most salient example of Megan's awareness of the greater system of inequalities in academic institutions is the way Megan reacted to her perception of how adjunct instructors were treated. As an adjunct instructor herself, Megan felt that they were underappreciated, undercompensated and invisible to their academic departments. An example of how invisible Megan felt as an adjunct was when she received an email from her department about a full-time professor in the department whose mother had passed away and realized that the department would probably have never sent such an email if she passed away because she was only an adjunct instructor (Excerpt 14). Furthermore, Megan also felt that adjunct faculty had little bargaining power because, as she claimed, there was a surplus of language teachers available to replace her. Thus, Megan did not attempt to make any major structural changes or confront the issue in large-scale ways (e.g. petitions and protests) to avoid any risk to her job security. Rather, she resisted the vicious cycle of mistreatment in her own small-scale approaches, such as arranging a farewell party for her co-workers who were leaving the department, a party that the department itself had not and would never have arranged for adjunct instructors (Figure 5.3, Excerpt 17).

While she was successful in resisting adjunct mistreatment at the individual level, the hopelessness for large-scale changes in terms of better treatment of adjunct instructors caused Megan to feel that she had no future career in academia. She noted that even if a full-time position opened up in the department she worked for, she would never be hired because she was a white woman and most of the department faculty were already white women; based on her prediction, the department would most likely hire based on the need for a more diverse faculty representative of the student body, in particular hiring faculty of color. Megan's awareness of the need for diversity in higher education faculty and her position in relation to that motivated her to consider career opportunities beyond academia, such as doing instructional design for a corporation (Excerpt 15).

However, Megan did not feel resentment toward her decreasing job opportunities because of diversity hiring needs. In fact, she respected diversity hiring as a positive approach to improving higher education because of her awareness of the greater systems of inequalities in higher education. This awareness also impacted her teaching, particularly in her FYC when she encouraged students to choose topics related to social inequalities such as urban homelessness (Figure 5.9, Excerpt 20) and valued the sense of community built in her classes among students of different backgrounds (Figure 5.6, Excerpt 19; Figure 5.7). Finally, her awareness of the greater systems of inequality also impacted her empathy for difficult situations that students might be going through in their personal lives and how that might be affecting their behavior in class. Megan had great empathy for students dealing with a range of issues, such as coming out to their parents, dealing with family pressure to excel academically (Excerpt 21), adjusting to life in the US as an international student (Excerpt 5) and coping with the death of a loved one. Megan's awareness of each student being situated within greater systems of inequality and struggle helped her approach students facing difficulties outside of her classroom with sensitivity and empathy.

6 Haruko's Narrative: Navigating Native-Speakerism as a TML

Haruko's Language Teaching Career Trajectory

Figure 6.1 presents an overview of the stages of Haruko's language teaching career. The version of her career described in this chapter spanned from 2010 to 2019. The following sections explain in detail each stage of Haruko's teaching career.

Stage 1: 'Chick stage' (2010–2011)

Haruko described her language teaching career trajectory using terms related to the developmental stages of a bird as a metaphor. She began her language teaching career trajectory during her first year of teaching in 2010. At the time, Haruko was still in the middle of studying for a master's in a teaching English to speakers of other languages (TESOL) graduate program at a university in the United States. During her graduate program in 2010, she was hired as a part-time English for academic purposes instructor in an intensive English program affiliated with the graduate program. The intensive English program offered one year of training and mentorship to new teachers and that year of training is what Haruko considered to be the 'chick stage'. Haruko started the 'chick stage' with 'no experience in teaching', so she spent most of the year 'trying to learn from observing other teachers and trying to do a lot of things with help from other teachers' (Interview 1, 3 June 2019). More specifically, the teacher training consisted of being paired with a mentor teacher, observing the mentor teacher's classes and gradually working toward teaching a full class session under the mentor teacher's supervision.

Stage 2: 'Juvenile bird stage' (2011–2016)

After finishing one year of training, Haruko began teaching her own classes as part of the intensive English program. This marked the beginning of the 'juvenile bird stage'. Haruko named this stage the 'juvenile bird stage' because it represented the stage of a bird's development between a chick and an adult. During this stage, Haruko was no longer

```
┌─────────────────────────────────────────────┐
│          Stage 1:"Chick Stage"               │
│            (2010-2011, 1 yr.)                 │
└─────────────────────────────────────────────┘
                      ▼
┌─────────────────────────────────────────────┐
│        Stage 2: "Juvenile Bird Stage"         │
│            (2011-2016, 5 yrs.)                │
└─────────────────────────────────────────────┘
                      ▼
┌─────────────────────────────────────────────┐
│         Stage 3: "Adult Bird Stage"           │
│            (2016-2019, 3 yrs.)                │
└─────────────────────────────────────────────┘
```

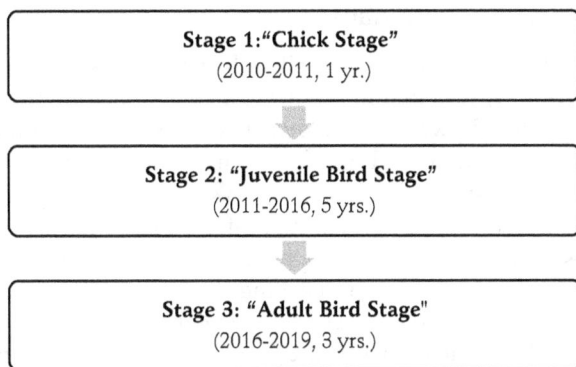

Figure 6.1 Stages of Haruko's career trajectory

under her mentor teacher's supervision. Instead, she taught her own classes. She explained that during this stage, she 'had more experience in teaching instead of just learning from others' and she 'also tried to do something new by incorporating new things' (Interview 1, 3 June 2019). Furthermore, she described her teaching during this time as 'trying to see what worked for [her] and what didn't work for [her] as a teacher' (Interview 1, 3 June 2019).

In a sense, this stage can be seen as a time of experimentation and exploration for Haruko not only because it was her first year teaching as a full-fledged teacher but also because of the diversity of teaching experiences she took on. In total, Haruko's 'juvenile bird stage' lasted five years and during this time, she took on three different teaching positions: teaching ESL in the intensive English program for three years (2010–2013), teaching Japanese at a local community temple for one year (2012–2013) and relocating to Japan to teach English as a foreign language (EFL) at a Japanese university for three years (2013–2016).

Stage 3: 'Adult bird stage' (2016–2019)

Stage 3 began after Haruko had returned to Japan teaching EFL at the university level for three years. After gaining enough experience teaching in various contexts, Haruko felt she had become an experienced teacher through changes in her teaching. She 'felt more relaxed in teaching' and 'could be more flexible in teaching' (Interview 1, 3 June 2019). This meant that she often 'didn't need to write lesson plans anymore' and was able to 'change as the classes go' (Interview 1, 3 June 2019). Because she no longer felt nervous about teaching and no longer had to worry about the minute details of teaching, Haruko's 'adult bird stage' consisted of refining the edges of her university teaching, such as trying out new ways of eliciting participation and feedback from students or implementing a new extensive reading program in her classes.

Epilogue: Possible future stages

Haruko described several possible future stages in her language teaching career: (1) teaching more new classes, (2) getting involved with training teachers, (3) writing her own textbook or curriculum materials and (4) starting her own English and/or Japanese language school in Japan or the US, respectively.

According to Haruko, the first idea of wanting to teach new classes was the most probable out of all the possible future stages. At the time of the interview, Haruko had been teaching the test of English as a foreign language (TOEFL) and reading classes for nearly five years at a Japanese university so she wanted to venture into new course subjects, such as teaching the test of English for international communication (TOEIC) or listening/speaking classes. Haruko noted that teaching the TOEIC would be more of a possibility for her in the near future, but teaching speaking and listening classes was 'almost impossible' because of 'an unwritten rule' in her department that speaking classes were only taught by native speaker (NS) English teachers (Interview 2, 10 July 2019). This was unfortunate because prior to returning to Japan, Haruko had already been teaching English as a second language (ESL) listening/speaking courses for several years in the intensive English program. Even though she was an experienced, qualified candidate, she felt that she could only 'follow the rules' and that she 'couldn't really say anything' (Interview 2, 10 July 2019). This led her to feeling certain that the underlying native-speakerism in her department would not allow her to teach any EFL listening/speaking classes.

Haruko also considered highly unlikely her second idea of being involved in training teachers, though she hoped for the opportunity. She noted that she had a co-worker who had been leading a teacher training seminar for students who wanted to become teachers. Haruko wanted to lead those types of seminars. However, when asked to estimate when in the future this might happen for her, she thought it might take another 10 years or so for her to get the opportunity to train teachers.

Haruko's third idea for a possible future stage in her language teaching career had to do with filling what she perceived to be a gap in the instructional materials she was required to use when teaching EFL at her university. At the time of the interview, her university department required textbooks and a set curriculum that Haruko must teach. While this enforced uniformity and consistency in course content, it also left little room for Haruko to teach using the material she wanted. Thus, one project she hoped to be able to do in the future was to write her own EFL textbook or create her own EFL course materials for Japanese students. Haruko specified that her intention would be primarily to create more suitable instructional materials to use in her classroom, but she was open to eventually publishing materials for other teachers to use as well.

One reason why Haruko was not already writing her own textbook at the time of the interview was because she was simply too busy teaching classes. Also, she was gathering observations and getting feedback from students about what kind of course materials would be more helpful to them than the textbook they already used.

Lastly, Haruko's final idea for a possible future stage of her language teaching career was opening her own English language school in Japan or her own English and/or Japanese language school in the US, respectively. If she opened an English language school in Japan, Haruko imagined her school to be geared toward young children, like a nursery school or a daycare with language lessons, because working with children had always been '[her] other dream' besides teaching at a university (Interview 2, 10 July 2019). If she opened a Japanese language school in the US, it would be geared toward children and adults who wanted to learn Japanese for conversation purposes, most likely for Japanese Americans or non-Japanese people. She imagined her Japanese language school as 'not very academic' and 'more informal, kind of a fun place to learn Japanese and Japanese culture' (Interview 2, 10 July 2019). Haruko noted that her language school in the United States might even be bilingual, that is, offering both Japanese and English language classes, but she specified that she would not start an English-only language school in the United States geared toward international students. She explained her reasoning in the following excerpt:

Excerpt 1

I feel like nobody wants to come to an English school owned by a Japanese person, right? I feel like if I go back to the US, I should probably take advantage of being Japanese so I should open a Japanese school. It's probably more popular that way. (Interview 2, 10 July 2019)

Haruko drew inspiration for owning a Japanese school in the United States from her prior experience working at a private Japanese/English language tutoring center in the United States. Haruko's experience at the private language school also sparked other ideas and considerations in terms of opening her own language school, such as location. She described how she took location into consideration in the following excerpt:

Excerpt 2

I'm thinking if I opened the school up in an area where Japanese people live, probably it will be popular, because the school I mentioned before, the Japanese lady opened a school in a Japanese community area where a lot of Japanese people stayed there for four years for work, so her students were all Japanese students from Japan who wanted to learn

English while they are staying in America. And also, I think there are also lots of Americans in that area who live in the Japanese community because they are either Japanese American or they like Japanese culture so if I open a school in that kind of area, it might be popular. (Interview 2, 10 July 2019)

Haruko mentioned that she wanted not only to own a language school but also to teach both English and Japanese at her own future language school. In some ways, the underlying desire for owning and teaching at her own language school was linked to her motivation to write her own textbook, that is, wanting to have more independence and creative control over her own teaching. She described her motivation to open her own language school in the following way:

Excerpt 3

I think but the most important thing for me is if I open my own school, I can just do anything I want, however I want to teach. So, for example, I can make my own rules to follow or I can choose my own teaching and I can decide my own materials or textbooks or syllabus, anything. I can decide everything. (Interview 2, 10 July 2019)

However, Haruko felt that if she were to teach Japanese, she would need to 'study more' and possibly 'go to school again' to learn how to teach Japanese. She compared this to her experience of going to a TESOL graduate program to learn how to teach English. In particular, she wanted to learn more about teaching grammar and Japanese culture. Even though Haruko is a NS of Japanese who was born and raised in Japan, she felt that she only had a surface level of knowledge about Japanese culture. She described this in the following way:

Excerpt 4

I know some Japanese culture, like the holidays and Japanese tea ceremony, that kind of stuff. But lots of times, when foreigners study Japanese, they already know a lot about Japan so they want to know details, like history, how something happened... I'm not really good at Japanese history. (Interview 2, 10 July 2019)

Finally, Haruko was aware that of the four possible future projects she might take on in her language teaching career, opening up her own language school would be the most difficult to achieve in a practical sense. She recognized that it would take a lot of time, effort and money to start her own language school and that any entrepreneurial investment would be a risk.

Haruko's Identities, Beliefs and Emotions as a TML

Language teacher identities as a TML

NS and NNS identities

One of the primary language teacher identities (LTIs) that impacted Haruko's teaching of multiple languages was being a NS of Japanese and a non-native speaker (NNS) of English. As mentioned in the section titled 'Language Teacher Emotions', one of the ways that the NS identity influenced Haruko's teaching was that she felt more stressed about teaching Japanese because she had a difficult time empathizing with the problems her learners of Japanese might have; on the contrary, since she had been an English language learner, it was easier for her empathize with her ESL and EFL students' difficulties. Also, Haruko noted that from teaching Japanese, she learned that 'it's important to study the target language well in order to teach it; just being a NS is not enough to teach the language' (Interview 3, 17 August 2019). These beliefs came from Haruko's experience teaching Japanese in the United States, when she experienced difficulties trying to explain Japanese grammar and culture to her students. This impacted her teaching because she found that she tended to 'spend more time on explanations rather than practicing the language' (Teaching philosophy, 19 June 2019). Sometimes, she could not come up with a good answer for a student's question about Japanese grammar so she often had to do some research after class and come back the following week with an appropriate answer to the student's question (Interview 1, 3 June 2019). What Haruko concluded from her experience as a NS teacher of Japanese in the United States was that she could not solely rely on her NS proficiency in Japanese and if she wanted to continue to teach Japanese, she would have to go through more schooling to learn about teaching Japanese.

Another way that Haruko's dual NS and NNS identity impacted her teaching of multiple languages was the way her students perceived her as their teacher and how that may have impacted their language learning. When teaching ESL in the United States and EFL in Japan, some of Haruko's students saw her as a role model, particularly the students who also came from Japan. Haruko mentioned that because she is a Japanese NNS and language learner of English, 'some of [her] current students often tell [her] that they want to speak English like [her] in the future' (Teaching philosophy, 19 June 2019). She sometimes heard 'students copying [her] English' because 'they want to speak English like [her]' (Interview 1, 3 June 2019). This influenced Haruko's teaching in that she 'shared [her] own learning experiences with students and spoke English as much as possible so that [she could] become their ideal English speaker' (Teaching philosophy, 19 June 2019). Some students even saw her as a role model not just as a NNS of English but also as a NNS *teacher* of English. Haruko explained this in more detail in the following excerpt:

Excerpt 5

When I was teaching at the intensive English program, there was a Japanese exchange student from Japan in my class. When she saw me teaching English in America as a Japanese, she was very impressed by how I could teach English, not my first language but second language, so she said she wanted to become a teacher just like me. So that was a high point for me, because I could encourage students to learn English and also gave me some confidence to teach English. (Interview 1, 3 June 2019)

Haruko had a vastly different experience of teaching Japanese in terms of the way she felt her students perceived her as a NS. Haruko felt that because she was a NS of Japanese, 'students probably expected [her] to answer all the questions they had', which made her more nervous when teaching Japanese (Interview 3, 17 August 2019). Furthermore, Haruko also felt that while some of her ESL/EFL students might have viewed her as a role model in speaking English, students in her Japanese class 'don't get motivated as much by seeing [her] speak Japanese because [she is] a native speaker of Japanese' (Teaching philosophy, 19 June 2019). What Haruko experienced in teaching Japanese in the United States was that her students expected a certain level of proficiency and cultural knowledge from her as a NS of Japanese and so she was no longer seen as a role model from the students' point of view.

An international teacher

Besides Haruko's NS and NNS identities impacting her language teaching, other significant LTIs were her identity as someone who had studied abroad and her identity as a teacher of both English and Japanese. Part of her identity as an international teacher developed in response to students' curiosity and interest about her background. She described an example of her students taking an interest in her past experience studying abroad.

Excerpt 6

They ask me, where I studied abroad, why I studied abroad, how long usually, how long it took for me to speak English. They really want to know. If they study one year, can they speak English or it has to be like two years or longer time. Also, they ask about where I lived and how was life in the US. I feel like I'm helping my students. Actually, not many teachers at our school have studied abroad because they're older teachers and they never studied abroad. I think for students, having study abroad experience is pretty positive for them. (Interview 3, 17 August 2019)

Haruko felt positive about her students' seeking advice about studying abroad. This was a special identity for Haruko because it was an aspect of who she was that set her apart from the more senior faculty members.

Although not necessarily directly related to being a language teacher, studying abroad was an aspect of her identity and background that could potentially impact students' motivation to learn a foreign language.

Thus, Haruko took advantage of her students' interest in her background by incorporating it into some of her lessons. For example, at the beginning of each semester when teaching EFL in Japan, Haruko often introduced herself to her students by talking about her experience studying abroad in the United States, as shown in Figure 6.2. She designed the slide in Figure 6.2 to show pictures from her past experiences studying abroad in the United States, including her graduation photo and pictures of Los Angeles and San Francisco. On the first day of class, she would typically have her students ask questions about the pictures and then she would talk about her experience studying abroad. Haruko chose to introduce herself in this way and focus on her experience studying abroad because she hoped it would 'give them motivation to study English [and] maybe some people would want to study abroad like [her] in the future' (Interview 3, 17 August 2019). Haruko also mentioned that this was not the only time during the school year when she would bring up her experiences of studying abroad. For example, during Halloween, she would wear her undergraduate cap and gown as her Halloween costume. She found that students were particularly interested in her graduation cap and gown because in Japan most students wear a suit or a traditional kimono rather than a cap and gown during graduation. Her Japanese

Figure 6.2 Haruko's self-introduction

students were familiar with the cap and gown because they had seen them in American movies so they often wanted to try them on when Haruko wore them at Halloween.

TML identity

In comparison to the other two participants, Haruko was the only one who expressed having an identity specifically based on teaching multiple languages, or what I refer to as a 'TML identity'. Haruko described the way her teacher of multiple languages (TML) identity played out in her interactions with her students:

> Excerpt 7
>
> So when I teach English in Japan right now, sometimes my students ask me about my background in college and my career. So I said, oh I used to teach Japanese in America and English. Students are really surprised that I can teach two languages. Some students actually now want to go abroad and teach Japanese but a lot of students are surprised that I can teach both languages because usually people teach one language, right? So for some students, that's really impressive to them. (Interview 3, 17 August 2019)

Haruko's identity as a TML was relatively new and came from sharing with her students in Japan her past experiences teaching in the United States. Yet, it presented itself as a cumulative identity integrating the other LTIs that Haruko had previously mentioned: as a type of role model for her students in terms of being successful as a language learner, a student who studied abroad and a language teacher. Aside from her students' positive impression of Haruko as a TML, it is interesting to note that none of Haruko's colleagues and co-workers knew about her past experiences teaching multiple languages. According to Haruko, they did not know that she had taught Japanese before and simply knew her as an EFL instructor because the topic had simply never come up. This shows the way identities are not fixed, stable entities, but rather, dynamic, multi-faceted and interactive. There is not only a single way others see Haruko or Haruko sees herself. Haruko's identities as an EFL instructor, Japanese instructor and/or TML emerge from the different ways that Haruko interacts and exists with different people and in different contexts and communities. With her students, Haruko proactively presents her TML identity as a source of credibility and rapport with her students, but with her colleagues, her TML identity is hidden.

Language teacher beliefs as a TML

Beliefs about language learning

Haruko described language learning using the metaphor of running a marathon, a long-term achievement that requires a lot of time and effort, but can also be very rewarding. She emphasized the need to 'practice using the target language every day in order to master it' and the important role of motivation in sustaining a language learner through the 'very long journey' (Teaching philosophy, 19 June 2019). Through this metaphor, Haruko seemed to place great emphasis on language learning as an extended and difficult process.

Haruko also explained how her beliefs about what exactly the process of language learning involves changed over time. Haruko described her experience learning English in Japan through primary and secondary education in this way:

Excerpt 8

Born and raised in Japan, where English is not an official language, I had been exposed to the traditional teaching approach that heavily relies on translation and memorization. At that time, I thought that learning a language was equal to memorizing a lot of words and phrases. Learning English in such a non-inspiring environment was nothing but a negative experience for me, and I did not have any motivation to learn English. (Teaching philosophy, 19 June 2019)

It was not until learning English in the US during college that her beliefs toward language learning began to change. Through communicative ESL classes, she realized that learning a language 'was not only knowing various words and phrases but also being able to use them' (Teaching philosophy, 19 June 2019). She found herself enjoying the experience of using English to communicate with others and her motivation to learn English increased. This bolstered her belief that communicative learning and motivation are two essential components of successful language learning.

Beliefs about language teaching

Haruko viewed her beliefs about language teaching as directly connected to her beliefs about language learning. She continued using the marathon metaphor, in which she compared language learning to running a marathon and language teaching to training a marathon runner. This meant that she viewed teaching as a form of coaching or training, or 'facilitators', in which 'a teacher should guide students so that they can keep learning a language and eventually become independent learners' (Teaching philosophy, 19 June 2019). Haruko's teaching 'always focuses on how to promote students' motivation to learn a language' (Teaching philosophy, 19 June 2019). To do so, first she 'heavily relied' on communicative language teaching (Teaching philosophy, 19 June 2019). This involved various types of communicative activities that could enhance real-life communication, such as pair work, group work, role play, group discussion and interviews. Another way she attempted to increase her students' motivation was to 'create a positive and enjoyable learning environment where students feel animated and comfortable' (Teaching philosophy, 19 June 2019). This involved establishing a good rapport with students (e.g. remembering students' names, pairing students up with different partners to get to know each other) and incorporating stress-free and enjoyable activities (e.g. Pictionary, Jeopardy).

Approaches to teaching English and Japanese

Haruko found that many of the teaching methods she had learned while going through mentorship and teacher training for teaching ESL in the intensive English program were transferrable to teaching Japanese at her local community temple in the United States. For example, when she taught Japanese in the US, she used the same self-introduction activity as shown in Figure 6.2, except she changed some of the photographs so that they were more suitable for whatever they were learning at the time (e.g. using photographs of her own family when students were learning the vocabulary for family members). Haruko explained that '[her] teaching style is similar for both languages' in that she emphasized the same key components of language teaching mentioned in the previous section: communicative language teaching and increasing students' motivation (Teaching philosophy, 19 June 2019). Her experience in being able to 'use similar methods in teaching both languages helped [her] gain confidence in [her] teaching' (Interview 3, 17 August 2019).

However, when it came to teaching EFL at universities in Japan, Haruko was not able to use communicative language teaching. In fact, even though she had always taught using English as the language of instruction in her teacher training and prior experience of teaching ESL in the US, she found that in Japan, she often had to teach EFL using Japanese. This is because Haruko's university students were required to pass a final exam based on their English skills and the only way to cover all of the content in class was to prioritize speed and efficiency over communicative learning by using Japanese to teach English. Therefore, when Haruko returned to Japan and began teaching EFL there for the first time, she had to readjust her teaching methodology, reverting to teaching English using mainly grammar translation, the way she learned English when she was a student in Japan.

Language teacher emotions as a TML

Teaching as a NS vs. NNS teacher

Haruko experienced very different emotions upon teaching English and Japanese that were influenced by her LTIs as a NS and NNS teacher as well as her teacher knowledge of the two languages. When teaching English, whether in the United States or Japan, Haruko felt confident and proud because students who were NNSs of English would express admiration for her as a NNS teacher of English. Haruko recalled a Japanese international student in the United States telling her that she was impressed that Haruko, a NNS of English, could be teaching English in the United States, and that she wanted to become a teacher like Haruko (Excerpt 5). Furthermore, Japanese students in Japan also expressed interest in and admiration for Haruko as their EFL teacher because of Haruko's extensive experience living, working and teaching in the United States (Excerpts 6 and 7). Thus, Haruko's NNS teacher identity had become a way for her to be seen as a role model for her EFL students as a level of proficiency and career success that they could also possibly achieve.

In contrast, Haruko felt stressed and anxious when teaching Japanese, mainly because she felt that she lacked sufficient teacher knowledge to teach Japanese. Haruko found teaching Japanese particularly difficult because she had not learned Japanese as a L2 learner nor had she taken any language teacher education (LTE) in teaching Japanese. Therefore, she found it difficult to understand the difficulties her students experienced. In addition, even though Haruko was a NS of Japanese, she did not feel that students looked up to her as a role model in the way that her EFL students did. If anything, it was because she was a NS of Japanese that her students expected her to speak Japanese fluently and did not express any sense of admiration for her. For Haruko, these emotions over teaching Japanese were related to her type of (or lack of) teacher knowledge. Overall, Haruko compared her emotional experiences of teaching English and Japanese in this way:

Excerpt 9

For me, transitioning from teaching English to Japanese was very different and difficult. For teaching Japanese, I never learned how to teach Japanese and Japanese is my native language so I never studied Japanese grammar so I couldn't really tell what was difficult for students and why they were having trouble. So for me, teaching Japanese was more stressful and difficult. Whereas when I'm teaching English, I learned English as a second language, so I could kind of tell why students were having trouble. So I would say it's less stressful and easier for me to teach English now. (Interview 3, 17 August 2019)

One might find it surprising that Haruko considered Japanese more stressful to teach than English because she considered herself to be a NS of Japanese and a NNS of English. However, the main reason she felt less stressed teaching ESL and EFL as a NNS teacher is because being a NNS teacher provided her with the ability to empathize with her students as she was once in their position as a language learner.

Teaching English in the United States vs. Japan

In addition to transitioning from teaching English to teaching Japanese, another transition Haruko experienced was teaching English in the US (i.e. ESL) to teaching English in Japan (i.e. EFL). In this scenario, the difference was not in her role as a NS or NNS teacher, but rather in adapting to the different educational contexts of the US and Japan. Haruko used Figure 6.3 to depict one of the challenges she faced in this transition and the emotions she experienced from this transition. For Haruko, one of the main differences when transitioning from teaching ESL in the United States to EFL in Japan was the use of her first language (L1; Japanese). When teaching ESL at an intensive English program in the US, Haruko did not use Japanese at all in her teaching. However, when she moved back to Japan and taught EFL, she found herself using Japanese more often. Haruko described how she felt about using Japanese in her EFL teaching in the following excerpt:

Excerpt 10

Since students all speak Japanese, I guess the good thing is I can use Japanese explanations to explain some grammar points. So I wrote on

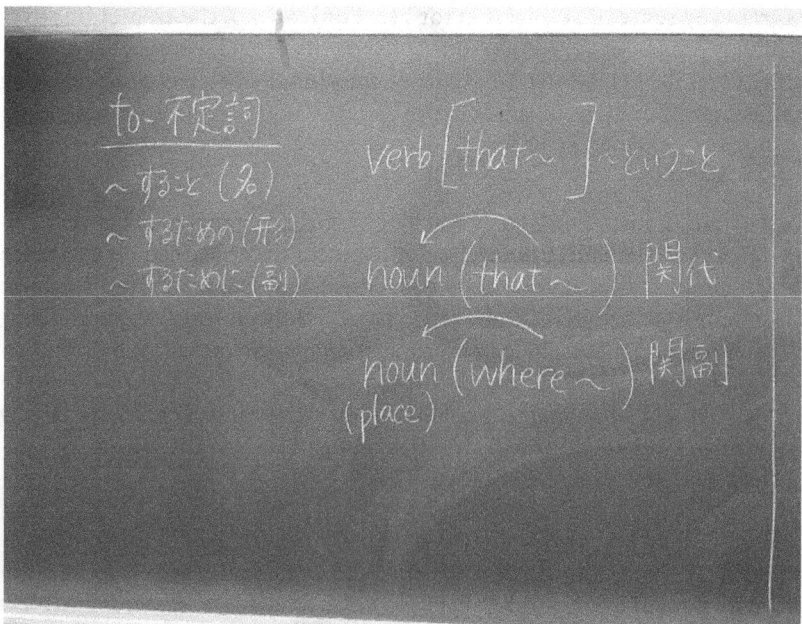

Figure 6.3 Using Japanese to teach EFL

the board that these are two infinitives, there are three different mean-
ings in two infinitives, and also students are really confused with the use
of that, or that clause, or it's a relative clause or a noun clause, so I can
write that in Japanese because we all share the same language. But at the
same time, I think this is kind of not good because we tend to do some
translation, a little bit, because just going over comprehension questions is not enough for them to understand the reading. So I use some
Japanese translations of words or some difficult phrases as we look at
the articles in the textbook because the textbook is written all in English
and sometimes students don't understand the exercise questions, what
they are asking in English, so we have to go through that in class as well.
(Interview 3, 17 August 2019)

From this excerpt, we can see that Haruko felt conflicted about using
Japanese in her EFL class. On the one hand, she recognized how using
Japanese can be helpful for students when understanding grammar explanations or difficult words and phrases. However, she also felt guilty about
using Japanese because she felt that she was reliant on translation. Overall,
Haruko acknowledged that using Japanese was actually helpful for her
students' learning and comprehension of course material because they
were all speakers of Japanese. In contrast, when teaching ESL in the United
States, Haruko's students were from a wide variety of different linguistic
and cultural backgrounds; therefore, using Japanese was not appropriate.

Empathy with language learners

Haruko mentioned empathy as an important factor not only in her
language teaching but also in students' language learning. In discussing
her experience teaching as a NS and NNS teacher, Haruko described
the difference in being able to empathize with her ESL and EFL students
because she had also once been an English language learner. This aided
Haruko's teaching, such as helping her answer students' questions or
explaining English grammar. In contrast, she was not able to empathize
with her students learning Japanese because she had never experienced
learning Japanese as a foreign language. This form of empathy mentioned by Haruko mainly focused on her ability to empathize with
language-based knowledge, such as grammar and vocabulary.

Another form of empathy mentioned by Haruko involved understanding the sociocultural environment of language learning in her classrooms. Part of being able to experience this form of empathy is having
insider knowledge of both the students and the sociocultural context
they are learning in. Haruko used Figure 6.4 to provide an abstract representation of a common pattern she had witnessed her students facing
for speaking English in her EFL class in Japan. She used colored magnets
to represent individual students. The green magnets represented students

Figure 6.4 Awareness of the sociocultural environment of the classroom

who wanted to speak English in class and the yellow magnets represented students who did not. Haruko noticed that students who wanted to speak English became socially isolated in class because they 'stand out'; thus, in order to avoid being cast out as 'different' or judged as 'showing off', students may have avoided speaking English during her EFL class even if they wanted to. Haruko saw this happen in discussion groups when a student might start off speaking English but revert to Japanese when other group members spoke Japanese.

Haruko explained that this even influenced students' English pronunciation in that students who might have had good English pronunciation intentionally used a Japanese accent because they did not want to 'stand out' or seem like they were 'showing off' (Interview 3, 17 August 2019). Haruko described her observations in the following excerpt:

Excerpt 11

There are some students who have very good English pronunciation but they try to speak like other Japanese people, you know what I mean? They have very good pronunciation and when I talk with them, they have very good pronunciation, but in class, when they read something, they try to read like Japanese English. There are a lot of people like that. Especially, our school has a lot of people who are half, like half American or half Japanese, or there are also some foreigners who moved from Taiwan or Vietnam. And, I know their English is good but they don't want to show off, so they just change it to Japanese-style English. (Interview 3, 17 August 2019)

Haruko's empathy for how her students experienced language learning provided her with a greater awareness of the students' experiences of language learning in her classroom. This allowed her to interpret different students' behaviors based on their social positioning as students with varying levels of proficiency and/or students of different ethnic identities, rather than more simplistic binaries of assuming certain students to be 'good' or 'bad'.

Other Aspects of Being a TML from the DFG Framework

The micro level of the DFG framework

The micro level of the Douglas Fir Group (DFG) framework focuses on the main internal mechanisms that build the foundation of Haruko's experience of becoming and being a TML. As with Megan and Ann, the three main internal mechanisms from Haruko's narratives are the development of teacher knowledge, the application of a range of semiotic resources and engagement with multiple emotions.

Teacher knowledge

Like Ann and Megan, Haruko's teacher knowledge also involved learning and understanding the linguistic differences and similarities between two languages and what implications that had for her teaching. Haruko's experience of developing this teacher knowledge was more similar to Ann's than Megan's experience, in that Haruko also had difficulty transitioning from the L1 she taught (i.e. English) to the second language (L2) she taught (i.e. Japanese), primarily because of the linguistic differences, such as grammar (Excerpt 8). One reason why the linguistic aspects of teaching Japanese were difficult for Haruko was because, unlike Ann, she did not receive any LTE in the L2 she taught. In this respect, Haruko's experience was more similar to Megan's, who also did not receive any LTE when it came to teaching German. Furthermore, because Haruko is a NS speaker of Japanese, she was unable to draw on any personal experiences of learning Japanese as a L2 learner, as Megan did, to help her predict or empathize with her Japanese learners' difficulties.

For Haruko, the inability to empathize with her students of Japanese as a NS of Japanese and her lack of LTE in teaching Japanese impacted her teaching efficacy. For example, Haruko recalled that she often did not know how to respond to students' questions about Japanese grammar because she had never taken any classes explicitly learning or teaching Japanese grammar. On the contrary, Haruko did not experience difficulty in explaining English grammar because not only had she taken pedagogical English grammar courses as part of her graduate TESOL program, but she also had the experience of explicitly learning English grammar as an EFL learner in Japan. Therefore, she was much better prepared to address grammar issues in English than in Japanese because she was able to draw from the knowledge she received from her LTE and her personal experience as an EFL learner in Japan. Because of the feeling that she did not have sufficient teacher knowledge to teach Japanese, she noted that if she wanted to pursue Japanese teaching in the future, such as opening her own Japanese language school in the United States (Excerpts 1–3), she would have liked to enroll in a graduate program that provided more LTE in teaching Japanese. This topic is discussed in further detail in the 'Meso Level' section.

Semiotic resources

When discussing the semiotic resources that mediated Ann's and Megan's experience of being a TML, I discussed the role that semiotic resources played in Ann's management of the linguistic differences in her teaching of English and Chinese as well as in Megan's use of technology in teaching English and German. In Haruko's case, I discuss the role semiotic resources played in Haruko's attempt to adjust and balance changes in her creative agency and independence as a language teacher when transitioning from teaching English to Japanese. Haruko taught ESL and Japanese in the United States as well as EFL in Japan and in each of these three positions, she experienced different degrees of creative agency in designing the curriculum and lessons.

When teaching ESL and Japanese in the United States, Haruko was expected to use communicative language teaching, and the curriculum did not depend on students' performance on standardized tests. Thus, she was also allowed more freedom in how she designed her courses and activities. However, when teaching EFL in Japan, Haruko was unable to use communicative language teaching because she was expected to cover a certain amount of content from the textbook in class in order for her students to effectively pass their department-mandated semester final exams. Furthermore, Haruko was unable to choose what textbook or final exam to use because both were issued by the department to maintain consistency between classes taught by different instructors. Despite the wide range of English proficiency levels of students from her TOEFL classes, she was required to use the same syllabus and the same textbook for all her classes because all of the students were required to take the same final exam. Having to use the same textbook made it difficult for Haruko when teaching lower-level students so she had to adjust her teaching to make the course content more level-appropriate. She described the adjustments she made in the following excerpt:

Excerpt 5

Well, I'm supposed to do all the exercises in the textbook, but for the lower classes I just don't do everything because I can't finish everything. So I will reduce the amount of exercises in the lower class levels, and for the quiz, I make it easier for the lower classes, so they have motivation to study. Like for example, for the higher level classes, I have them write the meaning of vocabulary in Japanese, but the lower level classes I have choices for students to choose the definition, which is much easier than writing it on your own. So something like that, I adjust my teaching to get my teaching to different levels. (Interview 3, 17 August 2019)

Even though Haruko experienced less creative agency in her EFL teaching in Japan, she was still able to apply new teaching approaches for her students as mediated by the use of various semiotic resources. For example, in order to help students with their English reading skills in her EFL class, Haruko had students use drawing as a way of creatively and holistically eliciting responses to questions from the textbook (Figure 6.5). Haruko asked students to draw a picture of a passage they had just read from the textbook. Figure 6.5 shows the drawings from two different groups. Students were organized into small groups and asked to discuss what kind of picture they should draw to represent what they had read in the textbook. The drawings are about a story in the textbook of a girl who survived the Haiti earthquake. Previously, Haruko would have asked students to write a paragraph-long summary of the reading to see if they understood what they had read. However, she found that

Figure 6.5 Having students to use drawing

many students did not do the assignment because it was too difficult, so she started to give the option of drawing a picture that summarized the reading. Haruko found that allowing students to draw pictures not only made it 'more fun' for the students but also allowed them to 'choose what they are good at' to show their understanding of the reading. Overall, she felt it was a more effective method of assessing whether or not students understood the reading.

Haruko also experimented with other more effective ways of covering textbook content, such as scanning and color-coding textbook pages onto PowerPoint slides (Figure 6.6) and creating multimodal videos based on textbook content (Figure 6.7). Figure 6.6 features the use of a PowerPoint slide to show a reading passage scanned from a textbook, which was a new technique that Haruko had begun to implement. As Haruko went over the answers to comprehension questions about the passage, she also highlighted where the answers could be found within the passage. Each color represented a different comprehension question from the textbook. By using different colors, Haruko found that students were more easily able to follow, take notes and review their notes. For Haruko, this was an improvement on the way she used to go over the answers to the textbook's comprehension questions, which was simply verbally saying the answers out loud. When she only relied on verbally saying the answers, some students had a difficult time keeping up. This

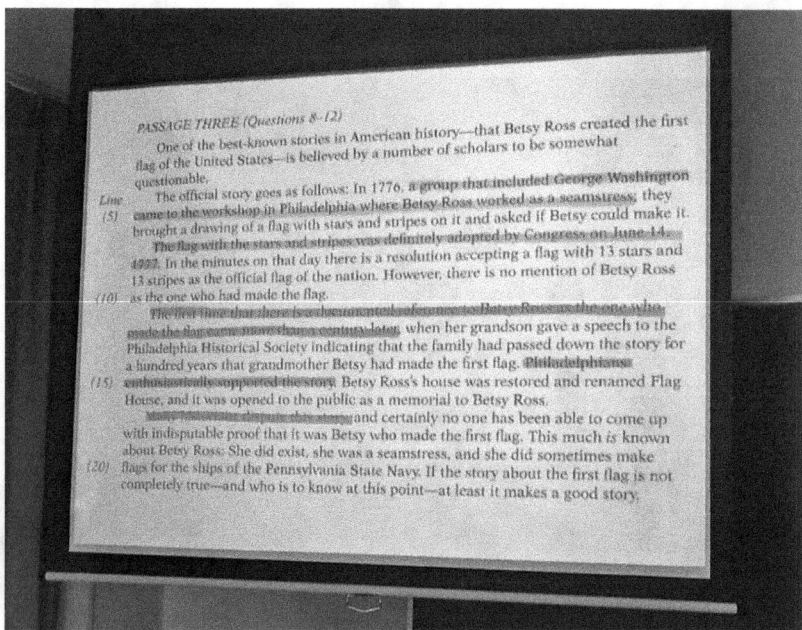

Figure 6.6 Digitally highlighting the textbook

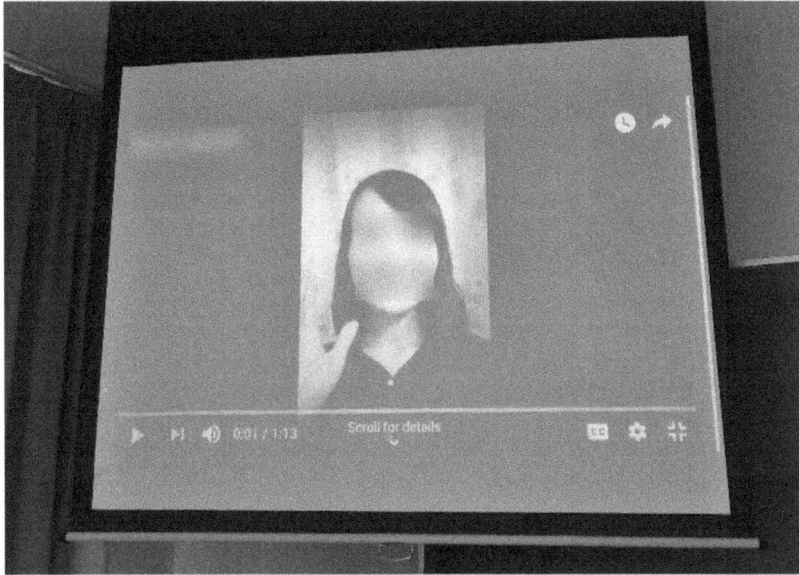

Figure 6.7 Creating a sample college application video

technique was inspired by a similar technique Haruko used in her Japanese class in the United States. In her Japanese class, there were no slide projectors or computers for her to use. Instead, she used colored chalk on a blackboard to make her teacher talk more visually clear.

Figure 6.7 features another use of digital technology to cover textbook content. In the textbook, there was a reading passage about a new method of applying for college in the United States – a college application video. Haruko said that the idea of submitting a video to apply for college was new to her students in Japan because Japanese students typically take exams to get into college. In order to help her students gain a better understanding of the topic, she made an example of a college application video as if she were a high school student applying for college and posted it on YouTube for her students to watch. She also had students make their own college application videos based on the content of the reading passage, such as the length and content of the video. Haruko felt that having students make their own videos was a good way of showing their understanding of the reading passage while also allowing them to practice speaking English.

Another way that Haruko used technology to cover textbook content was using a Jeopardy-based game as an alternative method of assessing student progress on textbook content (Figure 6.8). For the game, Haruko had students form small groups and compete in teams. She found that when using this game, 'everyone participates in the group, even the quiet

Figure 6.8 Reviewing textbook content

students participate to find answers together so it seemed like they really enjoy it, more than normal classes' (Interview 3, 17 August 2019). Finally, she even managed to introduce additional language learning opportunities that were supplementary to the required curriculum, namely through communicative ice-breaker activities (Figure 6.9) and optional extensive reading assignments (Figure 6.10). The extensive reading assignments, in particular, were part of a new extensive reading program that Haruko

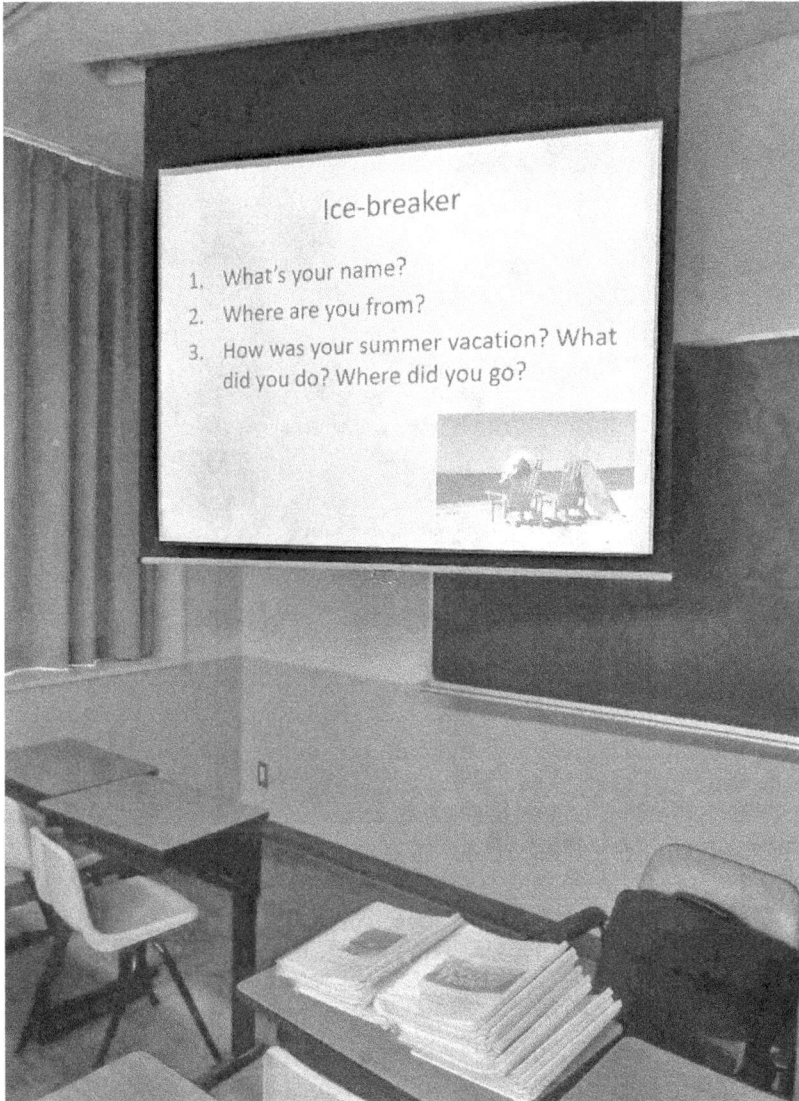

Figure 6.9 A communicative ice-breaker activity

had recently started in her EFL class in Japan. For the extensive reading assignment, students had to read 30,000 words over one semester outside of class. Her university used an online program where students can read selected ebooks and take comprehension quizzes online. When students passed a quiz, the book was added to a record of the books the student had read so far during the semester. Figure 6.10 is a screenshot of what the record of finished books looks like. Haruko's goal in implementing this

Figure 6.10 A new extensive reading program

extensive reading program was to 'create a learning environment where students could have more English input' (Interview 3, 17 August 2019).

Ultimately, Haruko was able to orchestrate a range of semiotic resources (e.g. visual, auditory, digital, multimodal, interactional) to customize those aspects of her classes that she could with the purpose of creating a more communicative and engaging learning experience for her students. She imagined that in the future, she might want to start her own language school with the main motivating reason being that she would be able to teach and design the curriculum the way she wanted to (Excerpt 3).

The meso level of the DFG framework

The meso level of the DFG framework focuses on how Haruko's participation and membership in certain sociocultural institutions and communities shaped the internal mechanisms discussed at the micro level. In Haruko's narratives, the two main sociocultural institutions and communities that were featured are additional LTE programs that Haruko would have liked to participate in and Haruko's prior experience living, studying and teaching in the United States.

The desire for additional LTE

As mentioned in the 'Micro Level' section, Haruko felt that she did not have adequate teacher knowledge to confidently teach Japanese. She felt that her LTE in the form of TESOL graduate courses had prepared her to teach ESL and EFL. It gave her a sense of confidence and reassurance because her teaching was guided by research and methodology. In contrast, she felt that her lack of LTE in teaching Japanese as a foreign language left her ill-prepared to teach Japanese in the United States, specifically when it came to explaining Japanese grammar. In fact, receiving formal LTE in teaching Japanese seemed so important to Haruko that when Haruko described the possibility of opening up her own bilingual English and Japanese school in the United States, she mentioned that she would need to go through some sort of Japanese LTE program first in order to feel sufficiently prepared. This is quite different from Ann's primary motivation for completing additional LTE in Chinese, which was focused on her understanding that in order to teach Chinese abroad, she needed to have a graduate degree in teaching Chinese to speakers of other languages (TCSOL). Haruko, on the other hand, was not facing any formal qualifications as mandated by an academic institution. Rather, Haruko focused more on the additional LTE as a source of teacher knowledge, self-confidence and social credibility when it came to expanding her Japanese teaching into a possible business venture.

Certainly, one can imagine that not all language teachers feel the same need for additional LTE; Megan certainly did not mention the need to receive further LTE when teaching German. This might be because some language teachers may have found their initial experience with LTE primarily negative or unhelpful. Other teachers may feel that they are already able to transfer what they had learned from the LTE they received for the L1 they taught to their teaching of an additional language, like Megan. However, Haruko's experience from teaching Japanese in the United States, including the emotions she felt, the reactions from her students and her own self-assessment of how well she did, made her feel that she needed to take additional LTE to be better prepared.

Living, studying and teaching abroad

One important aspect of Haruko's involvement in sociocultural institutions and communities that was similar to Ann's was her experience living, studying and teaching in the United States. Her participation in various academic and non-academic communities in the United States had a substantial influence on the development of her LTIs and her approaches to language teaching. Haruko lived in the United States for nearly 10 years, starting from her undergraduate studies and continuing through her graduate studies and part-time ESL teaching at various universities afterward. Throughout the 10 years, she not only took on the identity of a Japanese international student studying for her undergraduate and graduate degrees at reputable American universities, but she also took on the identity of a NNS teacher of English at American higher education institutions and a NS teacher of Japanese at a community temple.

These identities served to boost Haruko's self-confidence as a language teacher as well as motivate her students as language learners both in the United States and Japan. For example, at the beginning of each semester when teaching EFL in Japan, Haruko would introduce herself to her students by talking about her experience living, studying and teaching in the United States, as students often found this interesting (Figure 6.23). Haruko explained that she had students approach her for advice about how to apply to study abroad and advice about living in the United States. In this way, Haruko felt that she was not just a language teacher but also a counselor or life coach.

Another example of Haruko taking advantage of her identity as a language teacher who has lived, studied and taught abroad was during Halloween, when Haruko often used her university graduation cap and gown outfit as her costume. She explained that the cap and gown are a more Western style of dress for graduation and many Japanese universities do not use caps and gowns. However, her students recognized a graduation cap and gown from having seen them in movies or on the internet, so when Haruko wore them for Halloween, students often reacted with curiosity and fascination. In fact, many students asked to try on the cap and gown. This is an example of how the identities that Haruko developed from participating in the institutions and communities in the United States later served to bolster her identity as a language teacher. In other words, her 'lived/studied/taught abroad' identity reinforced her LTI just as her LTI reinforced her 'lived/studied/taught abroad' identity.

The macro level of the DFG framework

The macro level of the DFG framework focuses on how large-scale, societal ideologies influence the micro and meso levels of Haruko's development as a TML. The two ideologies that were particularly salient for Haruko are the native speaker fallacy and an awareness of 'the global language market'.

The native speaker fallacy

Compared to Ann and Megan, Haruko's narratives showed the strongest sense of (at least partially) believing in 'the native speaker fallacy' (Phillipson, 1992). The native speaker fallacy is a myth based on the NS/NNS dichotomy that claims that the ideal language teacher is the native speaker. NNS teachers have reported facing discriminatory hiring practices favoring NSs as by default more qualified language teachers. This is often referred to as 'native-speakerism' and stems from a belief in the native speaker fallacy.

One might find this to be a surprising aspect of Haruko's narratives because she expressed being proud that she had been a NNS ESL teacher in the United States and that she enjoyed being perceived as a role model of a successful NNS EFL teacher by her EFL students in Japan. These descriptions seemed to indicate that Haruko perceived herself as someone who had overcome the bias against NNS English teachers, particularly in an English-dominant teaching context such as the United States. Furthermore, Haruko's positive emotions around teaching ESL and EFL as well as her negative emotions around teaching Japanese seemed to suggest that she would challenge any claims that a language teacher would be more qualified based on their native-ness.

While all of the above observations were certainly true, Haruko's narratives actually presented more nuance about her views toward being a NNS teacher, notably a form of self-imposed native-speakerism. In particular, when Haruko described what she thought were possible career paths she might take in the future, she considered the idea of starting an English language school in the United States. However, she questioned the practicality of how financially successful a Japanese-owned English language school would be. She wondered, 'nobody wants to come to an English school owned by a Japanese person, right?' (Excerpt 1). Thus, Haruko suggested an alternative by proposing that she should take advantage of being Japanese by opening a Japanese language school (despite disliking her experience of teaching Japanese in the United States) or a bilingual English and Japanese language school. She also considered location and community to be important factors in the success of a possible English/Japanese language school, noting that she knew of a Japanese lady in the United States who had successfully run a Japanese language school that attracted both Japanese and American people from the local community.

Considering that Haruko disliked teaching Japanese and looked favorably on her LTI and success as a NNS teacher of English, one might wonder why she would feel hesitant to own an English language school as a Japanese person and feel the need to pair Japanese language teaching with English language teaching to make it more attractive to potential customers. A potential explanation could be that Haruko differentiated between two understandings of native-speakerism and her experience as a NNS English teacher: one based on her LTI and the other based on the global language market. In other words, as a LTI, Haruko felt proud and secure being a non-native speaker teacher (NNST) of English. However, in facing the global language market, she felt unsure and doubtful of how being a NNS as well as a Japanese person might affect potential customers' perceptions of her future language school. Haruko's understanding of the global language market is further elaborated in the next section.

Awareness of the global language market

Over the course of teaching multiple languages in her language teaching career, Haruko developed certain beliefs about how her experience of teaching certain languages granted her more opportunities in certain contexts than others. Haruko explained that she felt that Americans would not want to spend money taking an English course from a Japanese person. Also, in terms of opening a Japanese-only language school, she felt that not enough Americans were interested in learning Japanese. Therefore, she felt that offering both English and Japanese classes would be the more successful business idea.

From her experience teaching multiple languages in various institutions in the United States and Japan, Haruko had developed certain beliefs, or a 'neoliberal imaginary' that framed her language teaching skills as 'a commodity with market value' and thus language teachers as 'bundles of skills which can be marketed for productivity' (Shin & Park, 2016: 447). For Haruko, this impacted the way she perceived how marketable her English and Japanese language teaching skills as a NNS and NS teacher, respectively, would be in certain contexts as assessed by certain people within the global language market (Park & Wee, 2012). According to Park and Wee (2012: 154), 'speakers' work of negotiating the value of their linguistic capital is shaped by their own, socialized anticipations about what is possible and appropriate in the given market'.

This means that the way Haruko conceptualized how she would be perceived as a NNS English teacher led her to set negotiated self-limitations on the contexts and conditions under which she could advance her career as a TML. For example, Haruko believed that as a Japanese person, she would not be able to operate a language school that only taught English or Japanese because those would not be marketable enough in the American educational context. Instead, she believed that her language teaching skills in English and Japanese, when perceived as a commodity, had to be packaged together in order to be profitable enough to run a language school in the American educational context. Thus, the way Haruko positioned herself as a TML in the global language market molded how she imagined her future LTI and the possibilities that were open and closed to her in her future TML career trajectory.

There are some similarities and differences between Ann's and Haruko's understanding of her language teaching skills as part of a global language market. Both understood that how marketable their language teaching qualifications and skills were differed depending on which language they taught and the teaching context. Both had experience teaching the languages they perceived to be more marketable based on their own individual background in the United States (i.e. Chinese for Ann and Japanese for Haruko). Lastly, both sought to take advantage of what they perceived to be their advantages in the global language market (i.e. Ann teaching Chinese abroad and Haruko pairing Japanese teaching with English teaching) in order to achieve their own language teaching career goals. However, the main difference between Ann and Haruko is that the latter had actual experience teaching the language she perceived as less marketable, namely teaching English as a NNS in the United States; Ann, on the other hand, did not have such experience and thus, her understanding of how her language teaching skills would be received in the global language market was partially theoretical. This may suggest that Haruko felt greater hesitation and doubt about how financially successful a Japanese-owned English language school in the United States would be, possibly because influencing her beliefs were the actual experiences she had while teaching English in the United States as a NNS teacher.

7 Insights about TMLs

Chapters 4–6 presented Ann, Megan and Haruko's narratives with the aim of providing two different perspectives: (1) a broad look at how their teacher of multiple languages (TML) careers developed, beginning as teachers of a single language and expanding to teaching multiple languages; and (2) an in-depth look at their experience of being TMLs through exploring their identities, beliefs and emotions. The presentation of their narratives and subsequent analyses are part of my own interpretation of their stories, a form of re-storying (Barkhuizen *et al.*, 2014: 97), and their stories are interpretations of their experiences. Together, the collective processes of narrative inquiry involving Ann, Haruko, Megan and me can be described as 'narrative knowledging', defined by Barkhuizen (2011: 395) as 'the meaning making, learning, or knowledge construction that takes place during the narrative research activities of (co)constructing narratives, analyzing narratives, reporting the findings, and reading/watching/listening to research reports' (as cited in Barkhuizen, 2013). Although we cannot generalize the experiences of three participants as universal aspects of all TMLs, we can take their narratives as 'personal practical knowledge' (Clandinin, 2020) that can be used to further understand other possible experiences of TMLs. According to Clandinin (2020):

> We see personal practical knowledge as in the person's past experience, in the person's present mind and body and in the person's future plans and actions. It is knowledge that reflects the individual's prior knowledge and acknowledges the contextual nature of that teachers' knowledge. It is a kind of knowledge carved out of, and shaped by, situations; knowledge that is constructed and reconstructed as we live out our stories and retell and relive them through process of reflection. (Clandinin, 2020: 92)

Ann, Megan and Haruko's narratives provide us with a source of personal practical knowledge (in the form of narrative) to better understand the experience of teaching multiple languages.

Why a TML is a Specific Language Teacher

Ann, Megan and Haruko's journeys as TMLs show that the experience of teaching multiple languages is a specific kind of experience that 'refashions' (Kramsch & Zhang, 2018) language teachers, impacting their approaches to language teaching, their negotiations and understandings of who they are and their long-term career decisions. I argue that in applied linguistics research and real-world teaching contexts, we must not continue to overlook TMLs as the same kind of language teacher as those who have only taught a single language. *Teaching multiple languages is not simply an act of teaching an additional language or set of coursework, but also an act of developing additional ways of being through new identities, beliefs and emotions.* Thus, TMLs should be considered as a specific kind of language teacher, different than teachers of a single language, because the necessity of having to navigate multiple worlds from teaching multiple languages provides them with a specific kind of knowledge, experience and habitus different than that of teachers of a single language.

Another way to approach this is to say that TMLs are more than the sum of several teachers of a single language. This notion is inspired by holistic perspectives on bilingualism in psycholinguistics that recognized a bilingual individual as more than the sum of two monolingual individuals (Grosjean, 1985, 1989). This perspective meant that a bilingual individual was treated as 'a specific and fully competent speaker/hearer who has developed a communicative competence that is equal, but different in nature, to that of the monolingual' (Grosjean, 1994: 1657). In line with this perspective, the term *multicompetence* has also been used to describe second language (L2) learners as having fundamentally different systems of linguistic knowledge than monolinguals and thus should be seen as language users in their own right rather than as deficient monolinguals (Cook, 1991, 2016). Similarly, the Douglas Fir Group (DFG) (2016: 26) has referred to the competence of multilinguals as 'the holistic sum of their multiple-language capacities'.

The rest of this chapter focuses on detailing what exactly it is that makes the teaching of multiple languages more than the sum of teaching single languages. In the following sections, I discuss three claims about TMLs that show the complex ways in which teaching multiple languages involves the work of navigating various layers of identities, beliefs and emotions. In the second half of the chapter, I also present three dimensions of teaching multiple languages as a thematic summary of issues TMLs navigate in their teaching.

Claim 1: In teaching multiple languages, TMLs are engaged in 'identity-belief-emotion' work

In teaching multiple languages, TMLs are engaged with multiple identities, beliefs and emotions. I use the term 'identity-belief-emotion'

(IBE) work, inspired from the framing of language teachers' identity development as 'identity work' (Douglas Fir Group, 2016; Miller *et al.*, 2017; Yazan & Lindahl, 2020) and Barcelos' (2015) use of the term 'beliefs-emotions-identities', emphasizing the way the three concepts are interconnected. Thus, I use the term 'IBE work' to refer to language teachers' routine practice of negotiating, performing and making sense of multiple identities, beliefs and emotions involved with language teaching.

Indeed, IBE work is not solely limited to TMLs; in fact, one may argue that IBE work is a universal part of language teaching. What sets TMLs' engagement in IBE work apart from teachers of a single language is that with each additional language, it is likely that TMLs are dealing with IBE work that consists of many more moving parts. In other words, with each additional language taught, TMLs are developing new identities, experiencing new emotions and changing beliefs; they are performing, negotiating, comparing and juggling IBEs from each of the languages they teach.

Ann, Megan and Haruko's engagements with IBE work were evident throughout their narratives. Within the narratives, it is difficult to separate each of the individual concepts from each other. As Barcelos (2015: 315) has suggested, 'they are all part of one network and cannot be looked at separately; or rather, they are perhaps part of the same continuum, or parts of the same nucleus that forms our "selves"'. Furthermore, IBEs 'change and adapt in response to any changes within themselves within each other. They interact at different times but also simultaneously' (Barcelos, 2015: 315). However, from the narratives, we can observe a few recurring patterns in their experiences, which are explained in Claims 2 and 3.

Claim 2: For TMLs, IBE work may differ depending on the language being taught and the teaching contexts. Thus, TMLs are likely involved in multiple IBE work

As mentioned above, what sets TMLs' engagement in IBE work apart from teachers of a single language is that with each additional language, it is likely that TMLs will be dealing with additional IBE work. However, the *multiple* IBE work that TMLs are navigating is not simply a quantitative difference; the teaching of multiple languages requires navigating a greater qualitative complexity in the nature of IBE work. What I mean by a greater qualitative complexity is the sequencing and layering of multiple moving parts that make up IBE work, and the comparative nature of IBE work.

Both of the above characteristics of multiple IBE work can be seen in Ann, Megan and Haruko's narratives. One could imagine that in the simplest of scenarios, a language teacher would first embark on teaching one language before transitioning to teaching another language, with no direct overlap between them. While this may be the experience of some TMLs, this was not the case for Ann, Megan or Haruko. In all three narratives, there was some form of overlap in the teaching of multiple languages, and thus, in their IBE work. For Ann, this overlap occurred early in her teaching career during her undergraduate English as a foreign language (EFL) teacher education program when she had experience teaching both EFL and Chinese as a second language (CSL). She characterized this stage of her teaching career using the metaphor of two trees growing together. Megan experienced an overlap in teaching English and German when she began to teach German part-time at a company while continuing her English as a second language (ESL) teaching as an adjunct instructor. Her positive experience teaching German part-time at a company provided a stark contrast to the negative experience she had while teaching English as a part-time adjunct instructor. Finally, Haruko experienced an overlap in teaching English and Japanese when she began to teach Japanese at a community temple during her graduate master's (MA) teaching English to speakers of other languages (TESOL) program in the United States. Teaching Japanese provided her with the experience of being a native speaker (NS) teacher and how that differed from teaching ESL as a non-native speaker (NNS) teacher. Even for TMLs who may not be teaching multiple languages simultaneously but teaching each of the multiple languages separately, one after the other, there is still an unavoidable component of comparing the teaching of one language with another language, though the comparisons would be more retrospective in nature (i.e. comparing the current language they are teaching to a language they had taught in the past, rather than comparing languages they are currently teaching).

Thus, for Ann, Megan and Haruko, the teaching of multiple languages simultaneously was not only about teaching an additional subject or set of coursework, but also managing and making sense of additional IBEs. The simultaneous nature of their multiple language teaching put them in a situation where they were inevitably comparing their experiences and IBEs from teaching different languages. In this way, the IBE work of TMLs is qualitatively more complex than that of teachers of a single language because teaching different languages required them to juggle, manage, navigate and negotiate the various IBEs from the different languages they taught or were teaching.

Claim 3: IBE work is part of a greater ecology of factors that TMLs navigate

The discussions following each of the participants' narratives involve factors beyond those of IBEs because IBEs are part of a greater ecology of factors influencing the participants' teaching of multiple languages. As scholars have mentioned, IBEs are not confined to the inner self

(Barcelos, 2015; Douglas Fir Group, 2016), but are often socially and culturally constructed, interacting and changing the surrounding material and social environment. Ann, Megan and Haruko's narratives illustrate this through their discussions about their teaching practices and their teaching environments, their social interactions with colleagues and the institutional expectations and power dynamics in their workplaces. That is to say that it is often in conjunction with telling stories about their outer lives as TMLs that we gain access to explore their inner lives as TMLs.

What has proven useful in demonstrating the embedded nature of IBEs within a greater ecology is the DFG's framework (Douglas Fir Group, 2016), described in Chapter 3. Following each of the participants' narratives, the DFG framework was used to introduce 'other aspects of being a TML' beyond but interconnected with IBEs. In the rest of this section, I revisit the DFG framework as a guide toward gaining a broader understanding of how the experience of teaching multiple languages can be more complex than that of teaching a single language.

At the micro level of teaching multiple languages, TMLs must cognitively attend to the linguistic and pedagogical similarities and differences of the multiple languages they teach or have taught (i.e. 'teacher knowledge'). These similarities and differences lie on a spectrum and the way in which the relationships between the languages are negotiated by TMLs impacts their approaches to and beliefs about language teaching. Furthermore, at the micro level, TMLs' social interactions with others (e.g. students, colleagues, parents) are mediated by a wide range of semiotic resources they have at hand, particularly as multilingual individuals. However, the use of these semiotic resources may be withheld, restricted or selectively applied depending on the teaching context they are in, the language they are expected to use in their role as the language teacher and with whom they are interacting. For example, Haruko as a TML teaching English at a university in the United States was expected to teach using only English, while she was open to using both English and Japanese when teaching Japanese at a local community temple in the United States.

At the meso level of teaching multiple languages, TMLs must navigate the sociocultural institutions and communities (i.e. school, family, neighborhood) in which their teaching is situated. This becomes more complex for TMLs than teachers of a single language because teaching multiple languages often means teaching in contexts that involve multiple sociocultural institutions and communities. While in some cases these sociocultural institutions and communities may be related or overlap, many TMLs must also learn to adapt to completely different sociocultural institutions and communities. This means that as TMLs transition from teaching one language to another, they are not only changing the language they teach but also possibly shifting their language teaching methodologies and identities in accordance with the ideologies of the new institutions and communities. For example, Megan adapted to new language teacher identities (LTIs) and approaches to teaching when shifting from teaching English in higher education institutions as 'an invisible adjunct' to teaching German in a large corporation as a part-time employee jokingly working as 'employee retention'.

At the macro level, TMLs also navigate large-scale, society-wide ideological structures (i.e. beliefs about language use or language learning, cultural values, political values, etc.) that influence what they are expected to teach as well as how they are positioned as language teachers in their workplace. Again, navigating these ideological structures is more complex for TMLs because teaching multiple language often requires TMLs to transition between varying ideological structures. What this means is that the work of teaching multiple languages does not simply involve shifting between the different languages being taught, but also involves shifting between different beliefs about what variety of the language should be taught, what methodology should be used in teaching and what role the teacher plays in relation to the students and the classroom. What makes these factors difficult to navigate is that they are determined by society-wide forces, often cultural and political in nature, that are often not immediately apparent or in conflict with the beliefs of TMLs. For example, when Ann transitioned from teaching Chinese in Taiwan to the United States, she was required to change her Chinese accent to sound like the Beijing dialect because that is what was considered 'standard' at the American university where she taught. In other words, Ann, as a NS of Chinese, was not able to use her 'native' Taiwanese-based Chinese accent to teach Chinese and had to mimic a specific dialect of Chinese that was designated as the international 'standard' due to the large-scale ideological and political structures deriving from the People's Republic of China but reaching and influencing far beyond, even to American universities' Chinese language learning programs.

What the DFG framework is able to show about TMLs are the ways in which their careers are more complex and dynamic due to the need to navigate the multi-layered spaces, systems and ideologies that come with each language that TMLs teach. It shows that teaching multiple languages is more than simply adding on an additional subject of instruction, but that with each additional language taught, TMLs need to navigate an entire ecosystem of cognitions, emotions, identities, social interactions, communities, belief systems and ideologies operating at the micro, meso and macro levels. Using an ecological metaphor, we can compare the complexity, dynamism and variability that TMLs face in teaching multiple languages to that a farmer might face in deciding to cultivate multiple crops as opposed to only one. With each additional crop comes an entire ecology that the farmer must manage in relation to the original crop in order to achieve a successful harvest.

Dimensions of Teaching Multiple Languages

In this section, I present several dimensions of teaching multiple languages from Ann, Megan and Haruko's narratives. One can read this section as a thematic summary of issues that the participants brought up within their narratives and connect them to a broader discussion about teaching multiple languages. These dimensions are the topical spaces in which TMLs' IBE work occurs; that is, IBE work is interwoven within the way TMLs navigate each of these dimensions in their careers.

Navigating teacher knowledge as TMLs

An important dimension of teaching multiple languages is navigating teacher knowledge based on the linguistic and pedagogical similarities and differences between the different languages they have taught. Over the process of learning to teach multiple languages, TMLs inevitably compare their experiences of teaching different languages in terms of the different linguistic characteristics of the different languages they have taught (e.g. grammar, vocabulary, pronunciation) as well as the teaching methods used to teach the different languages (e.g. types of activities, use of specific methodologies, emphasis on particular language skills). The experience of teaching multiple languages provides TMLs with experience in navigating these differences. This means that in teaching multiple languages, each language does not exist in isolation from one another, and the teaching of one language influences the teaching of another language. In the following sections, I cover the two types of teacher knowledge that Ann, Megan and Haruko addressed.

Managing the relationship between languages

There are two ways we can think about how TMLs manage the relationship between language: the first is in relation to linguistic features and the second is in relation to identities and emotions. Primarily, part of the experience of teaching multiple languages is learning how the different linguistic features of the languages one has taught relate to one another. Research on multilingualism has found that, unlike monolingual speakers, multilingual speakers develop an increased awareness of the interaction among the languages they know, which has been referred to as 'multilingual awareness' (Jessner, 2008b, 2014). From LTE as well as teaching experience, each participant reported actively comparing and learning from their reflections about these differences. For example, Ann taught English first before transitioning to Chinese. As a NS of Chinese, Ann rarely explicitly thought about the grammatical features of Chinese. However, through her LTE and experience teaching Chinese, she learned what the grammatical features of Chinese were, how to explain them to her students using English and how the grammatical features of English relate to those of Chinese. In other words, by teaching *both* English and Chinese, her knowledge of the linguistic features of English and Chinese was expanded and refined. Megan and Haruko also followed the same pattern of developing teacher knowledge around the languages they taught.

At first, this may sound similar to the experience of a multilingual individual. Like TMLs, bilingual/multilingual speakers also develop a multilingual awareness from having to consider and compare the different linguistic features of the languages they know. However, an important difference is that TMLs are forced to consider the linguistic features of the languages they know *more explicitly* because they are not only expected to use the languages but also teach them. For example, a bilingual speaker who is able to fluently speak English and Chinese may have a general understanding of the linguistic features of English and Chinese, but they may not be able to explain those features explicitly because they have primarily used the two languages rather than taught them. This is what sets TMLs apart from a bilingual/multilingual speaker or a bilingual/multilingual language teacher. I elaborate further on the pedagogical role of managing linguistic relationships in the next section.

In addition to managing the *linguistic* features of the languages TMLs have taught, TMLs must also manage the *identity and emotional* features of the languages they have taught. For each TML, each language comes packed with multiple layers of meaning that are influenced by a range of factors, such as their cultural upbringing, their past experiences in language teaching or learning, or their perceptions of who they are. For example, for Haruko, the various identities (i.e. EFL learner, NNS, university instructor) and emotions (i.e. pride, familiarity) associated with teaching English were different than those of teaching Chinese (i.e. NS, community instructor; emotions: i.e. frustration, anxiety). The multiple layers of meaning that become associated with the different languages TMLs teach do not come pre-packaged; rather, they are developed over time through their experiences teaching multiple languages through social interactions with colleagues and students in various institutions and communities and exposure to ideological structures. Furthermore, gaining a greater awareness of the differences in identities and emotions associated with the languages they have taught can lead to TMLs taking these factors into consideration when making crucial decisions about their TML career, such as what language(s) and proficiency levels they prefer to teach and in what contexts they prefer to teach. Thus, developing an understanding of the multiple identities and emotions they come to associate with the languages they have taught becomes part of both the process and byproduct of being a TML.

Adjusting pedagogical practices

Managing the similarities and differences between the languages TMLs have taught leads to considering how those similarities and differences impact TMLs' approaches to language teaching. This manifests in two ways: broader language teaching methodologies and more specific instructional decisions.

First, when teaching multiple languages, TMLs consider whether the language teaching methodology they used in their initial language teaching experience is suitable for their next language teaching experience. Various factors are considered in order to determine whether a new language teaching methodology should be used when teaching a different language, such as the TML's LTE, the students' proficiency levels, the cultural context and the institution's expectations. For example, Megan first taught academic English to international students at a university in the United States using communicative language teaching. When teaching German, she taught beginning adult learners who were learning German out of personal interest rather than for academic achievement. Megan also felt less confident about teaching German than teaching English because she was a NNS of German. Thus, she decided to partially use communicative language teaching and partially use the direct method when teaching German. Ann and Haruko also implemented changes in their language teaching methodologies when transitioning to teaching a different language.

Second, in addition to considering changes in TMLs' broad language teaching methodologies, TMLs also consider changes in specific instructional decisions in their language teaching. Specifically, these instructional decisions may involve decisions such as the language of instruction, class activities, course materials and assessment types. Like decisions around which language teaching methodology to use, specific instructional decisions are also determined based on a multitude of factors, including LTE, course level, cultural context and institutional expectations. However, these decisions may be made separately from decisions regarding language teaching methodology. For example, when Haruko transitioned from teaching English and Japanese in the United States to teaching English in Japan, she had to switch from using communicative language teaching to a combination of communicative language teaching and grammar translation. However, despite this transition, there were certain instructional decisions she was able to maintain and others she had to change. Specifically, she was able to continue using some of her teaching techniques, such as icebreakers and pair work activities, but she had to change her language of instruction (i.e. using English to teach Japanese, using Japanese/English to teach English) and course materials as mandated by her institution's requirements. Thus, shifting from teaching one language to another requires adjusting to changes in both the broader teaching methodologies as well as the more specific aspects of language teaching, some of which TMLs have the ability to exercise agency over but others may be imposed by the rules and cultures of the teaching context.

Navigating habitus as TMLs

TMLs also navigate the relationship between the various layers, facets or versions of self from teaching multiple languages. While this section discusses LTIs, I also see this section as being broader than LTIs. Here, I refer to the concept of *habitus*; the notion of habitus is a core part of Bourdieu's (1990: 53) theory of practice and he defined habitus as a 'system of durable, transposable dispositions... principles which generate and organize practices and representations'. Habitus can be conceptualized as certain ways of acting and behaving instilled in our physical bodies through socialization by institutions (e.g. family, school) and ideologies over time and shaped by our socioeconomic positions in society. These ways of acting and behaving 'become "natural" ways of doing things with our bodies, what we do without rational or conscious calculation; it becomes part of our predisposition as a particular kind of member of society' (Park & Wee, 2012: 34). TMLs navigate a habitus shaped by their diverse experiences in teaching multiple languages to different demographics of students in different educational contexts. Language learners may recognize and respond to TMLs' unique habitus, which reinforces the way the habitus takes shape for TMLs both internally as self-perceptions and externally as how they are perceived. In the following sections, I discuss the ways the negotiation of habitus manifests in the teaching of multiple languages.

Being both NS teachers and NNS teachers

As TMLs, all three participants had experience of being both NS teachers and NNS teachers so they were able to compare their own self-perceptions and how others perceived or treated them as NS teachers and NNS teachers of different languages and different teaching contexts. Ann transitioned from being a NNS teacher of EFL in Taiwan to a NS teacher of Chinese in Taiwan, India and the United States. From this transition, she noticed that being a NNS teacher and a NS teacher afforded her different advantages and disadvantages. First, she noticed that as a NNS teacher of EFL, she was able to better empathize with her students because she had experienced the difficulties of being an EFL learner. When she was a NS teacher of Chinese, she noticed that she was less able to predict what difficulties her students might have and why they might be having those difficulties. Second, she noticed that as a NS teacher of Chinese, she felt a responsibility to represent and share 'her language' and 'her culture' properly, almost as if she had designated herself as a cultural ambassador. In fact, she described teaching Chinese as possibly a 'tool for diplomacy'. She realized the potential that she could be a cultural ambassador of the Chinese language and culture when she taught Chinese in India through a volunteer program and her students had a passionate desire to learn Chinese. This experience stood out to her because she was the first NS teacher of Chinese that school had ever had so she felt that they were interested not only in learning Chinese but also in getting to know her as an ethnically Chinese person.

Haruko had similar experiences to Ann when it came to being a NS and NNS teacher. Haruko started out as a NNS teacher of ESL in the United States, taught as a NS teacher of Japanese in the United States and then transitioned to being a NNS teacher of EFL in Japan. Like Ann, Haruko felt a sense of pride and responsibility that came from her experience as a NNS teacher of English in both the United States and Japan. To be specific, Haruko was not necessarily proud of being a NNS teacher at first, but it was through her experience of teaching as a NNS of English that the feelings of pride and responsibility arose. She recalls that in both the United States and Japan, several Japanese students taking her EFL class were so impressed with her English proficiency skills (specifically pronunciation) that they told Haruko they wanted to speak English just like her. In other words, Haruko's EFL students saw her as a role model and a highly proficient L2 user (Cook, 1991) in her own right rather than following a native speaker model and comparing their own language proficiency to that of a NS. Haruko felt proud that she was able to be a positive influence as a NNS teacher to her EFL students. In contrast, when teaching Japanese in the United States as a NS teacher, she did not feel the same kind of pride and honor. In fact, she felt that she was expected by default to have good pronunciation since she was a NS of Japanese and students did not see her as a role model. Furthermore, Haruko found it overall more difficult to teach Japanese as a NS teacher, particularly when trying to respond to students' questions about grammar. Unlike teaching EFL, when she taught Japanese, she was not able to refer to her LTE training in pedagogical grammar (because she did not receive any that was specific to Japanese) nor was she able to refer to her own experiences learning Japanese as a L2 (because she did not have any).

Megan started out teaching as a NS teacher of EFL in Germany, then a NS teacher of ESL in the United States and then a NNS teacher of German in the United States. Compared to Ann and Haruko, Megan had the least to say about being a NS and NNS teacher and thus, seemed least influenced by her NS and NNS LTIs. Megan certainly made observations about the differences between being a NS and NNS teacher. For example, she noted that teaching German as a NNS was harder because she could not depend on a NS's instinctual knowledge of German. As a NNS teacher, she had less confidence in herself and had to be much more careful about her teacher talk in class. This was the extent to which Megan considered her NS and NNS LTIs.

Being an adjunct or 'going corporate'

While Megan only briefly talked about being a NS and NNS teacher, she talked extensively about her experience of being an adjunct instructor at various higher education institutions. Fundamentally, this was a discussion about what kind of language teacher Megan originally saw herself as and desired to be, and how that perspective changed over time.

When Megan taught ESL and English composition at community colleges and universities in the United States, she was mostly hired as an adjunct instructor, which she felt was a position that was underappreciated by and invisible to higher education institutions. These had concrete impacts on Megan's attitudes toward her career as a language teacher, such as the number of unpaid hours Megan spent preparing for her classes and the lack of recognition for everyday personal aspects of teachers' lives (e.g. adjunct birthdays, adjunct's final days as part of the faculty). Megan felt strongly that the way adjunct instructors were treated as inferior members of the department was an injustice and this became a part of her LTI. Megan's passion for the plight of adjunct instructors not only came from her own personal experiences but also in witnessing the way her colleagues were treated. In fact, in one of Megan's stories, she recalled not being able to bear watching another of her colleagues leave the university department with no 'thank you' or 'goodbye', so Megan took matters into her own hands and arranged a farewell party for her colleague. For Megan, this was an act of resistance against an unjust system.

In contrast to Megan's experience of feeling that she was mistreated as an adjunct instructor of a higher education institution, her experience of being a part-time German teacher at a company was very positive. Specifically, she felt appreciated and acknowledged as a language teacher in the company. A particular moment for Megan was when she was teaching German at the company and her birthday was remembered and celebrated. She did not remember this happening in any of her adjunct positions. Megan's positive experience as a part-time employee in a large company and negative experience as an adjunct instructor in a higher education institution presented her with a scenario that defied her initial associations of what it meant to work in a higher education institution versus a corporate environment. It suffices to say that she was surprised that the large corporation seemed to treat her with more humanity as a language teacher than the higher education institutions did. While Ann and Haruko's LTIs remained largely within the language teaching context in higher education contexts, Megan's experience of teaching German exposed her to a language teaching context based in a corporate environment that may have initially conflicted with her LTI but later proved to actually bolster her LTI by acknowledging her work. The feeling that who she was and what she contributed as a language teacher was treated with respect and recognition was so important to Megan that it caused her to rethink her plans of pursuing a career in higher education and introduced a possible alternative career trajectory of 'going corporate', as she put it.

Bolstering personality, persuasiveness and charisma

Ann noticed that having taught English and Chinese in multiple countries and teaching contexts granted her a certain kind of 'persuasiveness' and 'charisma' with her students, as she put it. When Ann spoke of 'persuasiveness', she was referring to the sense that students believed and trusted her explanations and teaching as a language teacher. She felt that her experiences as a TML had made her a more persuasive language teacher because she was better able to make comparisons between students' native language and target language. Namely, when teaching Chinese in the United States, because she had previously taught EFL, she was able to explain Chinese vocabulary and grammar in relation to English. In addition, after she moved back to Taiwan and continued to teach EFL and CSL in Taiwan, she was able to explain EFL vocabulary and grammar in relation to Chinese. In these scenarios, Ann was using her pedagogical experience in teaching English and Chinese to make linguistic connections between those two languages in her teaching.

This idea that bridging her experiences of teaching multiple languages had a positive impact on the way students perceived her as a language teacher was not limited to her expertise and knowledge of the languages (i.e. persuasiveness), but was also applicable to her broader personality, what she calls 'charisma'. This manifested in her language classes when she was able to tell stories about her experience teaching different languages in different countries. She found that students were interested and impressed by these stories and it contributed to a sense of 'charisma' from her students' perspective of associating fascination and wonder with language learning. Similar to Ann's sense of 'charisma', Haruko noticed that her Japanese students were impressed by the fact that she had taught different languages in different countries. They thought that it was rare to meet a teacher from Japan who had taught both English and Japanese in the United States. From the narratives, what we see is Ann and Haruko reporting on the students' positive judgements of elements of their personality that came from teaching multiple languages in various contexts. In turn, their students' judgements further reinforced this habitus not just as something a student said about them, but also as characteristics that Ann and Haruko may inhabit or identify with more in their teaching careers.

Developing transnational competency

Ann felt that her persuasiveness and charisma after teaching Chinese in the United States developed into a certain kind of self-confidence. This can also be described as a kind of 'transnational competency' or the ability 'to participate effectively in activities that cut across two or more national boundaries' (Koehn & Rosenau, 2002: 114). For example, Ann noted that if she ever had an American student learning Chinese in

Taiwan in the future, she felt confident interacting with that student and that she 'knew' how to teach them. Haruko also noticed that her Japanese students were impressed by the fact that she had taught different languages in different countries. In particular, students would approach her to ask for advice about studying and teaching abroad because of her extensive experience living, studying and teaching in the United States. Also, when she shared her experiences teaching Japanese in the United States, her students were surprised that it was even a possibility and became interested in the possibility that they too could pursue a career teaching Japanese abroad. Haruko felt that one reason students sought her advice on teaching and studying abroad was because not many of the other faculty members had studied or taught abroad. In a sense, beyond simply seeing themselves as a language teacher, Ann and Haruko have also taken on the habitus of being a cultural ambassador or an embodied representative of their experiences drawing from 'two or more worlds of experience' (Li, 2000: 23) from teaching multiple languages in multiple countries.

Navigating language education contexts as TMLs

Another core dimension of teaching multiple languages is navigating multiple language education contexts that differ between the multiple languages that TMLs have taught. When teaching multiple languages, each language is often situated in different language education contexts that consist of multiple, overlapping social, political and economic factors that are often not immediately apparent. Thus, as TMLs transition from teaching one language to another, they become attuned and sensitive to the way changes in these contextual factors impact their teaching. This sensitivity grants TMLs the ability to make decisions and act within these varying contexts in ways that are most appropriate not only for their students in language learning but also for themselves in terms of teaching individual lessons as well as managing their teaching career. The two main contextual themes appearing in the three participants' narratives are the contextual expectations of TMLs and the global language markets for language teaching.

Contextual expectations of TMLs

As TMLs transition from teaching one language to another, they confront a wide range of expectations for what kind of teacher they should be, what aspects of language they should teach and what methods they should use to teach language. These expectations may vary from one context to another, so they may or may not align with the expectations TMLs had from a previous teaching position or the expectations TMLs were taught through their LTE programs. What this means is that teaching multiple languages is not simply about adding another subject to the list of languages one has taught; rather, teaching multiple languages involves a process of attuning to, sorting out and adapting to the changing expectations of their language teaching as a result of changes in context.

Ann experienced this shift most prominently when she attempted to apply for a government-sponsored program to teach Chinese classes as a foreign language teaching assistant at an American university. At the time, she was teaching large EFL cram school classes in Taiwan while also doing her master's in teaching Chinese to speakers of other languages (TCSOL). On her first attempt to apply for the government-sponsored program to teach Chinese in the United States, Ann was rejected after her interview and when she asked her interviewers why she had failed, the interviewers told her that her Chinese pronunciation was not 'accurate'. After asking for some specific examples, Ann realized that she was rejected because she did not speak Putonghua (普通話), 'the standard variety of Chinese' based on the Beijing dialect; instead, during the interview, she spoke Taiwanese Mandarin (Guoyu or 國語), the variety of Chinese she would normally use as a NS of Chinese in Taiwan. This made the interviewers (who were Taiwanese, like Ann) question whether or not she would be a suitable candidate to teach university Chinese classes in the United States where Putonghua is expected to be taught, even though Ann had already learned how to read and write simplified Chinese characters and use the Hanyu Pinyin Romanization system. Ann explained that once she realized her Taiwanese Mandarin accent was an issue, she practiced the Putonghua accent she was expected to use and in her second application attempt, she used Putonghua and passed the interview. When she taught university Chinese classes in the United States, she noted that indeed the department faculty expected her to consistently teach Chinese using Putonghua. Furthermore, to maintain a professional image in front of her colleagues and classmates, she avoided using Taiwanese Mandarin on campus.

In transitioning from the language education context in Taiwan to the United States, Ann realized that simply being a NS of Taiwanese Mandarin did not meet the expectations for teaching Chinese through the Fulbright Foreign Language Teaching Assistant (FLTA) program in the United States. Therefore, she adapted her accent to fit the linguistic expectations of the educational context she aspired to teach in. Since Ann expressed a desire to teach Chinese as a way for her to travel around the world, one can imagine that Ann may be expected to change her accent as she moves from one context to the next, while in other situations she may not be expected to, despite the fact that she is still consistently teaching the same language in all of those scenarios. As Ann gains more credibility and a higher reputation within her profession, she may gain greater bargaining power over what variety of Chinese she can teach; however, for now as a TML at the early stages of her career, she has learned to adapt to the expectations of certain contexts to the best of her ability. What Ann was learning to navigate were the dynamic changes that come with teaching across different contexts.

While Ann had to navigate contextual expectations set at the institutional level by gatekeepers of a national government-sponsored program and university departments abroad, Haruko and Megan had to navigate contextual expectations of their methods of language teaching as influenced by changes in student demographics and student learning needs. Haruko started out teaching academic English for international students at an American university where she was trained to use communicative language teaching. As she transitioned to teaching Japanese to adults at a local temple in the United States, even though it was certainly a different educational context, she was still able to use communicative language teaching methods because her students were learning Japanese for communicative purposes, rather than to pass a standardized test. However, when she moved back to Japan and taught university-level EFL courses, she was unable to continue using only communicative language teaching methods. She found herself using a combination of communicative language teaching and grammar translation methods because grammar translation methods were more familiar to Japanese students. Furthermore, Haruko felt that the curriculum and course materials that the department required her to use were not conducive to communicative language teaching and in order to help the students do well (i.e. pass the important final exam of the semester as issued by the department), using grammar translation methods was often more efficient. Haruko felt conflicted about this because she personally preferred to teach using communicative language teaching, and she felt that if she had been given more creative freedom as an instructor, she might have been able to integrate more communicative language teaching into the course.

Like Haruko, Megan also learned to adjust her language teaching methodology according to her students' learning needs. Megan transitioned from teaching academic ESL and freshman composition as an adjunct instructor at higher education institutions in the United States to a side-gig teaching German to the employees of a large corporation. The employees decided to enroll in Megan's class because they wanted to participate in an extracurricular activity offered at their workplace and learn practical German. This was very different from Megan's previous language teaching, which was mostly based on teaching academic skills. Like Haruko, Megan decided to adjust her teaching methods and used a combination of communicative language teaching and the direct method. Furthermore, while Haruko had little creative freedom to design her own curriculum and teaching materials when teaching EFL in Japan, Megan was given a lot of creative freedom while teaching German at the large corporation. Therefore, she utilized that creative freedom to design alternative language assessment methods that suited the students' learning goals. Rather than using a conventional paper and pen test, Megan used a Jeopardy-style game to test students' learning, which fit with the students' goals to learn practical German while also having fun. In adjusting her German teaching to fit the needs of her students within the particular context of teaching for a corporation, Megan was aware that transitioning from teaching one language to another also meant transitioning from one educational context to another, and thus, in the process of transitioning, she learned to navigate those differences by adapting her language teaching methods to the new context.

Global language markets for language teaching

The notion of a global language market (Park & Wee, 2012) was previously mentioned in the section titled 'Awareness of "the Language Market"' in Chapter 6, where I discussed Haruko's navigation of global language markets. Here, I aim to expand this notion to Ann and Megan to show how the other two participants also learned to navigate the global language markets for their respective language teaching careers.

As mentioned in Ann's discussion in the section titled 'Pursuit of Global and Local Mobility', Ann's decision to expand her career from teaching EFL to also teaching CSL was strongly based on her desire to be able to travel the world. She imagined having a career that would allow her to work and live in different countries and experience the cultures of those places. She mentioned that her goal was to have taught Chinese on every continent. At the time of this study, she had already taught Chinese in Taiwan, India and the United States. The reason why Ann believed that teaching CSL would be her ticket to global mobility was because of her awareness of the global language market. What this means is that she packaged the entirety of her language and teaching skills and experience (i.e. ability to teach classes using English; being a NS of Taiwanese Mandarin; getting a master's degree in TCSOL; having experience teaching Chinese in Taiwanese cram schools, Taiwanese university language centers and American university classes) as 'a commodity with market value' which she was able to leverage to achieve her goal (Shin & Park, 2016: 447). She felt that there was an increasing demand in the global language market for learning Chinese and so pursuing a career in teaching Chinese as a NS of Chinese with proficient English-speaking skills would give her the upper hand in getting jobs abroad. Thus, Ann ended up becoming a TML in order for her to play to her strengths in the global language market. She felt that if she had stayed solely as an EFL instructor (which is what she started her teaching career as), she would never have been able to travel abroad through her career. In trying to achieve her goal, she developed a sensitivity to the way English and Chinese were positioned in the global language teaching market and where career opportunities were available or constrained for her.

While Ann looked to a global language market, Megan's notion of a language market resided locally within the United States and was not necessarily about leveraging one language over the other but more about leveraging her skills and experience as a teacher to those who valued them. Megan started out teaching ESL at various universities but she realized that her career opportunities lay not solely within language teaching within academia and higher education, but also possibly in the private sector as an instructional designer. Megan had always wanted to be a language teacher in academic job settings; she prided herself in the idea that she was working among professors and other scholars. However, the difficulty of securing a tenure-track position in the field of ESL teaching and the mistreatment of adjunct instructors in the higher education institutions where she worked led her to consider alternative career opportunities that would provide her with more job security, better compensation and a sense of recognition and respect. Originally, she thought that this meant she would have to 'sell out' by 'going corporate'. However, it was through her positive experience teaching German for a corporation that she began to reconsider her negative associations of corporate workplaces and consider positions in 'instructional design' in the private sector. Megan felt that her language teaching skills and experience were not being valued in the academic job market in terms of both monetary compensation and respect. Therefore, she sought out the kind of job market (in the private sector) that did provide the kind of compensation and treatment she needed.

8 Future Directions: Rethinking the Language Teachers We Think We Know

I began Chapter 1 with the notion that *no teacher begins their teaching with a blank slate*, inspired by a similar quote from Wolff and De Costa (2017). The 'blank slate' is the default setting we can unconsciously impose on language teachers if we are not careful. We might take a look at a language teacher of a certain language and forget to take into consideration what we may not see, unknowingly assuming that this language teacher has always only been a teacher of the language indicated by their position or course title. The 'blank slate' can also be the misguided belief in ahistorical neutrality; we might be aware that language teachers' teaching is informed by and developed from their histories and past experience, but also believe to some degree that the past is not that important to understand or recognize. Overall, when we do not challenge ourselves to develop a critical eye to consider the possibility and significance of a language teacher having taught multiple languages, we risk discounting a significant portion of a language teacher's teaching experience that likely has had an impact on their current language teaching practices.

It is also important to remember that this sense of awareness of teachers of multiple languages (TMLs) applies not only to the way we see other language teachers, but also the way we see ourselves as language teachers. I think back to the first few years of my academic career, originally as a lecturer in the Department of English Instruction at the University of Taipei. Our department focused on preparing undergraduate students to become elementary school English teachers in Taiwan, and therefore, the students who wanted to pursue a career in teaching saw themselves as prospective English teachers. It was only after having taught in the department for a couple of years that I realized that many of the students who successfully obtained teaching positions after graduating from our English instruction department did not end up teaching English. While there had always been an overall national demand for English teachers in Taiwan, the number of English classes arranged at an individual elementary school was fewer than that of other 'standard' subjects, like Mandarin Chinese or mathematics. Thus, getting assigned to teach an English class was a competitive endeavor and quite often, the elementary school teachers with seniority had priority in choosing what classes to teach. New teachers, like those just graduating from our department, were left teaching the classes other teachers did not want to teach. In Taiwan, this often included being a 'homeroom teacher', which meant teaching all the 'general subjects' (i.e. Mandarin Chinese, mathematics, history) and taking on the responsibility of being the main disciplinarian if students misbehaved.

Having only lived and worked in Taiwan for a few years, I double-checked this information with my Taiwanese colleagues, who confirmed the stories that I had heard from our department alumni. From an outsider perspective, I was baffled by the situation my students were facing. They had gone through four years of undergraduate coursework preparing them to be English teachers, obtained an undergraduate degree in English education and developed identities as prospective English teachers, only to enter a system where, with little choice, they expected to teach completely different subjects in their first years as teachers, which often included teaching languages and subjects other than English. Eventually, many of these teachers were able to get English classes to teach, but only after gaining enough seniority to choose classes earlier than newer teachers. For such teachers, I wonder how they thought about their experiences teaching multiple languages. Did they consider themselves to be more than simply the English teachers they had set out to become during their undergraduate years? Did they consider the breadth of knowledge and experience they gained from teaching multiple languages to be legitimate and valuable?

It is my hope that there will be more research bringing attention to, reflecting on and recognizing the importance of TMLs. This includes developing an explicit awareness of TMLs on the part of institutions, researchers, employers and fellow language teachers in all possible situations, including research agendas, job postings, research design, everyday conversations and more. To begin such an endeavor, I propose a set of reflective questions that can help language teachers and researchers become more aware of the simplistic assumptions we may often make, and guide us through rethinking the languages teachers we think we know:

(1) Have you ever asked a language teacher (e.g. a friend, colleague, student) whether they have previously taught other languages? If so, how did the conversation come about?
(2) How might a language teacher's previous experience of teaching other languages influence their current teaching?

(3) With regard to any research you have conducted on language teachers, how would the knowledge of a participant's prior experience teaching multiple languages influence the study?

(4) On a more personal level, how would learning that a language teacher you know has taught or is currently teaching other languages influence your perception of them?

(5) What are aspects of your own language teaching career that are not immediately apparent to others?

(6) The idea that 'no teacher begins their teaching with a blank slate' can sound nice but remain abstract. In what concrete ways does the recognition of teachers' past experiences inform policies, procedures, decisions or interactions at your institution? In other words, how does the idea that 'no teacher begins their teaching with a blank slate' manifest at your institution?

With these reflective questions in mind, I hope that this book and the participants' narratives encourage researchers and educators to take a second look at the assumptions we make about the language teachers we interact with and write about in research. In the rest of this chapter, I broaden the discussion about TMLs to explore the implications that TML research has for language teacher education (LTE) and possible directions for research.

Implications for Language Teacher Education

The necessity of LTE programs for TMLs

When considering the implications this study has for LTE, a few questions come to mind. First, *is there a need to design LTE programs specifically geared toward TMLs (i.e. 'TML programs')?* As noted in the Introduction, LTE programs already exist in various parts of the world, though they are still relatively uncommon and certainly not mainstream. Ann, Megan and Haruko's narratives suggest that TMLs are dealing with unique issues that arise from the fact that they are teaching more than one language, such as learning how to navigate the relationship between multiple languages. As discussed in Chapter 7, in trying to manage the relationship between the languages they teach, they have to consider the linguistic similarities and differences between languages, the different roles and identities they may need to take on that are associated with the different languages they teach, and the different spaces and contexts they may need to inhabit from the different languages they teach and how that impacts the opportunities afforded to them in their teaching careers. These insights suggest that TMLs indeed do experience situations and dilemmas unique to the teaching of multiple languages that may not be adequately addressed in current LTE programs that assume that all teachers have only taught a single language or do not explicitly discuss the impact of any additional languages taught.

Issues TML programs should address

If we take seriously the suggestion that LTE programs geared for TMLs are necessary, then a second question must be asked: *what issues do TML programs need to address that current LTE programs do not address?* The dimensions of teaching multiple languages presented in Chapter 7 suggest that there are three topics relevant to the experiences of TMLs that LTE programs can address. First, TML programs should help TMLs understand that teaching multiple languages requires them to develop a deeper understanding and awareness of the linguistic similarities and differences across the different languages they teach. Furthermore, TML programs should have TMLs consider and plan for how those linguistic similarities and differences may affect their language teaching beliefs and practices.

Second, TML programs should help TMLs understand that teaching multiple languages is not only about managing the different linguistic systems among the multiple languages they teach but also managing new ways of being, including identity-belief-emotion (IBE) work and developing a new habitus. TML programs should address the fact that each additional language taught may introduce complex relationships between the multiple IBE associated with the different languages taught. TML programs should help TMLs understand the ways in which the new IBE may integrate holistically or be in conflict with existing IBE and how the negotiation of those dynamics may impact their approaches to language teaching.

Third, TML programs should help TMLs understand that teaching multiple languages also means managing new workplaces, sociocultural contexts and communities, and that these contextual factors may have a large impact on a language teacher's career trajectory over time. Teaching multiple languages means transitioning and adjusting to new expectations and ideologies of what should be taught, how languages should be taught and what role language teachers should play in the classroom. TML programs should help TMLs develop a critical awareness of the way in which these contextual expectations are informed by the greater sociocultural ideologies of the institutions and communities of which they become a part.

It is important to note that neither Ann, Megan nor Haruko attended TML programs. Nor were they explicitly taught the issues they would need to confront in transitioning from teaching one language to teaching multiple languages. While each of the participants certainly received LTE for at least one of the languages they taught, these LTE programs assumed that they would be teaching a single language. In other words, the LTE programs did not address how TMLs should manage any of the three issues mentioned above: (1) the pedagogical relationships, (2) the IBE work and (3) the various educational contexts between the different languages they had previously taught and/or were possibly going to teach. Instead, this knowledge was gradually developed over time through their experience of having taught multiple languages. That is, they were essentially 'thrown in to the deep end', so to speak. It was through the experience of teaching multiple languages that TMLs figured out how to navigate each of the issues mentioned above.

It is beyond the scope of this study and impossible to know how Ann, Megan and Haruko would have developed as TMLs if they had attended a TML program. While all three TMLs did figure out on their own ways to navigate the teaching of multiple languages, they would most likely have benefitted from LTE that specifically addressed issues relevant to TMLs. Specifically, the role of TML programs should be to raise awareness of and familiarity with these issues that TMLs may possibly face and help pre-service and in-service TMLs better prepare for their future careers by engaging in critical reflection on the issues that arise from teaching multiple languages.

Future Directions for Research

This book has only introduced the notion of TMLs as a particular demographic of language teachers and some of the issues relevant to teaching multiple languages, so a plethora of potential research topics have yet to be covered. Next are some possible future directions for research.

Researching the teaching of multiple languages

When it comes to researching the teaching of multiple languages, future research could focus on a number of different pedagogical issues. First, scholars may be interested in investigating the use of different approaches when teaching multiple languages, including established pedagogical approaches (e.g. task-based language teaching, computer-assisted language teaching) as well as pedagogical approaches that are still considered 'new' or 'innovative' (e.g. translanguaging, post-method). Calafato (2021a, 2021b) presents a good example of such research, in which he examined the implementation of multilingual teaching practices in teaching multiple languages. Finally, research on the pedagogical approaches in teaching multiple languages may also address the way a pedagogical approach might evolve when adapted for the teaching of multiple languages.

Another possible avenue for future research on the teaching of multiple languages would be the different combinations of languages that TMLs might possibly be teaching and how different combinations may impact TMLs' language teaching. In my study, Ann, Megan and Haruko each taught English with a globally dominant language (i.e. Chinese, Japanese and German). Researchers might want to study the experiences of TMLs teaching a globally dominant language and a lesser-known language or minority language.

Finally, researchers may want to take a broader look at the social contexts in which the teaching of multiple languages takes place. In particular, previous research as well as the study featured in this book have examined TMLs who taught multiple languages in a variety of circumstances, such as through an international exchange program (e.g. Ann) or teaching multiple languages domestically (e.g. Megan) (see also 'How and Why Language Teachers Become TMLs' in Chapter 2). Future research can examine and compare the impact of different social contexts on the teaching of multiple languages.

Researching TMLs

Building on the research presented in this book, future research on TMLs would focus on aspects of TMLs as multi-faceted, agentive language teachers. There is certainly a need for more narratives from TMLs of other demographic populations. Ann, Megan and Haruko are all female, under 40 years old and from developed countries or the Global North. Narratives featuring TMLs from a greater diversity of backgrounds, such as gender, age, class, geographic region or language learning experiences, would provide the opportunity for a broader understanding of the state of TMLs.

On the flipside, rather than focusing on TMLs' backgrounds, future research could focus on how language teachers' awareness and understanding of themselves as TMLs may have positive or negative impacts on their identities, emotions and overall teacher wellbeing. Furthermore, this line of research could also explore students' and parents' perceptions of TMLs.

Researching TML programs

Finally, future directions of TML research could focus on LTE programs for TMLs, or TML programs. One area of focus could be surveying the current approaches and topics covered when preparing language teachers to become TMLs in current LTE programs or other forms of professional development. Knowing what methods are being used and what topics are being discussed in TML programs will provide the foundation for future studies that can explore new ways of implementing TML LTE programs. Similarly, future research could also take a discourse analysis approach and survey the ways TML programs describe and frame TMLs, the teaching of multiple languages or TML careers in promotional materials, such as institutional websites, advertisements or job postings.

In addition, another important line of research on TML programs would be the impact of having professional development in teaching multiple languages, such as TML programs. Essentially, this would compare TMLs who had professional development with those who did not in relation to other factors, such as their approaches to teaching or their language teacher identities/emotions/beliefs.

Conclusion

My journey in conducting this study with Ann, Megan and Haruko and writing this book has been a continuous process of learning, discovery and understanding. In fact, this research was born out of realizing my own ignorance and biases in overlooking a major part of who some of the students and colleagues I had been working with nearly every day are as TMLs. Ann, Megan and Haruko's narratives in this book end at a certain point and I present recurring, overarching themes that contribute to language teaching research and from which readers can gain insight. But Ann, Megan and Haruko's actual language teaching careers will continue to grow and evolve in unexpected ways, as will the identities, emotions and beliefs they develop over time. Similarly, TML research is undoubtedly still in its infancy and there remains a lot to catch up on as we adapt new perspectives in language teaching research, re-examining prior research using a TML lens while also advancing new directions unique to TML research. For many scholars like me, this may begin with a re-examination of our very own personal and professional communities and searching for the ways TMLs are already part of our everyday lives. This is the connection I hope Ann, Megan and Haruko's narratives can make with readers – a spark inspiring the first steps toward greater awareness of TMLs and recognition of TML research in its own right.

Appendix A: Semi-Structured Interview Guide

Interview Session 1 (Past and Present Teaching Experiences)

(1) Please begin by thinking about *your whole teaching career so far* as if it were a book or novel with multiple chapters in it. Please describe very briefly what the main chapters in the book might be. Please give each chapter a title, tell me just a little bit about what each chapter is about and say a word or two about how we get from one chapter to the next.

(2) Please describe a moment that you would consider as *the high point* of your *teaching career*. This should be a moment when you felt particularly *positive*.

(3) Please describe a moment that you would consider as *the low point* of your *teaching career*. This should be a moment when you felt particularly *negative*.

(4) Please describe a moment that you would consider as *the turning point* of your *teaching career*.

(5) Please describe a moment in *your teacher training* that stands out as an especially *positive* experience.

(6) Please describe a moment in *your teacher training* that stands out as an especially *negative* experience.

(7) Please describe a moment in *your teaching career* that stands out as an especially *important, memorable or meaningful* experience.

(8) Please describe a moment in *your teaching career* in which you feel you displayed wisdom, perhaps acting in a wise way, making a wise decision or giving good advice.

(9) Please describe a moment in *your teaching career* in which you felt anxious, worried or doubtful of yourself as a teacher.

Interview Session 2 (Future Teaching Plans and Follow-Up Questions)

(10) Last week, you told me about the key chapters and scenes from your teaching career so far. Please describe what you see to be the next

chapters in your life. What is going to come next in your teaching career?

(11) Please describe your plans, dreams and hopes for the future. What do you hope to accomplish in the future in your teaching career?

(12) Are there any projects you are working on as part of your teaching career? This can be a project you are working on as part of your job (ex: establishing a new tutoring program for the university) or it can be something personal that you've created for yourself (ex: trying to use new materials this semester). Please describe any project that you are currently working on or plan to work on in the future. Tell me what the project is, how you got involved in the project or will get involved in the project, how the project might develop and why you think this project is important for you and/or for other people.

Appendix B: Guidelines for Written Teaching Philosophy Statement

The goal of the teaching philosophy is to describe your beliefs about language teaching and learning and how you've implemented those beliefs in your teaching.

Instructions

(1) Please use the following questions to write your teaching philosophy.
(2) Your teaching philosophy can be written in any language you prefer.
(3) Your teaching philosophy should be written in paragraph form (like the format of an essay), rather than answering the questions individually. It should be separated into three sections:
　　(a) your beliefs about language learning;
　　(b) your beliefs about language teaching;
　　(c) how your beliefs are connected to your teaching.
(4) Be sure to answer all of the 'required' questions. You can also answer the 'optional' questions if you like.
(5) There is no page limit. However, your teaching philosophy should include all three sections.

Approaches to Writing about Your Beliefs about Language Learning

- Think of your personal experiences as a language learner and teacher for all of the languages you have learned and/or taught.
- Describe specific examples of teaching strategies, assignments or lessons that give a detailed picture of your teaching.
- Using metaphors (e.g. learning a language is a journey) can be a way to help you describe abstract concepts of learning and teaching.

Content of the Teaching Philosophy

(1) Your beliefs about *language learning*
- Main questions (required):
  - What does 'learning a language' mean to you?

- – Have your beliefs about language learning changed over time? How?
- – How has teaching multiple languages influenced your beliefs about language learning?
- Other questions to consider (optional):
  - – In your opinion, what is 'effective learning'?
  - – How do you know when a student has successfully learned something?
  - – What has the biggest impact on your beliefs about language learning?

(2) Your beliefs about *language teaching*
- Main questions (required):
  - – What does 'teaching a language' mean to you?
  - – Have your beliefs about language teaching changed over time? How?
  - – How has teaching multiple languages influenced your beliefs about language teaching?
- Other questions to consider (optional):
  - – In your opinion, what is 'effective teaching'?
  - – How do you know when a teacher has successfully taught something?
  - – What has the biggest impact on your beliefs about language teaching?

(3) How your beliefs are *connected* to your teaching
- Main questions (required):
  - – How would you describe your teaching style? What is unique about your teaching?
  - – What teaching methods have been most effective for you?
  - – How is your teaching similar and/or different when you are teaching your T1 (the first language you ever taught) compared to your T2/T3 (the second/third language you taught)?
  - – How are your teaching styles/methods connected to your beliefs about learning and teaching?
- Other questions to consider (optional):
  - – What teaching strategies do you most often rely upon? Why?
  - – What are your strengths and skills as a teacher?
  - – What skills do you think are most important to teach in your classes and why?
  - – Which teaching tasks do you find most challenging?
  - – What are new teaching strategies or methods that you are experimenting with?
  - – What strategies have you used to evaluate and gather feedback on the effectiveness of your teaching?
  - – What areas of your teaching require improvement? Why? How do you intend to improve?
  - – What have you learned about yourself as a teacher?

Appendix C: Guidelines for Participant Photographs

Topic: Take a set of 6–12 photographs that represent your everyday life as a language teacher. This includes people, places, objects, actions, feelings or ideas that play a role in your daily routines as a language teacher.

Instructions

- Photographs do not necessarily have to be restricted to your classroom. You can take photographs outside the classroom as well, as long as they are related to your life as a language teacher.
- Photographs do not necessarily have to be restricted to images of teaching. You can take photographs of other activities that are related to your life as a language teacher.
- Photographs can be literal images of your everyday life as a teacher (e.g. a photograph of a classroom) or your photographs might be abstract representations of your everyday life as a teacher (e.g. a photograph of road traffic as a representation of the workload with which a teacher may be dealing).
- You are encouraged to take new photographs, though the use of existing photographs is allowed.
- Photographs can be taken using any method or device (e.g. smartphones, digital cameras, disposable cameras or polaroid cameras).

References

Adams, N.J. (2004) *Bilingualism and the Latin Language*. Cambridge: Cambridge University Press.

Adams, N.J., Janse, M. and Swain, S. (eds) (2002) *Bilingualism in Ancient Society: Language Contact and the Written Text*. Oxford: Oxford University Press.

Ahns, H. and Delesclefs, D. (2020) Insecurities, imposter syndrome, and native-speakeritis. In P. Stanley (ed.) *Critical Autoethnography and Intercultural Learning* (pp. 95–99). London: Routledge.

Ajayi, L. (2011) How ESL teachers' sociocultural identities mediate their teacher role identities in a diverse urban school setting. *The Urban Review* 43 (5), 654–680. https://doi.org/10.1007/s11256-010-0161-y.

Alleyne, B. (2014) *Narrative Networks: Storied Approaches in a Digital Age*. London: SAGE Publications.

Aneja, G.A. (2016) (Non)native speakered: Rethinking (non)nativeness and teacher identity in TESOL teacher education. *TESOL Quarterly* 50 (3), 572–596. https://doi.org/10.1002/tesq.315.

Ansah, G.N. (2014) Re-examining the fluctuations in language in-education policies in post-independence Ghana. *Multilingual Education* 4 (12), 1–15. https://doi.org/10.1186/s13616-014-0012-3.

Aoyama, R. (2021) Language teacher identity and English education policy in Japan: Competing discourses surrounding 'non-native' English-speaking teachers. *RELC Journal* https://doi.org/10.1177/00336882211032999.

Arias, M.B. and Fee, M. (eds) (2018) *Profiles of Dual Language Education in the 21st Century*. Bristol: Multilingual Matters.

Aronin, L. and Singleton, D. (2008) Multilingualism as a new linguistic dispensation. *International Journal of Multilingualism* 5 (1), 1–16.

Aslan, E. (2015) When the native is also a non-native: 'Retrodicting' the complexity of language teacher cognition. *Canadian Modern Language Review* 71 (3), 244–269.

Aydarova, E. (2017) 'I want a beautiful life': Divergent chronotopes in English language teacher education. *Critical Inquiry in Language Studies* 14 (4), 263–293.

Bagnoli, A. (2009) Beyond the standard interview: The use of graphic elicitation and arts-based methods. *Qualitative Research* 9 (5), 547–570. https://doi.org/10.1177/1468794109343625.

Banda, F. (2009) Critical perspectives on language planning and policy in Africa: Accounting for the notion of multilingualism. *Stellenbosch Papers in Linguistics PLUS* 38, 1–11.

Banks, M. and Zeitlyn, D. (2015) *Visual Methods in Social Research* (2nd edn). Thousand Oaks, CA: SAGE Publications.

Barcelos, A.M.F. (2003) Researching beliefs about SLA: A critical review. In P. Kalaja and A.M.F. Barcelos (eds) *Beliefs about SLA: New Research Approaches* (pp. 7–33). New York: Springer.

Barcelos, A.M.F. (2015) Unveiling the relationship between language learning beliefs, emotions, and identities. *Studies in Second Language Learning and Teaching* 5 (2), 301–325.

Barcelos, A.M.F. (2017) Identities as emotioning and believing. In G. Barkhuizen (ed.) *Reflections on Language Teacher Identity Research* (pp. 145–150). New York: Routledge.

Barcelos, A.M.F. and Kalaja, P. (2011) Introduction to beliefs about SLA revisited. *System* 39 (3), 281–289.

Barkhuizen, G. (2009) An extended positioning analysis of a pre-service teacher's better life small story. *Applied Linguistics* 31 (2), 282–300. https://doi.org/10.1093/applin/amp027.

Barkhuizen, G. (2011) Narrative knowledging in TESOL. *TESOL Quarterly* 45 (3), 391–414.

Barkhuizen, G. (2013) Introduction: Narrative research in applied linguistics. In G. Barkhuizen (ed.) *Narrative Research in Applied Linguistics* (pp. 1–17). Cambridge: Cambridge University Press.

Barkhuizen, G. (2016) Narrative approaches to exploring language, identity and power in language teacher education. *RELC Journal* 47 (1), 25–42. https://doi.org/10.1177/0033688216631222.

Barkhuizen, G. (2017) Language teacher identity research: An introduction. In G. Barkhuizen (ed.) *Reflections on Language Teacher Identity Research* (pp. 1–11). New York: Routledge.

Barkhuizen, G. (2018) The centrality of story in teacher inquiry. In D. Xerri and C. Pioquinto (eds) *Becoming Research Literate: Supporting Teacher Research in English Language Teaching* (pp. 110–115). Sursee: ETAS.

Barkhuizen, G. and Mendieta, J. (2020) Teacher identity and good language teachers. In C. Griffiths and Z. Tajeddin (eds) *Lessons from Good Language Teachers* (pp. 3–16). Cambridge: Cambridge University Press.

Barkhuizen, G., Benson, P. and Chik, A. (2014) *Narrative Inquiry in Language Teaching and Learning Research*. Abingdon: Routledge.

Basturkmen, H. (2012) Review of research into the correspondence between language teachers' stated beliefs and practices. *System* 40, 282–295.

Bates, E.A., McCann, J.J., Kaye, L.K. and Taylor, J.C. (2017) 'Beyond words': A researcher's guide to using photo elicitation in psychology. *Qualitative Research in Psychology* 14 (4), 459–481. https://doi.org/10.1080/14780887.2017.1359352.

Benesch, S. (2017) *Emotions and English Language Teaching: Exploring Teachers' Emotion Labor*. New York: Routledge.

Benesch, S. (2018) Emotions as agency: Feeling rules, emotion labor, and English language teachers' decision-making. *System* 79, 60–69.

Benesch, S. (2019) Feeling rules and emotion labor: A poststructural-discursive approach to English language teachers' emotions. In X. Gao (ed.) *Second Handbook of English Language Teaching* (pp. 1111–1130). Cham: Springer.

Benesch, S. (2020) Theorising emotions from a critical perspective: English language teachers' emotion labour when responding to student writing. In C. Gkonou, J.M. Dewaele and J. King (eds) *The Emotional Rollercoaster of Language Teaching* (pp. 53–69). Bristol: Multilingual Matters.

Benson, P. (2014) Narrative inquiry in applied linguistics research. *Annual Review of Applied Linguistics* 34, 154–170. https://doi.org/10.1017/S0267190514000099.

Bernat, E. (2008) Towards a pedagogy of empowerment: The case of 'impostor syndrome' among pre-service non-native speaker teachers of TESOL. *English Language Teacher Education and Development Journal* 11, 1–8. http://www.elted.net/issues/volume-11/1%20Bernat.pdf.

Biville, F. (2002) The Graeco-Romans and Graeco-Latin: A terminological framework for cases of bilingualism. In J.N. Adams, M. Janse and S. Swain (eds) *Bilingualism in Ancient Society: Language Contact and the Written Text* (pp. 77–102). Oxford: Oxford University Press.

Blachford, D.R. and Jones, M. (eds) (2011) Trilingual education policy ideals and realities for the Naxi in Rural Yunnan. In A. Feng (ed.) *English Language Education Across Greater China* (pp. 228–259). Bristol: Multilingual Matters.

Blair, A. (2012) Who do you think you are? Investigating the multiple identities of speakers of other languages teaching English. Unpublished doctoral dissertation, University of Sussex.

Blair, A. (2015) Evolving a post-native, multilingual model for ELF-aware teacher education. In Y. Bayyurt and S. Akcan (eds) *Current Perspectives on Pedagogy for English as a Lingua Franca* (pp. 89–102). Berlin: De Gruyter.

Block, D. (2015) Researching language and identity. In B. Paltridge and A. Phakti (eds) *Research Methods in Applied Linguistics* (pp. 527–540). London: Bloomsbury.

Borg, S. (2003) Teacher cognition in language teaching: A review of research on what teachers think, know, believe and do. *Language Teacher* 36, 81–109.

Borg, S. (2011) The impact of in-service teacher education on language teachers' beliefs. *System* 39 (3), 370–380.

Borg, S. (2018) Teachers' beliefs and classroom practices. In P. Garrett and J.M. Cots (eds) *The Routledge Handbook of Language Awareness* (pp. 75–91). New York: Routledge.

Bouchard, J. (2018) Native-speakerism in Japanese junior high schools: A stratified look into teacher narratives. In S.A. Houghton and K. Hashimoto (eds) *Towards Post-Native-Speakerism: Dynamics and Shifts* (pp. 17–40). Singapore: Springer.

Bourdieu, P. (1990) *The Logic of Practice* (trans. R. Nice). Stanford, CA: Stanford University Press.

Brandão, A.C.L. (2019) Imagining second language teaching in Brazil: What stories do student teachers draw? In P. Kalaja and S. Melo-Pfeifer (eds) *Visualizing Multilingual Lives: More than Words* (pp. 197–213). Bristol: Multilingual Matters.

Brandão, A.C.L. (2021) First experiences of teaching EFL in metaphors. *Teaching and Teacher Education* 97, 103214.

Bronfenbrenner, U. (1979) *The Ecology of Human Development: Experiments by Nature and Design.* Cambridge, MA: Harvard University Press.

Brown, H. (2014) Contextual factors driving the growth of undergraduate English medium instruction programmes at universities in Japan. *The Asian Journal of Applied Linguistics* 1 (1), 50–63.

Bureau of Educational and Cultural Affairs Exchange Programs (2021) Participant story: Blind student finds new confidence teaching in a foreign country. *Bureau of Educational and Cultural Affairs Exchange Programs.* See https://exchanges.state.gov/non -us/program/fulbright-foreign-language-teaching-assistant-flta/stories/blind-student -finds-new-confidence-teaching-foreign-country (accessed 23 October 2021).

Cabrera, M.V. (2017) The construction of teacher candidates' imaginaries and identities in Canada, Colombia, and Chile: An international comparative multiple narrative case study. Unpublished doctoral dissertation, University of Toronto.

Calafato, R. (2019) The non-native speaker teacher as proficient multilingual: A critical review of research from 2009–2018. *Lingua* 227, 1–25.

Calafato, R. (2020) Language teacher multilingualism in Norway and Russia: Identity and beliefs. *European Journal of Education* 55 (4), 602–617.

Calafato, R. (2021a) 'I feel like it's giving me a lot as a language teacher to be a learner myself': Factors affecting the implementation of a multilingual pedagogy as reported by teachers of diverse languages. *Studies in Second Language Learning and Teaching* 11 (4), 579–606.

Calafato, R. (2021b) Teachers' reported implementation of multilingual teaching practices in foreign language classrooms in Norway and Russia. *Teaching and Teacher Education* 105, 103401.

Canagarajah, S. and Liyanage, I. (2012) Lessons from pre-colonial multilingualism. In M. Martin-Jones, A. Blackledge and A. Creese (eds) *The Routledge Handbook of Multilingualism* (pp. 49–65). London: Routledge.

Celani, M.A.A. (2010) Perguntas ainda sem resposta na formação de professores de línguas. In T. Gimenez and M.C. de G. Monteiro (eds) *Formação de professors de língua na América Latina e transformação social* (pp. 57–67). Campinas: Pontes Editores.

Cenoz, J. (2013) Defining multilingualism. *Annual Review of Applied Linguistics* 33, 3–18.

Cenoz, J. and Gorter, D. (2019) Multilingualism, translanguaging, and minority languages in SLA. *The Modern Language Journal* 103 (S1), 130–135. https://doi.org/10.1111/modl.12529.

Chang, Y.J. (2018) Certified but not qualified? EFL pre-service teachers in liminality. *Journal of Language, Identity & Education* 17 (1), 48–62. https://doi.org/10.1080/15348458.2017.1401929.

Chen, S.C. (2006) Simultaneous promotion of indigenisation and internationalisation: New language-in-education policy in Taiwan. *Language and Education* 20 (4), 322–337. https://doi.org/10.2167/le632.0.

Cheung, Y.L. (2015) Teacher identity in ELT/TESOL: A research review. In Y.L. Cheung, S.B. Said and K. Park (eds) *Advances and Current Trends in Language Teacher Identity Research* (pp. 175–185). London: Routledge.

Christian, D. (2016) Dual language education: Current research perspectives. *International Multilingual Research Journal* 10 (1), 1–5.

Clandinin, D.J. (2016) *Engaging in Narrative Inquiry*. Abingdon: Routledge.

Clandinin, D.J. (2020) *Journeys in Narrative Inquiry: The Selected Works of D. Jean Clandinin*. London: Routledge.

Clandinin, D.J. and Connelly, F. (2000) *Narrative Inquiry: Experience and Story in Qualitative Research*. San Francisco, CA: Jossey-Bass.

Clandinin, D.J. and Rosiek, J. (2007) Mapping a landscape of narrative inquiry: Borderland spaces and tensions. In D.J. Clandinin (ed.) *Handbook of Narrative Inquiry: Mapping a Methodology* (pp. 35–76). Thousand Oaks, CA: SAGE Publications.

Clandinin, D.J. and Caine, V. (2008) Narrative inquiry. In L.M. Given (ed.) *The SAGE Encyclopedia of Qualitative Research Methods* (pp. 542–544). Thousand Oaks, CA: SAGE Publications.

Clark, E. and Paran, A. (2007) The employability of nonnative speaker teachers of EFL: A UK survey. *System* 35, 407–430. https://doi.org/10.1016/j.system.2007.05.002.

Clarke, M. (2008) *Language Teacher Identities: Co-constructing Discourse and Community*. Clevedon: Multilingual Matters.

Classen, A. (2013) Multilingualism in the middle ages and the early modern age: The literary-historical evidence. *Neophilologus* 97 (1), 131–145.

Collier Jr, J. (1957) Photography in anthropology: A report on two experiments. *American Anthropologist* 59, 843–859.

Connelly, F.M. and Clandinin, D.J. (1990) Stories of experience and narrative inquiry. *Educational Researcher* 19 (5), 2–14. https://doi.org/10.3102/0013189X019005002.

Cook, V. (1991) The poverty-of-the-stimulus argument and multicompetence. *Second Language Research* 7 (2), 103–117. https://doi.org/10.1177/026765839100700203.

Cook, V. (1999) Going beyond the native speaker in language teaching. *TESOL Quarterly* 33 (2), 185–209. https://doi.org/10.2307/3587717.

Cook, V. (2016) Premises of multi-competence. In V. Cook and Li Wei (eds) *The Cambridge Handbook of Linguistic Multi-competence* (pp. 1–25). Cambridge: Cambridge University Press.

Cooper, A.C. and Bryan, K.C. (2020) Reading, writing, and race: Sharing the narratives of black TESOL professionals. In B. Yazan and K. Lindahl (eds) *Language Teacher Identity in TESOL: Teacher Education and Practice as Identity Work* (pp. 125–142). Abingdon: Routledge.

Cortazzi, M. and Jin, L.X. (1996) English teaching and learning in China. *Language Teaching* 29, 61–80.

Cox, M.I.P. and Assis-Peterson, A.A. (2008) O drama do ensino de inglês na escola pública brasileira. In A.A. Assis-Peterson (ed.) *Línguas estrangeiras: para além do método* (pp. 19–54). Cuiabá: EdUFMT.

Creswell, J.W. (2008) *Educational Research: Planning, Conducting, and Evaluating Quantitative and Qualitative Research* (2nd edn). Upper Saddle River, NJ: Pearson.

Creswell, J.W. (2013) *Qualitative Inquiry and Research Design: Choosing among Five Approaches* (3rd edn). Thousand Oaks, CA: SAGE Publications.

Creswell, J.W. and Poth, C.N. (2018) *Qualitative Inquiry and Research Design: Choosing Among Five Approaches* (4th edn). Thousand Oaks, CA: SAGE Publications.

Critten, R.G. and Dutton, E. (2021) Medieval English multilingualisms. *Language Learning* 71 (S1), 12–38.

Cross, D.I. and Hong, J.Y. (2009) Beliefs and professional identity: Critical constructs in examining the impact of reform on the emotional experiences of teachers. In P.A. Schultz and M. Zembylas (eds) *Advances in Teacher Emotion Research: The Impact of Teachers' Lives* (pp. 273–296). New York: Springer.

Darvin, R. and Norton, B. (2015) Identity and a model of investment in applied linguistics. *Annual Review of Applied Linguistics* 35, 36–56. https://doi.org/10.1017/S0267190514000191.

Davies, A. (2003) *The Native Speaker: Myth and Reality*. Clevedon: Multilingual Matters.

De Costa, P.I. (2015) Tracing reflexivity through narrative and identity lens. In Y.L. Cheung, S.B. Said and K. Park (eds) *Advances and Current Trends in Language Teacher Identity Research* (pp. 135–147). London: Routledge.

De Costa, P. (2019) Elite multilingualism, affect and neoliberalism. *Journal of Multilingual and Multicultural Development* 40 (5), 453–460.

De Costa, P.I. and Norton, B. (2016) Identity in language learning and teaching: Research agendas for the future. In S. Preece (ed.) *The Routledge Handbook of Language and Identity* (pp. 586–601). London: Routledge.

De Costa, P.I. and Norton, B. (2017) Introduction: Identity, transdisciplinarity, and the good language teacher. *The Modern Language Journal* 101 (S1), 3–14. https://doi.org/10.1111/modl.12368.

De Costa, P., Park, J. and Wee, L. (2016) Language learning as linguistic entrepreneurship: Implications for language education. *The Asia-Pacific Education Researcher* 25 (5), 695–702.

De Costa, P.I., Li, W. and Rawal, H. (2019) Language teacher emotions. In M.A. Peters (ed.) *Encyclopedia of Teacher Education* (pp. 1–4). New York: Springer.

De Costa, P.I., Park, J.S.Y. and Wee, L. (2021) Why linguistic entrepreneurship?. *Multilingua* 40 (2), 139–153.

Dewaele, J. (2010) *Emotions in Multiple Languages*. Basingstoke: Palgrave Macmillan.

Dewaele, J.M. (2018) Why the dichotomy 'L1 versus LX user' is better than 'native versus non-native speaker'. *Applied Linguistics* 39 (2), 236–240.

Dewaele, J.M., Gkonou, C. and Mercer, S. (2018) Do ESL/EFL teachers' emotional intelligence, teaching experience, proficiency and gender affect their classroom practice? In J.D.M. Agudo (ed.) *Emotions in Second Language Teaching* (pp. 125–141). Cham: Springer.

Dobinson, T. and Mercieca, P. (2020) Seeing things as they are, not just as we are: Investigating linguistic racism on an Australian university campus. *International Journal of Bilingual Education and Bilingualism* 23 (7), 789–803. https://doi.org/10.1080/13670050.2020.1724074.

Domínguez-Fret, N. and Oberto, E.E. (2022) Untapped potential: The current state of dual language education in Chicago public schools. *Bilingual Research Journal* 45 (1), 61–81. https://doi.org/10.1080/15235882.2022.2095541.

Douglas Fir Group (2016) A transdisciplinary framework for SLA in a multilingual world. *The Modern Language Journal* 100 (S1), 19–47. https://doi.org/10.1111/modl.12301.

Dovchin, S. (2020) The psychological damages of linguistic racism and international students in Australia. *International Journal of Bilingual Education and Bilingualism* 23 (7), 804–818. https://doi.org/10.1080/13670050.2020.1759504.

Duff, P.A. (2019) Social dimensions and processes in second language acquisition: Multilingual socialization in transnational contexts. *The Modern Language Journal* 103 (S1), 6–22. https://doi.org/10.1111/modl.12534.

Early, M., Kendrick, M. and Potts, D. (2015) Multimodality: Out from the margins of English language teaching. *TESOL Quarterly* 49 (3), 447–460. https://doi.org/10.1002/tesq.246.

Edwards, E. and Burns, A. (2016) Language teacher–researcher identity negotiation: An ecological perspective. *TESOL Quarterly* 50 (3), 735–745. https://doi.org/10.1002/tesq.313.

Ellis, C. (2004) *The Ethnographic I: A Methodological Novel about Autoethnography.* Oxford: Rowman & Littlefield.

Ellis, E.M. (2004) The invisible multilingual teacher: The contribution of language background to Australian ESL teachers' professional knowledge and beliefs. *International Journal of Multilingualism* 1 (2), 90–108.

Ellis, E. (2016) *The Plurilingual TESOL Teacher: The Hidden Languaged Lives of TESOL Teachers and Why They Matter.* Boston, MA: De Gruyter Mouton.

Elmquist, A.M. (1970) Professional attitudes of high school modern language teachers in Texas. Unpublished doctoral dissertation, Texas A&M University.

Elsheikh, A. and Yahia, E. (2020) Language teacher professional identity. In C. Coombe, N.J. Anderson and L. Stephenson (eds) *Professionalizing Your English Language Teaching* (pp. 27–38). Cham: Springer.

Ely, M., Anzul, M., Friedman, T., Garner, D. and Steinmatz, A.M. (1991) *Doing Qualitative Research: Circles within Circles.* London: The Falmer Press.

Faez, F. (2011) Reconceptualizing the native/nonnative speaker dichotomy. *Journal of Language, Identity & Education* 10 (4), 231–249. https://doi.org/10.1080/15348458.2011.598127.

Fairley, M.J. (2020) Conceptualizing language teacher education centered on language teacher identity development: A competencies-based approach and practical applications. *TESOL Quarterly* 54 (4), 1037–1064.

Fan, F. and de Jong, E.J. (2019) Exploring professional identities of nonnative-English-speaking teachers in the United States: A narrative case study. *TESOL Journal* 10 (4), e495.

Farrell, T.S. and Bennis, K. (2013) Reflecting on ESL teacher beliefs and classroom practices: A case study. *RELC Journal* 44 (2), 163–176.

Farrell, T.S. and Ives, J. (2015) Exploring teacher beliefs and classroom practices through reflective practice: A case study. *Language Teaching Research* 19 (5), 594–610.

Flores, N. and Rosa, J. (2019) Bringing race into second language acquisition. *The Modern Language Journal* 103 (S1), 145–151. https://doi.org/10.1111/modl.12523.

Flowerdew, J. and Miller, L. (2013) Narrative inquiry in a second language context: Stories from Hong Kong. In G. Barkhuizen (ed.) *Narrative Research in Applied Linguistics* (pp. 41–61). Cambridge: Cambridge University Press.

Flynn, K. and Gulikers, G. (2001) Issues in hiring nonnative English-speaking professionals to teach English as a second language. *CATESOL Journal* 13 (1), 151–161.

Fogle, L.W. and Moser, K. (2017) Language teacher identities in the Southern United States: Transforming rural schools. *Journal of Language, Identity & Education* 16 (2), 65–79.

Free University of Bozen-Bolzano (2021) *Laurea magistrale a ciclo unico in Scienze della Formazione primaria.* See https://www.unibz.it/it/faculties/education/master-primary-education/ (accessed October 2021).

Fresacher, C. (2016) Why and how to use positive psychology activities in the second language classroom. In P.D. MacIntyre, T. Gregersen and S. Mercer (eds) *Positive Psychology in SLA* (pp. 344–358). Bristol: Multilingual Matters.

Fulbright Foreign Student Program (2021) Fulbright Foreign Language Teaching Assistant (FLTA) Program. *Fulbright Foreign Student Program.* See https://foreign.fulbrighton-line.org/about/flta-program (accessed 23 October 2021).

Gagné, A., Herath, S. and Valencia, M. (2018) Exploring privilege and marginalization in ELT: A trioethnography of three diverse educators. In B. Yazan and N. Rudolph (eds) *Criticality, Teacher Identity, and (In)equity in English Language Teaching* (pp. 237–256). Cham: Springer.

Gao, X. (2019) The Douglas Fir Group framework as a resource map for language teacher education. *The Modern Language Journal* 103, 161–166. https://doi.org/10.1111/modl.12526.

García, O. (2009) *Bilingual Education in the 21st Century: A Global Perspective.* Chichester: Wiley-Blackwell.

García, O. and Li, W. (2014) *Translanguaging: Language, Bilingualism and Education.* Basingstoke: Palgrave Macmillan.

Gaskell, G. and Bauer, M.W. (2000) Towards public accountability: Beyond sampling, reliability and validity. In M.W. Bauer and G. Gaskell (eds) *Qualitative Researching with Text, Image and Sound* (pp. 336–350). Thousand Oaks, CA: SAGE Publications.

Gimenez, T., Ferreira, A.D.J., Alves Basso, R.A. and Carvalho Cruvinel, R. (2016) Policies for English language teacher education in Brazil today: Preliminary remarks. *Profile: Issues in Teachers' Professional Development* 18 (1), 219–234.

Giroir, S. (2014) Narratives of participation, identity, and positionality: Two cases of Saudi learners of English in the United States. *TESOL Quarterly* 48 (1), 34–56. https://doi.org/10.1002/tesq.95.

Gkonou, C. and Mercer, S. (2017) Understanding emotional and social intelligence among english language teachers. *British Council.* See https://www.teachingenglish.org.uk/sites/teacheng/files/pub_G211_ELTRA_Gkonou%20and%20Mercer%20paper_FINAL_web.pdf (accessed 26 January 2023).

Golombek, P. and Jordan, S.R. (2005) Becoming 'Black Lambs' not 'Parrots': A poststructuralist orientation to intelligibility and identity. *TESOL Quarterly* 39 (3), 513–533. https://doi.org/10.2307/3588492.

Gor, K. and Vatz, K. (2009) Less commonly taught languages: Issues in learning and teaching. In M.H. Long and C.J. Doughty (eds) *The Handbook of Language Teaching* (pp. 234–249). Malden, MA: Wiley-Blackwell.

Graham, K.M. and Yeh, Y.F. (2022) Teachers' implementation of bilingual education in Taiwan: Challenges and arrangements. *Asia Pacific Education Review.* https://doi.org/10.1007/s12564-022-09791-4.

Gregersen, T., MacIntyre, P.D. and Meza, M. (2016) Positive psychology exercises build social capital for language learners: Preliminary evidence. In P.D. MacIntyre, T. Gregersen and S. Mercer (eds) *Positive Psychology in SLA* (pp. 147–167). Bristol: Multilingual Matters.

Gregersen, T., Mercer, S., MacIntyre, P., Talbot, K. and Banga, C.A. (2020) Understanding language teacher wellbeing: An ESM study of daily stressors and uplifts. *Language Teaching Research* 27 (4), 1–22.

Grosjean, F. (1985) The bilingual as a competent but specific speaker–hearer. *Journal of Multilingual and Multicultural Development* 6 (6), 467–477. https://doi.org/10.1080/01434632.1985.9994221.

Grosjean, F. (1989) Neurolinguists, beware! The bilingual is not two monolinguals in one person. *Brain and Language* 36 (1), 3–15. https://doi.org/10.1016/0093-934X(89)90048-5.

Grosjean, F. (1994) Individual bilingualism. In R.E. Asher (ed.) *The Encyclopaedia of Language and Linguistics* (pp. 1656–1660). Oxford: Pergamon Press.

Guskey, T.R. (2002) Professional development and teacher change. *Teachers and Teaching* 8 (3), 381–391.

Hall, J.K. (2019a) *Essentials of SLA for L2 Teachers: A Transdisciplinary Framework.* New York: Routledge.

Hall, J.K. (2019b) The contributions of conversation analysis and interactional linguistics to a usage-based understanding of language: Expanding the transdisciplinary framework. *The Modern Language Journal* 103 (S1), 80–94. https://doi.org/10.1111/modl .12535.

Hallman, H. (2015) Teacher identity as dialogic response: A Bakhtinian perspective. In Y.L. Cheung, S.B. Said and K. Park (eds) *Advances and Current Trends in Language Teacher Identity Research* (pp. 3–15). London: Routledge.

Haneda, M. and Sherman, B. (2016) A job-crafting perspective on teacher agentive action. *TESOL Quarterly* 50 (3), 745–754. https://doi.org/10.1002/tesq.318.

Harper, D. (2002) Talking about pictures: A case for photo elicitation. *Visual Studies* 17 (1), 13–26. https://doi.org/10.1080/14725860220137345.

Harrison, B. (2002) Photographic visions and narrative inquiry. *Narrative Inquiry* 12 (1), 87–111. https://doi.org/10.1075/ni.12.1.14har.

Hashimoto, K. (2018) 'Mother tongue speakers' or 'native speakers'?: Assumptions surrounding the teaching of Japanese as a foreign language in Japan. In S.A. Houghton and K. Hashimoto (eds) *Towards Post-Native-Speakerism: Dynamics and Shifts* (pp. 61–78). Singapore: Springer.

Haukås, Å. (2016) Teachers' beliefs about multilingualism and a multilingual pedagogical approach. *International Journal of Multilingualism* 13 (1), 1–18.

Hayes, D. (2013) Narratives of experience: Teaching English in Sri Lanka and Thailand. In G. Barkhuizen (ed.) *Narrative Research in Applied Linguistics* (pp. 62–84). Cambridge: Cambridge University Press.

Hayes, D. (2017) Narratives of identity: Reflections on English language teachers, teaching, and educational opportunity. In G. Barkhuizen (ed.) *Reflections on Language Teacher Identity Research* (pp. 145–150). New York: Routledge.

Helgesen, M. (2017) Jobs, careers and callings: Adapting positive psychology tasks for use in ESL/EFL and other language classes and teacher education. In T.S. Gregersen and P.D. MacIntyre (eds) *Innovative Practices in Language Teacher Education: Spanning the Spectrum from Intra- to Inter-personal Professional Development* (pp. 165–183). Cham: Springer. https://doi.org/10.1007/978-3-319-51789-6_8.

Hesse-Biber, S.N. (2007) The practice of feminist in-depth interviewing. In S.N. Hesse-Biber and P.L. Leavy (eds) *Feminist Research Practice* (pp. 111–148). Thousand Oaks, CA: SAGE Publications.

Higgins, C. and Ponte, E. (2017) Legitimating multilingual teacher identities in the mainstream classroom. *The Modern Language Journal* 101 (S1), 15–28.

Hiver, P. (2016) The triumph over experience: Hope and hardiness in novice L2 teachers. In P.D. MacIntyre, T. Gregersen and S. Mercer (eds) *Positive Psychology in SLA* (pp. 168–192). Bristol: Multilingual Matters.

Holliday, A. (2015) Native-speakerism: Taking the concept forward and achieving cultural belief. In A. Swan, P. Aboshiha and A. Holliday (eds) *(En)Countering Native-Speakerism: Global Perspectives* (pp. 11–25). London: Palgrave Macmillan.

Horwitz, E.K., Horwitz, M.B. and Cope, J. (1986) Foreign language classroom anxiety. *The Modern Language Journal* 70 (2), 125–132.

Houghton, S.A. and Hashimoto, K. (eds) (2018) *Towards Post-Native-Speakerism: Dynamics and Shifts.* Singapore: Springer.

Hu, G. (2002) The People's Republic of China Country report: English language teaching in the People's Republic of China. In R. Silver and G. Hu (eds) *English Language Education in China, Japan, and Singapore* (pp. 1–77). Singapore: National Institute of Education, Nanyang Technological University.

HU University of Applied Sciences Utrecht (2021a) During the [teacher education in French] programme. See https://www.internationalhu.com/bachelor-programmes/teacher-education-in-french/during-the-programme (accessed 1 October 2021).

HU University of Applied Sciences Utrecht (2021b) During the [teacher education in German] programme. See https://www.internationalhu.com/bachelor-programmes/teacher-education-in-german/during-the-programme (accessed 1 October 2021).

HU University of Applied Sciences Utrecht (2021c) During the [teacher education in Spanish] programme. See https://www.internationalhu.com/bachelor-programmes/teacher-education-in-spanish/during-the-programme (accessed 1 October 2021).

Hurst, N. (2018) Learning teaching: Research and reporting in the post-graduate language teaching practicum at the Faculty of Letters, the University of Porto, Portugal. In Å. Carvalho, J.D.D. Almeida, N. Hurst, R. Ponce de León and S. Tomé (eds) *As línguas estrangeiras no ensino superior: Balanço, estratégias e desafios futuros* (pp. 161–172). Porta: FLUP e-DITA.

Jain, R. (2014) Global Englishes, translingual practices, and translinguistic identities in a community college ESL classroom: A practitioner researcher reports. *TESOL Journal* 5 (3), 490–522. https://doi.org/10.1002/tesj.155s.

Jain, R. (2018) Alternative terms for NNESTs. In J.I. Liontas (ed.) *The TESOL Encyclopedia of English Language Teaching* (pp. 1–5). New York: John Wiley & Sons.

Jenkins, J. (2003) *World Englishes: A Resource Book for Students*. New York: Psychology Press.

Jessner, U. (2008a) A DST model of multilingualism and the role of metalinguistic awareness. *The Modern Language Journal* 92 (2), 270–283.

Jessner, U. (2008b) Teaching third languages: Findings, trends and challenges. *Language Teaching* 41 (1), 15–56. https://doi.org/10.1017/S0261444807004739.

Jessner, U. (2014) On multilingual awareness or why the multilingual learner is a specific language learner. In M. Pawlak and L. Aronin (eds) *Essential Topics in Applied Linguistics and Multilingualism: Studies in Honor of David Singleton* (pp. 175–184). Dordrecht: Springer.

Jin, J., Mercer, S., Babic, S. and Mairitsch, A. (2021) 'You just appreciate every little kindness': Chinese language teachers' wellbeing in the UK. *System* 96, 1–12.

Johnson, K.E. (2019) The relevance of a transdisciplinary framework for SLA in language teacher education. *The Modern Language Journal* 103, 167–174. https://doi.org/10.1111/modl.12524.

Jørgensen, J.N. (2008) Polylingual languaging around and among children and adolescents. *International Journal of Multilingualism* 5, 161–176.

Kachru, B. (1992) *The Other Tongue: English across Cultures*. Urbana, IL: University of Illinois Press.

Kadowaki, K. (2018) Japanese native speaker teachers at high schools in South Korea and Thailand. In S.A. Houghton and K. Hashimoto (eds) *Towards Post-Native-Speakerism: Dynamics and Shifts* (pp. 97–112). Singapore: Springer.

Kagan, D.M. (1992) Implications of research on teachers' belief. *Educational Psychologist* 27 (1), 65–90.

Kalaja, P., Barcelos, A.M.F., Aro, M. and Ruohotie-Lyhty, M. (eds) (2016) *Beliefs, Agency and Identity in Foreign Language Learning and Teaching*. Basingstoke: Palgrave Macmillan.

Kamiya, N. (2018) Teacher and student beliefs. In J. Liontas (ed.) *TESOL Encyclopedia of English Language Teaching Vol. II* (1st edn, pp. 1–6). New York: John Wiley & Sons.

Kang, D.M. (2020) An elementary school EFL teacher's emotional intelligence and emotional labor. *Journal of Language, Identity & Education* 21 (1), 1–14.

Kanno, Y. and Stuart, C. (2011) Learning to become a second language teacher: Identities-in-practice. *The Modern Language Journal* 95 (2), 236–252. https://doi.org/10.1111/j.1540-4781.2011.01178.x.

Kayi-Aydar, H. (2015a) Multiple identities, negotiations, and agency across time and space: A narrative inquiry of a foreign language teacher candidate. *Critical Inquiry in Language Studies* 12 (2), 137–160. https://doi.org/10.1080/15427587.2015.1032076.

Kayi-Aydar, H. (2015b) Teacher agency, positioning, and English language learners: Voices of pre-service classroom teachers. *Teaching and Teacher Education* 45, 94–103.

Kayi-Aydar, H. (2019) Language teacher identity. *Language Teaching* 52 (3), 281–295. https://doi.org/10.1017/S0261444819000223.

Kim, E.G. (2017) English medium instruction in Korean higher education: Challenges and future directions. In B. Fenton-Smith, P. Humphreys and I. Walkinshaw (eds) *English Medium Instruction in Higher Education in Asia-Pacific: From Policy to Pedagogy* (pp. 53–69). Cham: Springer.

Kim, J. and Smith, H.Y. (2019) Beyond nativeness versus nonnativeness in the construction of teacher identity in the context of Korean as a foreign language. *The Sociolinguistic Journal of Korea* 27 (2), 25–50.

Kim, J. and Smith, H.Y. (2020) Negotiation of emotions in emerging language teacher identity of graduate instructors. *System* 95, 1–10.

Kioko, A.N., Ndung'u, R.W., Njoroge, M.C. and Mutiga, J. (2014) Mother tongue and education in Africa: Publicising the reality. *Multilingual Education* 4 (18), 1–11. https://doi.org/10.1186/s13616-014-0018-x.

Kirkpatrick, A. (2010) English as an Asian Lingua Franca and the multilingual model of ELT. *Language Teaching* 44 (2), 212–224. https://doi.org/10.1017/S0261444810000145.

Kocabaş-Gedik, P. and Ortaçtepe Hart, D. (2021) 'It's not like that at all': A poststructuralist case study on language teacher identity and emotional labor. *Journal of Language, Identity & Education* 20 (2), 103–117.

Koehn, P.H. and Rosenau, J.N. (2002) Transnational competence in an emergent epoch. *International Studies Perspectives* 3 (2), 105–127. https://doi.org/10.1111/1528-3577.00084.

Kramsch, C. (2014) Teaching foreign languages in an era of globalization: Introduction. *The Modern Language Journal* 98 (1), 296–311.

Kramsch, C. and Zhang, L. (2018) *The Multilingual Instructor*. [Ebook version.] Oxford: Oxford University Press. https://global.oup.com/academic/product/the-multilingual-instructor-9780194217378?lang=en&cc=au.

Krashen, S. (1982) *Principles and Practice in Second Language Acquisition*. New York: Prentice-Hall International.

Krawczyk-Neifar, E. (2017) Bilingual teacher training: Failure or success? A students' and teachers' perspective. In D. Gabryś-Barker, D. Gałajda, A. Wojtaszek and P. Zakrajewski (eds) *Multiculturalism, Multilingualism and the Self* (pp. 171–184). Cham: Springer.

Ku, E.K. (2020) *Dear Eric*: An autoethnodrama of exploring professional legitimacy as a transnational EFL instructor. In B. Yazan, S. Canagarajah and R. Jain (eds) *Autoethnographies in ELT: Transnational Identities, Pedagogies, and Practices* (pp. 88–106). New York: Routledge.

Ku, E.K. and Liu, Y-T. (2021) Integrating language teacher identity into competency-based language teacher education. In A.Y. Wang (ed.) *Competency-Based Teacher Education for English as a Foreign Language: Theory, Research and Practice* (pp. 39–56). Abingdon: Routledge. https://doi.org/10.4324/9781003212805.

Kurihara, Y. and Samimy, K. (2007) The impact of a U.S. teacher training program on teaching beliefs and practice: A case study of secondary school level Japanese teachers of English. *JALT Journal* 29 (1), 99–121.

Lander, R. (2018) Queer English language teacher identity: A narrative exploration in Colombia. *Profile: Issues in Teachers' Professional Development* 20 (1), 89–101.

Langmann, S. and Pick, D. (2018) *Photography as a Social Research Method*. Singapore: Springer.

Larsen-Freeman, D. (2019) On language learner agency: A complex dynamic systems theory perspective. *The Modern Language Journal* 103 (S1), 61–79. https://doi.org/10.1111/modl.12536.

LaScotte, D. and Tarone, E. (2019) Heteroglossia and constructed dialogue in SLA. *The Modern Language Journal* 103 (S1), 95–112. https://doi.org/10.1111/modl.12533.

Lawrence, L. and Nagashima, Y. (2020) The intersectionality of gender, sexuality, race, and native-speakerness: Investigating ELT teacher identity through duoethnography. *Journal of Language, Identity & Education* 19 (1), 42–55.

Lee, J.J. (2005) The native speaker: An achievable model? *Asian EFL Journal* 7 (2), 152–163. https://www.asian-efl-journal.com/main-journals/the-native-speaker-an-achievable-model/.

Lemberger, N. (1997) *Bilingual Education: Teachers' Narratives*. Mahwah, NJ: Lawrence Erlbaum.

Leonet, O., Cenoz, J. and Gorter, D. (2017) Challenging minority language isolation: Translanguaging in a trilingual school in the Basque Country. *Journal of Language, Identity & Education* 16 (4), 216–227.

Li, W. (2000) Dimensions of bilingualism. In Li Wei (ed.) *The Bilingualism Reader* (pp. 3–25). Abingdon: Routledge.

Li, Z. and Lai, C. (2022) Identity in ESL-CSL career transition: A narrative study of three second-career teachers. *Journal of Language, Identity & Education*. https://doi.org/10.1080/15348458.2022.2065992.

Liao, F.Y. (2020) When my professor tells me to write poetry in my second language: A poetic autoethnography. In B. Yazan, S. Canagarajah and R. Jain (eds) *Autoethnographies in ELT: Transnational Identities, Pedagogies, and Practices* (pp. 57–74). New York: Routledge.

Lin, A., Grant, R., Kubota, R., Motha, S., Sachs, G.T., Vandrick, S. and Wong, S. (2004) Women faculty of color in TESOL: Theorizing our lived experiences. *TESOL Quarterly* 38 (3), 487–504. https://doi.org/10.2307/3588350.

Lincoln, Y.S. and Guba, E.G. (1985) *Naturalistic Inquiry*. Thousand Oaks, CA: SAGE Publications.

Llurda, E. and Calvet-Terré, J. (2022) Native-speakerism and non-native second language teachers: A research agenda. *Language Teaching*, 1–17. https://doi.org/10.1017/S0261444822000271.

Lo Bianco, J. and Aronin, L. (eds) (2020) *Dominant Language Constellations: A New Perspective on Multilingualism*. Cham: Springer Nature.

Loh, J. (2013) Inquiry into issues of trustworthiness and quality in narrative studies: A perspective. *The Qualitative Report* 18 (33), 1–15.

Luo, H. and Gao, P. (2017) A study of Chinese Fulbright TAs in the U.S.: Implications for second language teacher education. *Journal of the National Council of Less Commonly Taught Languages* 22, 67–102.

MacIntyre, P.D., Gregersen, T. and Mercer, S. (2019) Setting an agenda for positive psychology in SLA: Theory, practice, and research. *The Modern Language Journal* 103 (1), 262–274.

Maddamsetti, J. (2020) Intersectional identities and teaching practice in an elementary general classroom: A case study of a plurilingual teacher candidate. *Journal of Language, Identity & Education* 19 (5), 342–358.

Mahboob, A. and Golden, R. (2013) Looking for native speakers of English: Discrimination in English language teaching job advertisements. *Voices in Asia Journal* 1 (1), 72–81.

Mahboob, A., Uhrig, K., Hartford, B. and Newman, K. (2004) Children of a lesser English: Nonnative English speakers as ESL teachers in English language programs in the United States. In L.D. Kamhi-Stein (ed.) *The State of the Non-Native Teachers in the United States* (pp. 100–120). Ann Arbor, MI: University of Michigan Press.

Makoni, S. and Pennycook, A. (eds) (2007) *Disinventing and Reconstituting Languages.* Clevedon: Multilingual Matters.

Mannay, D. (2010) Making the familiar strange: Can visual research methods render the familiar setting more perceptible? *Qualitative Research* 10 (1), 91–111. https://doi.org /10.1177/1468794109348684.

Marshall, S. and Moore, D. (2018) Plurilingualism amid the panoply of lingualisms: Addressing critiques and misconceptions in education. *International Journal of Multilingualism* 15 (1), 19–34.

Mastrella-de-Andrade, M.R. and Pessoa, R.R. (2019) A critical, decolonial glance at language teacher education in Brazil: On being prepared to teach. *DELTA: Documentação de Estudos em Lingüística Teórica e Aplicada* 35 (3), 1–28.

McAdams, D.P. (2008) The life story interview. See https://cpb-us-e1.wpmucdn.com/ sites.northwestern.edu/dist/4/3901/files/2020/11/The-Life-Story-Interview-II-2007.pdf (accessed 5 October 2021).

McAlinden, M. (2014) Can teachers know learners' minds? Teacher empathy and learner body language in English language teaching. In K. Dunworth and G. Zhang (eds) *Critical Perspectives on Language Education: Australia and the Asia Pacific* (pp. 71–100). Cham: Springer.

McGill University (2021) B.Ed. Teaching English as a second language: TESL elementary and secondary; Teaching Greek language and culture option. See https://www.mcgill .ca/dise/teachercert/teslgreek (accessed 9 October 2021).

Medgyes, P. (1992) Native or nonnative: Who's worth more? *ELT Journal* 46 (4), 340–349. https://doi.org/10.1093/elt/46.4.340.

Menard-Warwick, J. (2008) The cultural and intercultural identities of transnational English teachers: Two case studies from the Americas. *TESOL Quarterly* 42 (4), 617–640. https://doi.org/10.2307/40264491.

Menard-Warwick, J., Masters, K.A. and Orque, R. (2019) The translingual identity development of two California teachers: Case studies of self-authoring. *Journal of Language, Identity & Education* 18 (2), 110–125. https://doi.org/10.1080/15348458 .2018.1505516.

Mercer, S. (2011) Language learner self-concept: Complexity, continuity and change. *System* 39 (3), 335–346.

Mercer, S. (2016) Seeing the world through your eyes: Empathy in language learning and teaching. In P.D. MacIntyre, T. Gregersen and S. Mercer (eds) *Positive Psychology in SLA* (pp. 91–111). Bristol: Multilingual Matters.

Mercer, S. (2020) The wellbeing of language teachers in the private sector: An ecological perspective. *Language Teaching Research.* https://doi.org/10.1177/1362168820973510.

Merriam, B.S. and Tisdell, E.J. (2016) *Qualitative Research: A Guide to Design and Implementation* (4th edn). San Francisco, CA: Jossey-Bass.

Middlebury Institute of International Studies (2021a) Teaching English to speakers of other languages certificate and specialization. See https://www.middlebury.edu/ institute/academics/additional-programs/certificates/tesol (accessed 1 October 2021).

Middlebury Institute of International Studies (2021b) Teaching foreign language certificate and specialization. See https://www.middlebury.edu/institute/academics/additional -programs/certificates/tesol (accessed 1 October 2021).

Mignolo, W. (2018) The decolonial option. In W. Mignolo and C. Walsh (eds) *On Decoloniality: Concepts, Analytics and Praxis* (pp. 105–257). Durham, NC: Duke University Press.

Miller, E.R., Morgan, B. and Medina, A.L. (2017) Exploring language teacher identity work as ethical self-formation. *Modern Language Journal* 101 (S1), 91–105. https:// doi.org/10.1111/modl.12371.

Mischler, E.G. (1990) Validation in inquiry-guided research: The role of exemplars in narrative studies. *Harvard Educational Review* 60 (4), 415–442.

Moore, C. (2014) Screenshots as virtual photography. In P.L. Arthur and K. Bode (eds) *Advancing Digital Humanities: Research, Methods, Theories* (pp. 141–160). Basingstoke: Palgrave Macmillan.

Morgan, B. (2004) Teacher identity as pedagogy: Towards a field-internal conceptualisation in bilingual and second language education. *International Journal of Bilingual Education and Bilingualism* 7 (2–3), 172–188.

Morgan, B. (2016) Language teacher identity as critical social practice. In G. Barkhuizen (ed.) *Reflections on Language Teacher Identity Research* (pp. 211–217). New York: Routledge.

Morrison, J.A., McBride, L. and González, A. (2020) Writing narratives, shifting identities: Developing language teacher identity and practice in working with students with limited/interrupted formal education. In B. Yazan and K. Lindahl (eds) *Language Teacher Identity in TESOL: Teacher Education and Practice as Identity Work* (pp. 31–45). Abingdon: Routledge.

Motha, S. (2006) Racializing ESOL teacher identities in U.S. K-12 public schools. *TESOL Quarterly* 40 (3), 495–518. https://doi.org/10.2307/40264541.

Motha, S., Jain, R. and Tecle, T. (2012) Translinguistic identity-as-pedagogy: Implications for teacher education. *International Journal of Innovation in English Language Teaching and Research* 1 (1), 13–28.

Moussu, L. and Llurda, E. (2008) Non-native English-speaking English language teachers: History and research. *Language Teaching* 41 (3), 315–348.

Mutlu, S. and Ortaçtepe, D. (2016) The identity (re) construction of nonnative English teachers stepping into native Turkish teachers' shoes. *Language and Intercultural Communication* 16 (4), 552–569.

Negueruela-Azarola, E. (2011) Beliefs as conceptualizing activity: A dialectical approach for the second language classroom. *System* 39 (3), 359–369.

New York University (2021) Master of Arts world language education/ Teaching English to speakers of other languages dual certification. See https://steinhardt.nyu.edu/degree/ma-foreign-language-education-teaching-english-speakers-of-other-languages (accessed 1 October 2021).

Nikula, T. and Pitkänen-Huhta, A. (2008) Using photographs to access stories of learning English. In P. Kalaja, V. Menezes and A.M.F. Barcelos (eds) *Narratives of Learning and Teaching EFL* (pp. 171–185). Basingstoke: Palgrave Macmillan.

Nomura, K. and Mochizuki, T. (2018) Native-speakerism perceived by 'non-native-speaking' teachers of Japanese in Hong Kong. In S.A. Houghton and K. Hashimoto (eds) *Towards Post-Native-Speakerism: Dynamics and Shifts* (pp. 79–96). Singapore: Springer.

Nonaka, C. (2018) 'They were American but shy!': Japanese university students' encounter with local students in Hawai'i. In S.A. Houghton and K. Hashimoto (eds) *Towards Post-Native-Speakerism: Dynamics and Shifts* (pp. 41–60). Singapore: Springer.

Norton, B. (2013) *Identity and Language Learning: Extending the Conversation.* Bristol: Multilingual Matters.

Norton, B. (2017) Learner investment and language teacher identity. In G. Barkhuizen (ed.) *Reflections on Language Teacher Identity Research* (pp. 80–86). New York: Routledge.

Norton, B. and De Costa, P.I. (2018) Research tasks on identity in language learning and teaching. *Language Teaching* 51 (1), 90–112. https://doi.org/10.1017/S0261444817000325.

O'Rourke, B. and Pujolar, J. (2013) From native speakers to "new speakers"–Problematizing nativeness in language revitalization contexts. *Histoire Épistémologie Langage* 35 (2), 47–67.

Ortega, L. (2014) Ways forward for a bi/multilingual turn in SLA. In S. May (ed.) *The Multilingual Turn: Implications for SLA, TESOL and Bilingual Education* (pp. 32–52). New York: Routledge.

Ortega, L. (2019) SLA and the study of equitable multilingualism. *The Modern Language Journal* 103 (S1), 23–38. https://doi.org/10.1111/modl.12525.

Otheguy, R., García, O. and Reid, W. (2015) Clarifying translanguaging and deconstructing named languages: A perspective from linguistics. *Applied Linguistics Review* 6 (3), 281–307.

Otsuji, E. and Pennycook, A. (2009) Metrolingualism: Fixity, fluidity, and language in flux. *International Journal of Multilingualism* 7, 240–254.

Oxford, R. (2020) The well of language teachers' emotional well-being. In C. Gkonou, J.M. Dewaele and J. King (eds) *The Emotional Rollercoaster of Language Teaching* (pp. 247–268). Bristol: Multilingual Matters.

Oxford, R.L. and Jain, R. (2010) 'Taking the arrogance out of English' and 'letting go of imperialistic beliefs': New perspectives on World Englishes, non-native English speakers, and non-native English speaking teachers from a graduate course. In A. Mahboob (ed.) *The NNEST Lens: Non Native English Speakers in TESOL* (pp. 239–262). Newcastle: Cambridge Scholars.

Paine, L., Blömeke, S. and Aydarova, O. (2016) Teachers and teaching in the context of globalization. In D.H. Gitomer and C.A. Bell (eds) *Handbook of Research on Teaching* (pp. 717–786). Washington, DC: American Education Research Association.

Pajares, M.F. (1992) Teachers' beliefs and educational research: Cleaning up a messy construct. *Review of Educational Research* 62 (3), 307–332.

Park, G. (2006) Unsilencing the silenced: The journeys of five East Asian women with implications for TESOL teacher education programs. Unpublished doctoral dissertation, University of Maryland, College Park.

Park, G. (2015) Situating the discourses of privilege and marginalization in the lives of two East Asian women teachers of English. *Race, Ethnicity and Education* 18 (1), 108–133. https://doi.org/10.1080/13613324.2012.759924.

Park, G. (2017) *Narratives of East Asian Women Teachers of English: Where Privilege Meets Marginalization*. Bristol: Multilingual Matters.

Park, J.S.Y. and Wee, L. (2012) *Markets of English: Linguistic Capital and Language Policy in a Globalizing World*. London: Routledge.

Patton, M.Q. (2015) *Qualitative Research and Evaluation Methods: Integrating Theory and Practice* (4th edn). Thousand Oaks, CA: SAGE Publications, Inc.

Pavlenko, A. (2003) 'I never knew I was a bilingual': Reimagining teacher identities in TESOL. *Journal of Language, Identity & Education* 2 (4), 251–268. https://doi.org/10.1207/S15327701JLIE0204_2.

Pavlenko, A. (2005) *Emotions and Multilingualism*. Cambridge: Cambridge University Press.

Pennington, M.C. and Richards, J.C. (2016) Teacher identity in language teaching: Integrating personal, contextual, and professional factors. *RELC Journal* 47 (1), 5–23.

Pennycook, A. and Makoni, S. (2020) *Innovations and Challenges in Applied Linguistics from the Global South*. Abingdon: Routledge.

Pessoa, R.R., Andrade, M.E.S.F. de and Ferreira, E.P. (2018) A critical teacher education experience in the State of Goiás, Brazil. *Revista Brasileira de Linguística Aplicada* 18 (2), 339–366.

Phan, L.H. (2008) *Teaching English as an International Language: Identity, Resistance and Negotiation*. Clevedon: Multilingual Matters.

Phillipson, R. (1992) *Linguistic Imperialism*. Oxford: Oxford University Press.

Phipps, S. (2007) What difference does DELTA make? *Cambridge ESOL: Research Notes* 29, 12–16.

Pineda, I. and Tsou, W. (2021) Understanding CLIL from an ELF perspective: Language in Taiwanese primary bilingual education. *Journal of English as a Lingua Franca* 10 (2), 209–233.

Piri, R. (2002) Teaching and learning less widely spoken languages in other countries. See https://rm.coe.int/teaching-and-learning-less-widely-spoken-languages-in-other-countries/1680886eb4 (accessed 24 January 2022).

Polkinghorne, D.E. (2007) Validity issues in narrative research. *Qualitative Inquiry* 13 (4), 471–486.

Pomerantz, A. (2013) Narrative approaches to second language acquisition. In C.A. Chapelle (ed.) *The Encyclopedia of Applied Linguistics* (pp. 4144–4157). Cambridge: Wiley-Blackwell.

Porto, M. and Zembylas, M. (2020) Pedagogies of discomfort in foreign language education: Cultivating empathy and solidarity using art and literature. *Language and Intercultural Communication* 20 (4), 356–374.

Racelis, J.V. and Matsuda, P.K. (2015) Exploring the multiple identities of L2 writing teachers. In Y.L. Cheung, S.B. Said and K. Park (eds) *Advances and Current Trends in Language Teacher Identity Research* (pp. 203–216). London: Routledge.

Rajagopalan, K. (2005) Nonnative speaker teachers of English and their anxieties: Ingredients for an experiment in action research. In E. Llurda (ed.) *Nonnative Language Teachers: Perceptions, Challenges and Contributions to the Profession* (pp. 283–303). New York: Springer.

Rampton, M.B.H. (1990) Displacing the 'native speaker': Expertise, affiliation, and inheritance. *ELT Journal* 44 (2), 97–101. https://doi.org/10.1093/eltj/44.2.97.

Reis, D.S. (2012) '*Being underdog*': Supporting nonnative English-speaking teachers (NNESTs) in claiming and asserting professional legitimacy. *Journal on Excellence in College Teaching* 23 (3), 33–58.

Reis, D.S. (2015) Making sense of emotions in NNESTs' professional identities and agency. In Y.L. Cheung, S.B. Said and K. Park (eds) *Advances and Current Trends in Language Teacher Identity Research* (pp. 31–43). London: Routledge.

Richardson, V. and Placier, P. (2001) Teacher change. In V. Richardson (ed.) *Handbook of Research on Teaching* (pp. 905–947). Washington, DC: American Educational Research Association.

Riessman, C.K. (2008) *Narrative Methods for the Human Sciences*. Thousand Oaks, CA: SAGE Publications.

Rivers, D.J. (2018) Foreword. In S.A. Houghton and K. Hashimoto (eds) *Towards Post-Native-Speakerism: Dynamics and Shifts* (pp. v–xv). Singapore: Springer.

Roiha, A. and Iikkanen, P. (2022) The salience of a prior relationship between researcher and participants: Reflecting on acquaintance interviews. *Research Methods in Applied Linguistics* 1 (1), 100003.

Rose, G. (2016) *Visual Methodologies: An Introduction to Researching with Visual Materials*. London: SAGE Publications.

Rostami, F., Yousefi, M.H. and Amini, D. (2021) How shifting from teaching Arabic or Persian to English prompts the professional identity: A thematic study. *Journal of Applied Linguistics and Applied Literature: Dynamics and Advances* 9 (1), 123–144.

Rubio, B., Palmer, D.K. and Martínez, M. (2021) Si no estás defendiendo tus alumnos, que estás haciendo en el salón? A Mexican immigrant teacher's journey to critical consciousness. *Journal of Language, Identity & Education* 20 (1), 45–57.

Rudolph, N.J. (2012) Borderlands and border crossing: Japanese professors of English and the negotiation of translinguistic and transcultural identity. Unpublished doctoral dissertation, University of Maryland, College Park.

Ruohotie-Lyhty, M. (2013) Struggling for a professional identity: Two newly qualified language teachers' identity narratives during the first years at work. *Teaching and Teacher Education* 30, 120–129.

Salovey, P., Mayer, J.D., Caruso, D.E. and Yoo, S.H. (2011) The positive psychology of emotional intelligence. In S.J. Lopez and C.R. Snyder (eds) *The Oxford Handbook of Positive Psychology* (pp. 237–248). Oxford: Oxford University Press.

Sang, Y. (2020) Research of language teacher identity: Status quo and future directions. *RELC Journal* 53 (3). https://doi.org/10.1177/0033688220961567.

Schutz, P.A. and Lee, M. (2014) Teacher emotion, emotional labor and teacher identity. In J.d.D.M. Agudos (ed.) *English as a Foreign Language Teacher Education* (pp. 167–186). Leiden: Brill.

Schutz, P.A., Cross, D.I., Hong, J.Y. and Osbon, J.N. (2007) Teacher identities, beliefs, and goals related to emotions in the classroom. In P.A. Schutz and R. Pekrun (eds) *Emotion in Education* (pp. 223–241). London: Academic Press.

Schwandt, T.A. (2007) *The SAGE Dictionary of Qualitative Inquiry* (3rd edn). Thousand Oaks, CA: SAGE Publications.

Scott, M. and Tiun, H.K. (2007) Mandarin-only to Mandarin-plus: Taiwan. *Language Policy* 6 (1), 53–72.

Scovel, T. (1978) The effect of affect on foreign language learning: A review of the anxiety research. *Language Learning* 28 (1), 129–142.

Seidman, I. (2006) *Interviewing as Qualitative Research: A Guide for Researchers in Education and the Social Sciences* (3rd edn). New York: Teachers College Press.

Seligman, M.E.P. and Csikszentmihalyi, M. (2000) Positive psychology: An introduction. *American Psychologist* 55, 5–14.

Selvi, A.F. (2010) 'All teachers are equal, but some teachers are more equal than others': Trend analysis of job advertisements in English language teaching. *WATESOL NNEST Caucus Annual Review* 1, 156–181.

Selvi, A.F. (2014) Myths and misconceptions about nonnative English speakers in the TESOL (NNEST) movement. *TESOL Journal* 5 (3), 573–611. https://doi.org/10.1002/tesj.158.

Shaw, D. (2013) A new look at an old research method: Photo-elicitation. *TESOL Journal* 4 (4), 785–799. https://doi.org/10.1002/tesj.108d.

Shin, H. and Park, J.S.Y. (2016) Researching language and neoliberalism. *Journal of Multilingual and Multicultural Development* 37 (5), 443–452. https://doi.org/10.1080/01434632.2015.1071823.

Simon-Maeda, A. (2004) The complex construction of professional identities: Female EFL educators in Japan speak out. *TESOL Quarterly* 38 (3), 405-436. https://doi.org/10.2307/3588347.

Skott, J. (2015) The promises, problems, and prospects of research on teachers' beliefs. In H. Fives and M.G. Gill (eds) *International Handbook of Research on Teachers' Beliefs* (pp. 13–30). New York: Routledge.

Skutnabb-Kangas, T. (2015) 'Linguicism'. In C. Chapelle (ed.) *The Encyclopedia of Applied Linguistics* (pp. 1–6). Cambridge: Wiley.

Slabakova, R. (2019) 'L' stands for language. *The Modern Language Journal* 103 (S1), 152–160. https://doi.org/10.1111/modl.12528.

Song, J. (2016) Emotions and language teacher identity: Conflicts, vulnerability, and transformation. *TESOL Quarterly* 50 (3), 631–654. https://doi.org/10.1002/tesq.312.

Song, J. (2018) Critical approaches to emotions of non-native English speaking teachers. *Chinese Journal of Applied Linguistics* 41 (4), 453–467.

Song, S.Y. (2015) Teachers' beliefs about language learning and teaching. In M. Bigelow and J. Ennser-Kananen (eds) *The Routledge Handbook of Educational Linguistics* (pp. 263–275). New York: Routledge.

Spector-Mersel, G. (2010) Narrative research: Time for a paradigm. *Narrative Inquiry* 20 (1), 204–224. https://doi.org/10.1075/ni.20.1.10spe.

Stake, R. (2010) *Qualitative Research: Studying How Things Work.* New York: Guilford Press.

Suarez, J. (2000) 'Native' and 'non-native': Not only a question of terminology. *Humanizing Language Teaching* 2 (6).

Talbot, K. and Mercer, S. (2018) Exploring university ESL/EFL teachers' emotional well-being and emotional regulation in the United States, Japan and Austria. *Chinese Journal of Applied Linguistics* 41 (4), 410–432.

Tavares, V. (2022) Teaching two languages: Navigating dual identity experiences. *Pedagogies: An International Journal*, 1–22. https://doi.org/10.1080/1554480X.2022.2065996.

Taylor, S.K. and Snoddon, K. (2013) Plurilingualism in TESOL: Promising controversies. *TESOL Quarterly* 47 (3), 439–445.

Teachers College (2021a) TCSOL/TESOL summer dual certificate program in Macau. See https://www.tc.columbia.edu/arts-and-humanities/tcsol-certificate/program-offerings/tcsoltesol-summer-dual-certificate-program-in-macau--online/ (accessed 1 October 2021).

Teachers College (2021b) TCSOL/TESOL summer dual certificate program in Osaka. See https://www.tc.columbia.edu/arts-and-humanities/tcsol-certificate/program-offerings/tcsoltesol-summer-dual-certificate-program-in-osaka--online/ (accessed 1 October 2021).

Tsao, F. (2008) The language planning situation in Taiwan: An update. In R.B. Kaplan and R.B. Baldauf Jr (eds) *Language Planning and Policy in Asia, Vol. 1: Japan, Nepal and Taiwan and Chinese Characters* (pp. 285–300). Bristol: Multilingual Matters.

Tsui, A. (2007) Complexities of identity formation: A narrative inquiry of an EFL teacher. *TESOL Quarterly* 41 (4), 657–680. https://doi.org/10.1002/j.1545-7249.2007.tb00098.x.

Umino, T. and Benson, P. (2016) Communities of practice in study abroad: A four-year study of an Indonesian student's experience in Japan. *The Modern Language Journal* 100 (4), 757–774.

Umino, T. and Benson, P. (2019) Study abroad in pictures: Photographs as data in life-story research. In P. Kalaja and S. Melo-Pfeifer (eds) *Visualizing Multilingual Lives: More than Words* (pp. 173–193). Bristol: Multilingual Matters.

Universidade do Estado de Mato Grosso (2022) *Matriz curricular do curso de letras*. See http://www.unemat.br/caceres/letras/?link=matriz (accessed 24 January 2022).

Universidade Federal do Triângulo Mineiro (2022) Languages – Portuguese/English. See http://www.uftm.edu.br/en/undergraduate/letters-portuguese-english (accessed 24 January 2022).

Urmston, A. (2003) Learning to teach English in Hong Kong: The opinions of teachers in training. *Language and Education* 17 (2), 112–137.

Varghese, M. (2001) Professional development as a site for the conceptualization and negotiation of bilingual teacher identities. In B. Johnson and S. Irujo (eds) *Research and Practice in Language Teacher Education: Voices from the Field* (pp. 213–232). Minneapolis, MN: Center for Advanced Research on Language Acquisition.

Varghese, M., Morgan, B., Johnston, B. and Johnson, K. (2005) Theorizing language teacher identity: Three perspectives and beyond. *Journal of Language, Identity & Education* 4, 21–44.

Varghese, M., Motha, S., Park, G., Reeves, J. and Trent, J. (eds) (2016) Language teacher identity in (multi)lingual educational contexts [Special Issue]. *TESOL Quarterly* 50 (3), 541–783.

Vélez-Rendón, G. (2010) From social identity to professional identity: Issues of language and gender. *Foreign Language Annals* 43 (4), 635–649. https://doi.org/10.1111/j.1944-9720.2010.01113.x.

Wang, L. and Kirkpatrick, A. (2019) *Trilingual Education in Hong Kong Primary Schools*. Cham: Springer.

Wernicke, M. (2018) Plurilingualism as agentive resource in L2 teacher identity. *System* 79, 91–102.

White, C.J. (2018) The emotional turn in applied linguistics and TESOL: Significance, challenges and prospects. In J.D.M. Agudo (ed.) *Emotions in Second Language Teaching: Theory, Research and Teacher Education* (pp. 19–34). Cham: Springer.

Wolff, D. and De Costa, P.I. (2017) Expanding the language teacher identity landscape: An investigation of the emotions and strategies of a NNEST. *The Modern Language Journal* 101 (S1), 76–90. https://doi.org/10.1111/modl.12370.

Woodley-Baker, R. (2009) Private and public experience captured: Young women capture their everyday lives and dreams through photo-narratives. *Visual Studies* 24 (1), 19–35. https://doi.org/10.1080/14725860902732694.

Xiong, T. and Xiong, X. (2017) The EFL teachers' perceptions of teacher identity: A survey of 'Zhuangang' and 'non-Zhuangang' primary school teachers in China. *English Language Teaching* 10 (4), 100–110.

Yang, S.Y. (1987) What is expected of English instructors in China. *TESOL Newsletter* 21 (3), 29.

Yazan, B. (2018a) A conceptual framework to understand language teacher identities. *Journal of Second Language Teacher Education* 1 (1), 21–48.

Yazan, B. (2018b) Identity and NNESTS: Non-native English-speaking teachers (NNESTs). In J.I. Liontas (ed.) *The TESOL Encyclopedia of English Language Teaching* (pp. 1–7). New York: John Wiley & Sons.

Yazan, B. (2018c) TESL teacher educators' professional self-development, identity, and agency. *TESL Canada Journal* 35 (2), 140–155.

Yazan, B. and Lindahl, K. (2020) Language teacher learning and practice as identity work: An overview of the field and this volume. In B. Yazan and K. Lindahl (eds) *Language Teacher Identity in TESOL: Teacher Education and Practice as Identity Work* (pp. 1–10). Abingdon: Routledge.

Yoshihara, R. (2018) Accidental teachers: The journeys of six Japanese women from the corporate workplace into English language teaching. *Journal of Language, Identity & Education* 17 (6), 357–370.

Zembylas, M. and Chubbuck, S. (2009) Emotions and social inequalities: Mobilizing emotions for social justice education. In P.A. Schultz and M. Zembylas (eds) *Advances in Teacher Emotion Research: The Impact of Teachers' Lives* (pp. 343–363). Boston, MA: Springer.

Zheng, X. (2017) Translingual identity as pedagogy: International teaching assistants of English in college composition classrooms. *The Modern Language Journal* 101 (S1), 29–44. https://doi.org/10.1111/modl.12373.

Index

accidental teachers 33
adjunct instructor 3, 104-114, 116,
    125, 128-131, 163, 165,
    170-171, 177 (*See also* social
    justice/mistreatment of adjunct
    instructors)
agency 48-49, 58, 73, 97, 148-149, 168
Arabic
  - learning 116
  - teaching 9, 20, 27
Aslan, E. 8, 11, 18, 20-21, 52, 87
assessment 118, 124, 126-128, 151,
    168, 175

Barcelos, A.M.F. 13-16, 162, 164
Barkhuizen, G. 16, 50-51, 55, 58-59,
    160
beliefs, language teacher
  - benefits of being multilingual
    23-24
  - benefits of previous teaching
    experience and training 21-22,
    143
  - benefits of teaching multiple
    languages 23, 30-32, 88-89
  - definitions 13-14
  - difficulty of being a native
    speaker teacher 21, 87-88, 142-
    143
  - language learning beliefs, 116-
    121, 140-141
  - new teaching methods 22, 94,
    167-168
  - relationship with emotions and
    identities 16, 92 (*See also*
    identity-belief-emotion work)

bilingualism 4, 37, 64, 68-69, 94, 135,
    155, 157, 161, 167
Brazil 9, 19, 35, 37, 40, 119
brokering, language and knowledge
    17, 29

Calafato, Raees 2, 8, 23, 68, 182
Canada 9, 35
career transition 3, 14, 17, 20, 24-25,
    29-33, 38, 173
China, People's Republic of 9, 18-20,
    24, 32-33, 38, 41, 66-67, 97,
    99, 103, 165
  - China-Soviet relations 38
Chinese (Mandarin)
  - phonemic awareness 78, 93
  - Pinyin 78, 93-94, 174
  - Putonghua (普通話) 81, 87, 97,
    174
  - Taiwanese Mandarin (Guoyu,
    國語), 1, 33, 41-42, 63, 69, 81,
    99, 165, 174, 176, 179
  - teaching (*See* Teaching Chinese as
    a Second Language)
  - writing 83-84, 94
code-switching 64
communicative language teaching 88,
    141-142, 148, 152, 154, 168,
    175,
community 41-42, 85, 102, 109, 114,
    118-120, 125, 131, 157
corporate workplaces 3, 33, 109-110,
    114-116, 128-129, 170-171 (*See
    also* identities, language teacher/
    corporate identities)
cosmopolitan 20, 82, 138-139

- when non-native speakers become native speaker teachers 17-18, 20-21, 24-25, 87, 89, 142-147, 169-170

natural method 107, 116

Netherlands 35

Norway 3, 8, 23

Ortaçtepe, Deniz 9, 18-22, 24-27, 39, 87

Pavlenko, A. 4, 12, 15, 69

Pennycook, A. 63-66

Persian 9, 20, 27

personality 89, 172

photo-elicitation
- advantages 56
- data collection 57
- definition 55
- photographs in narrative research 55
- photo-narratives 57

photographs in language teaching 139, 142

plagiarism 16, 123,

Poland 36-37

Portuguese
- teaching 9, 19, 21-22, 24, 30-31, 35, 37, 40

positive learning environment 119-120

positionality 62

power 5, 15, 18, 25, 46, 48, 56, 68, 131, 164, 174

professional development 6, 9, 47, 111-112, 183-184 (*See also* teacher development)

rapport 51, 140, 142

reflexivity 62

Rose, G. 56, 57

rural schools 33, 41-42

Russia 8, 23, 38-39

Russian (language) 8, 38-39, 66

second career teachers (*See* career transition)

second language acquisition 44-46, 50

semiotic resources 45-47, 93-96, 126-128, 148-154, 164

Smith, Hye Young 17-18, 20-21, 24-26, 28, 38, 87

social justice
- in language teaching 12, 15, 118, 120-121, 130-131
- mistreatment of adjunct instructors 112-114, 125, 128, 131, 171, 177

South Korea 8, 21, 25

Southern Min
- teaching, 1, 41, 98-99

Spanish 3, 8-9, 23, 27, 35-37, 65

status 27, 31, 63, 67, 110-111

story
- definition 50
- photographs as stories 56, 60
- storytelling for children 73-74, 77, 94

study abroad 55, 73, 138-140, 155-156, 173

Taiwan 5, 31-32, 41, 52, 62-63, 70-71, 73-74, 76, 78, 81-82, 86-88, 90, 94, 96-99, 146, 165, 169, 172-174, 176, 178-179

Taiwanese
- identity 63, 91, 97
- teaching (language) (*See* Southern Min)

teacher agency 12, 48, 58, 73, 97, 148-149, 168

teacher burnout 125

teacher development 16, 106 (*See also* professional development)

teacher knowledge 4, 10, 17, 20, 22-26, 29-30, 50, 75, 79, 89-90, 92-93, 96, 104, 125-126, 128, 136, 138, 143, 145, 147-148, 154-155, 161, 164, 166-167, 170, 172, 182

teacher resilience 30, 87, 106

teacher talk 29, 94, 116, 122, 126, 128, 130, 151, 170

teacher training 20-22, 25, 34, 36-37, 39, 42, 96, 101-102, 104-105, 132, 134, 142, 170, 175

For Product Safety Concerns and Information please contact our EU Authorised Representative:

Easy Access System Europe

Mustamäe tee 50

10621 Tallinn

Estonia

gpsr.requests@easproject.com

www.ingramcontent.com/pod-product-compliance
Lightning Source LLC
Chambersburg PA
CBHW050432280326
41932CB00013BA/2090